PRAISE FOR WOMEN À LA MODE

"I love this book! Women À La Mode is not just a memoir about women. It's a book that encompasses all of life.

And there is something lovely and transporting and unhurried about the prose and the experiences Blaisdell charts here. When I read her words, it feels like I'm a Parisian pigeon standing on her shoulder during a joyful exploration of the city's romantic and cultural pleasures. We follow along with her through the tunnels of the Metro and into highfalutin whiskey bars. We stroll through the galleries of the Musee d'Orsay, catch up with Judy Chicago, have brunch at the Cafe Rendezvous, charter a golf cart through the grounds of Versailles, and get to know a mysterious, ingratiating woman who was an intimate of both Jean Paul Sartre and Simone de Beauvoir.

The book is hard to put down, and it keeps drawing me back to revisit it. The narrator comes to Paris to explore some of her life's biggest questions: what does a feminist look like? Is it possible to pursue creative and personal independence and embrace sisterhood and still hold out for a "fairytale" happy ending? Can feminism be beautiful, fashionable, glamorous? The book, as Blaisdell says, is no stilted "five paragraph essay" but a warm and comforting quilt for readers to wrap around their shoulders. With an enigmatic friend and mentor, Claudine, at its center, and many fascinating side trails (from the origins of high heels to the possibilities of French obscenities) this book holds surprises on every page. And it has a narrative momentum that is undeniable and also mysterious. Blaisdell has dispensed with an obvious chronological through-line and replaced it with something beautiful and associative. The reader reads on, not to discover the 'next big happening' but to trace her evolving thought processes, listen in on good conversations, and chart her adventures.

I read this book during the hideous events of early January, and I found that Women À La Mode was exactly what I needed to break that feedback loop. Life has become so regimented, broken up, hurried, frenzied. And this book invites us all to slow down, notice, and take it all in. The book wrestles with serious issues, including sex trafficking and domestic violence, and yet the book is refreshingly optimistic, with an intoxicating sense of freedom and possibility."

—Dan White, author of *Under The Stars* and *The Cactus Eaters*

∼

"Who has the luxury of time to contemplate women's condition?" asks Augustine Blaisdell in her charming memoir Women À La Mode. At once serious and romantic, this is a madcap and magical book that confronts how class intersects with gender and race. Blaisdell upends our expectations of the American in Paris narrative, taking the reader on a whirlwind journey through feminist history while sharing moments of vulnerability and personal discovery. Women À La Mode celebrates the power of intergenerational female friendship, showing us how these bonds can bring us together and carry us into a bright future."

—Doretta Lau, author of *How Does a Single Blade of Grass Thank the Sun?* and *Cause and Effect*

WOMEN À LA MODE

A MEMOIR OF WRITING A BOOK ABOUT FEMINISTS IN PARIS

AUGUSTINE BLAISDELL

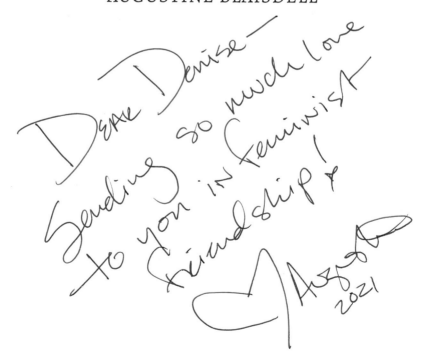

Dear Denise—
Sending so much love
to you in feminist
friendship!

2021

A BLAZE IMPRINT
www.ablazeimprint.com

Ordering Information:
Quantity sales. Special discounts are available on quantity purchases by corporations, associations, and others. For details, contact the publisher at the address above.

A BLAZE IMPRINT organizes lively discussions, speaking engagements and events. To have our authors come to your book club or gathering, contact business@ablazeimprint.com.

Cover Design by Nicole Caputo
Author Photo by Karen Blaisdell
Interior Design by Sandy Kreps

BLAZE

IMPRINT

CONTENTS

PART I

Meeting Claudine   3
An Education   18
Like Any Other -ism?   21
An Experience   26
Butter and Tartare   28
Camaraderie   33
Work It   36
Financially Independent Woman   40
A Breakthrough   48
The Torch is You: Body as Power   52
The Bravery of Becoming Known   56
What is Women À La Mode?   58
The Weight of Eating and Praying and Loving   60
Apologies for Versailles   64
A Rendezvous   66
Becoming Parisienne   72
Talkin' Bout My Generation   77
Getting Over Heartbreak   78
Turkish and French Alliances   80
Courage   82
Woolf's Sentence Continues   87
We Are a Mineral Resource   90
Tiens au Courant?   101

PART II

This Is Where Simone Died   107
Growing Up Hollywood   116
Code Blue   121
The Social Currency of Influence   124
Useful Phrases in French   129
Brunch at Mariage Frères   133
Il m'aime, un peu, beaucoup…   135

At The Place des 'Voyages'   138
Female Equivalents   142
Her Story   147
Two Steps Back   150
One Step Forward   153
The First Thing, CEDAW   156
A Sense of Urgency   160
Five-Paragraph Essay   161
Bac à Glaces   164
Which Identity is Your Priority?   166
Let the Man Carry the Money   171
Au Relais-Relay   173
Au Marché   176
Two Months Later   178
Writing a Book is like Falling in Love   180
Sheroes   182
Pretty Woman   184
An Object of Vision   187
My Italian Doppelgänger   195
18 Million Cracks   200
Americans in Paris   204
From Russia with Love   206
When Feminism Becomes Fashionable   209
Transitions   210

PART III
Egyptian Red Ring   215
My Interview at the Backstage Cafe   217
A More Serious Tone   222
Della   224
Brunch at Cafe Rendezvous   226
Fromages et Ramages   233
Beyond the Dinner Party   234
Back to "Work"   245
Asking the Inevitable   248
Christmas Day at the Sacré-Coeur   250
A New Transcendentalism   254
An Evening in a Montmartre Café   257
Le Jardin Secret   261

Marriage, Istanbul, Turkey   264
Decisions Set You Free   269
Between Floors   274
Bac à Glaces   281
Having It All   284
Bienvenue en France!   288
It's NOT a Man's World. Why?   292
Witch Hunt   295
Least Violent Time for Women   297
Birth Control   299
Contraception is the Answer   301
Actual Costs of Giving Birth, Aside From the Obvious   303
Clinique Joan of Arc   305

PART IV
Becoming a Mama   309
First Smile   311
A Regulatory Substance?   312
Rééducation Périnéale   314
Femme Potomitan   319
Solo Adventures   323
It's in the Book   325
Je Suis et Je Ne Suis Pas Charlie   329
Stop Saying Violence Against Women   332
Letter to Zohra D   336
Trumped   338
What Would Hillary Have Done?   340
Le Choix du Roi   345
A Book about Writing a Book   348
Rendez-vous with Dr. W   349
Madame President   356
CODEPINK   358
Talk About It!   361
Passion   364
The Future is Female: Women's March in Paris   366
Migrant Misconceptions   369
Feminists in the City   372
Diving In   374
The End of My Body   376

Hélène de Beauvoir in Strasbourg   378
Passover, A Love Story   380
Climax   383
Why I Write   385
Mamie Gâteau   387

Afterword   390
Works Consulted   395
Acknowledgments   401
About the Author   405

To my mother Karen,
To my aunt Relissa,
To my father Don,
To my mentor Claudine,
To my husband Eric,

With Love,

In honor of my Nana Eva,
Without whom I would not have come to France.

PART I

MEETING CLAUDINE

I arrive in Paris at seven in the morning.

It is gray, rainy, and cold. In my excitement, I realize I've forgotten to get euros out of the ATM machine, and when the cab drops me off in front of the apartment, I have to persuade him to take $20 US. He is unhappy, but there is nothing I can do—except repeatedly say sorry and please, *desolée*, and *s'il vous plaît*, in unfamiliar French, and he takes the money.

I've swapped my fifth floor (fourth floor by French standards) one-bedroom East Village apartment for Barbara's third floor (fourth floor by American standards) *appartement*. This Parisian photographer's space is much larger than mine, three rooms, but by any standards, it's an even trade. I am just two stops outside of Paris, in an immigrant/artist community called Montreuil, metro stop Robespierre on line 9.

The moment you enter the apartment you want to shout FREEDOM! Free from your obligations, free from your family, free from your ex who you risked your best friend for, free from your broken heart, free to do whatever you want—freedom. It's 2009, you are twenty-eight years old, and you are alone. The apartment is sparsely decorated. It's cold inside, but not cold in feeling. It looks exactly like the pictures you saw many months ago, with the classic French windows that go all the way from floor to ceiling. There are those three rooms.

First a living room with a small couch and tiny TV on a stool not much higher than the floor with a few orchid plants surrounding it. There is an office, an actual office, with a long, clean white desk going the length of the room, and then the bedroom with a modest bed and another window. You don't think you've ever been so happy in your entire life. Surely, it occurs to you, you must have been, but standing there in a place not your own, you are home.

You may have noticed I switched to second person there. It was me, firmly rooted in that apartment, but then it was you. Why? Because I want you to feel as I felt then, because when I switch it to the you, there is a universality there. It just sounds better in you form. And because Hemingway did it. I didn't know he would switch to the second person in his classic Paris memoir *A Moveable Feast* when I first started writing, I hadn't read it yet, but he does, so I do it. It's a nod to my imagined writerly kinship with Hemingway and adventure, I suppose. Jokes aside, I imagine I have your attention now, just in case I didn't before.

I call Claudine, and we agree to meet at Place St. Placide. Even understanding where this square is is difficult. Nothing in France is pronounced the same as in America. The stresses are on different letters, and even English words take on an unknown sound. I practice saying Placide. I'm very America-centric, but I'm too America-centric to know it yet.

Your heart is racing when you leave the apartment, because you are in a foreign place on not a lot of sleep and can't understand anything anyone says. Even getting money from the ATM is a heroic feat, which it will take you months to learn the word for, *distributeur*. It makes sense, but you never remember it. There are several people standing around the one you've found, but it looks as if it's not working. You try anyway and realize this is a bad idea, as now you can't read what it says on the screen and your card is in the machine and again, your heart is racing because perhaps you won't get your card back, your only passport to money anywhere. You'll ask yourself later how could you be so stupid, but instead you're just thinking *oh fuck, oh fuck, fuck* (you should say *merde,* heavy on the ending *d* sound, or rather *putain,* meaning whore, or even more so a combo of the two, *putain merde,* but you'll never curse that way) while frantically pushing the button with a red X for *annuler.* The card is thankfully returned, but with no brightly colored euros along with it. Still shaking from the experience and your good fortune of at least getting back your bank card, you walk to the metro. Now you have to hope to be able to buy tickets at the counter with said bank card. On the way past a graffiti-filled street (graffiti seems to make the unknown more menacing) you practice saying *Bonjour, je voudrais dix billets, s'il vous plaît.* It sounds all right, but your voice is shaky, anyway.

The woman gives you ten tiny tickets, each one the size of two postage stamps. Later you'll learn there is a particular bikini wax called the *ticket de metro,* so called for the size of the strip of hair you keep, but you don't know that yet. Buying ten tickets is cheaper than buying them individually: eleven euros for the bunch.

Now on the metro, you *regard* the map. The directions are easy: go into Paris and change at Strasbourg St. Denis, a rundown and very popular interchange to the line 4 that will take me to St. Placide. This is where I will meet the woman on whom my whole future depends.

Eight months before, I'd emailed Claudine without a second thought after finding her website through a quote about Simone de Beauvoir on Wikipedia. She responded within a few hours. We spoke the next day, and she instantly agreed to be my mentor (I needed a mentor because I was applying for a Fulbright grant, which would pay me to live in France for a year and write a book on "women.")

"It's very important for me to transmit the wisdom I learned from Simone," she had said in her lovely French accent. "You understand, I have a full-time job as well, which has absolutely nothing to do with my work on Simone, but I will do my best to help you." I didn't ask any questions about her "real job," as it was dismissed as boring and not important enough to discuss.

That was the only time we spoke to each other until this brisk April morning when we agreed to meet at the kiosk in front of the metro, and I told her I would be wearing a black coat with brightly colored flowers.

"Hello, my dear!" she says enthusiastically when I exit the metro. "But Augustine, you look fantastic. Barely jet lagged at all, all fresh faced and shiny."

"So do you," I say, and she does, her blonde hair cut short in what I'll come to know as a quintessential Parisian style for *une femme d'un certain age*—a nice way of saying she's sixty. She has bright pink lipstick and skin like Bible paper, though, being an atheist, she would find this comparison amusing. Claudine is short, and I am tall, we hug, and then do the French *bises*—air kiss on both cheeks. All is fast around us. The sound of speed from the passing cars creates the sensation of everything spinning. We are on the major four-lane boulevard of Rue de Rennes, which leads from Tour Montparnasse straight down to Saint-Germain-des-Prés, the area known for the cafes made famous by Simone and Sartre.

I'm always inclined to call Simone de Beauvoir just *Simone* and Jean-Paul Sartre just *Sartre*. Why is it that so many famous women are known by their first names, whereas men tend to be known by their last names? Somewhere, I'm sure, this could be construed as condescending to women. Maybe I should be referring to Simone as simply *Beauvoir*, and yet it seems more personal to use her first name, whereas with Sartre, I'd rather keep my distance. Or is it that, together, Simone and Sartre have such a symbiotic synergy in the alliteration of the sensual S? Searching for Simone just sounds better than searching for Beauvoir. But I will also have to use Beauvoir because part of the struggle of women who make brilliant contributions to society is to be called by their last name.

Monteil is not Claudine's real last name, but I don't know that yet.

From the moment I meet Claudine, I believe it is fate: fate we found each other; fate I am here, fate I am doing what I'm supposed to be doing—writing a book on women in Paris. We try to go to one small tea room, Mamie Gâteau, but it is full and noisy, and they haven't guarded her table, so we continue on, the streets out of focus as we walk quickly in the damp afternoon mist. Claudine moves fast, and as I come to learn her idiosyncrasies, it is her speed that comes as quickly in memory as it does in real life.

We have tea and ice cream on rue du Cherche Midi, a fancy street in the 6th arrondissement. I don't know where we are, won't remember the name of the street until a year or two later. Paris is divided by *arrondissements*, 1 to 20, starting at the center and spiraling out like an *escargot*; the snail they eat is the structure of the city. What could be a better symbol for a city obsessed with food than an actual favorite dish? Running through it all is the River Seine, dividing the Left Bank (south side) and the Right Bank (north side). The Left, where we are, is historically known as the intellectual side, which is why the restaurant we stop at is called Le Rousseau. It's named after Jean-Jacques Rousseau, the 18th century philosopher whose writing triggered French Revolutionist thought, and who is also known for his scandalous book, *Confessions*. It was based on another scandalous book: my namesake, *St. Augustine's Confessions*. Confessional writing was taboo then. Now, it seems commonplace—necessary, even. *Obligatoire*.

Le Rousseau is a gorgeous restaurant with red leather couches and the type of soft warm lighting that lulls one into comfort. And all feminists —well, at least the three I know most intimately (Claudine Monteil, Simone de Beauvoir, and Virginia Woolf)—say women should eat comfortably. A feminist is well fed, Claudine will tell me Simone was always telling her, and Woolf writes a whole essay about it.

Self-care isn't a thing yet, isn't a trend. This isn't to say you can't be a feminist if you're not well fed. On the contrary, we need feminism to ensure women, and all people who consider themselves female, are well nourished. Historically, girls were the last one to be served; brothers got the food first. Girls are the more malnourished explicitly because they are girls.

But this is not what I'm thinking about over ice cream. I've come to France frustrated by feminism, but eating *glaces pistache,* pistachio ice cream, in this fancy cafe meeting this formidable feminist, I think that perhaps feminism isn't so annoying after all.

Claudine is French, but she spent the autumns of her youth in Princeton, New Jersey, where her father taught as a mathematician. She met Simone in 1970, when she was twenty and Simone was sixty-two. Since then, Claudine has dedicated her life and work not only to "all things Beauvoir," as she would say, but also to the fight for women's rights. Claudine begins our discussion and many of her speeches about Simone in the same way: "I am a child of *The Second Sex,* as my mother was reading it at the time she was pregnant with me." My mother was born the same year. An easy way to remember the publication date of 1949. Exactly sixty years before I arrived in France.

When Claudine finally tells me what she does, it does indeed have everything to do with women's rights. She is an international Legion of Honor diplomat working at the ministry of Foreign Affairs for the French government. "Augustine, I am in charge of the forced marriages in France. These fourteen-year-old girls, who are French citizens, were born here, go to school, have boyfriends. What their family does is tell them they are going to visit their grandparents' homeland, and once there, they force them to marry, steal their passports, and leave them in the middle of nowhere. This is one of the things I do all day. We find them and bring them back to France."

I don't have time to ask why as Claudine looks at me with all seriousness and says, "Did you know there are over thirty thousand illegal female circumcisions a year in France?"

No, I do not know this.

"They are primarily immigrants," Claudine says, her voice coming down to a whisper. "But you have to be careful and not focus your book too much on the immigrant population in France, as it is only ten percent. You need to talk about the other ninety percent."

"OK," I agree easily. I don't know any better. This sounds reasonable, but who are these French people? It will be years before I learn that, because of World War II, France doesn't keep statistics on race, which, like gender, they view as a social construct. It is illegal to keep track of the demographics of ethnicity and religion because they have seen the flip side, that those types of lists can be used to round people up. Obviously, the Jews. France is very sensitive to this. And they are very investigative also. How did this happen? How did we ship those Jewish children to their deaths? There are many plaques dedicated to the Jews that France sent to the Germans. Turn on French TV, and I could bet good money there would be a program on World War II on, at any time of day. The war is still quite close.

I am essentially an immigrant in France, but I don't usually think of myself that way, nor do others. Usually I'm grouped together with the more romantic term "expat." There has been a lot of investigation into why, but the simple reason is that I'm white. White people are expats, while Black people and people of color are immigrants. However, those are not quite the lines. I believe there's an element of intellectual prowess at play, a certain intellectual elitism that accounts for why James Baldwin, Nina Simone, Josephine Baker, and Bessie Coleman were all considered expats, too. There seems to be something there about contributing to the society you're joining. Nevertheless, I do consider myself both immigrant and expat. Perhaps "immigrant" suggests a lack of choice, akin to the migrants who risk their lives entering France, Italy, or Greece from across the Mediterranean. "Expat," on the other hand, implies choice—that you've left your country of origin purposely, that you were forced out by poverty or war, and that you've chosen this place to take up residency.

In a dramatic moment, Claudine says, "Augustine, you will never be the same after your time here in France. This is the reality, not just the fantastic notions of Women's Liberation and being an independent woman, of French women and romance. This is the reality. The world will not be at peace until the violence against women has stopped. We must take back the power, change attitudes." Claudine is intense when she speaks this way. She repeatedly takes off her glasses and leans in closer to make her point.

She continues, "This is not the romantic ideals of French women. This is the real world. This is what I deal with every day. It is not philosophy, but activism." I prefer the romance of salons and art and beauty and sexy stockings to mutilated vaginas, though I don't say this at the time. Her presence permeates the space of our table. She exudes that grand, commanding force I imagine Simone must've possessed.

Claudine is petite, measuring in at five foot two, the same height as Simone. We forget Simone was short because in pictures of her and Sartre, she seems to be towering over him, because he was even shorter. Their height, however, is of no consequence to their force. Claudine says, "Simone spoke like a machine gun, rattling off ideas faster than one could keep up."

Claudine is tough but sensitive, and when she speaks of Simone, her eyes sparkle. It's as if she becomes smaller, like a child looking up. I think this is because she is reminded of being "a kid" when she first met Simone. She becomes her twenty-year-old self, full of ambition and naiveté and a relentless drive to fight justly for the cause. Ever humble though, Claudine never wanted it to seem like she was using Simone for her fame—subsequently she has few pictures of them together.

Claudine will always make sure we take pictures. Here is us the day after we met.

"Now when you are writing your book, you can't use my real name, you understand; for my job, you see. This is very important. That is why I have the pen name for my novels, as everything must be kept separate. It would never do for my job to know I was an extreme feminist in league with Simone, you understand."

I don't fully understand this, but I take her word for it. Over the years, the French government will take an interest in her work with Simone, and her worlds will collide such that I am now able to use her name in print, but here in 2009, it's very hush hush. Have I mentioned Claudine has a flair for drama? To this day, I'm not sure if she does it for my benefit or her own.

When I ask her how she became a diplomat, how she learned to handle the negotiations she does every day, she is quick to say with a laugh, "It is from the feminist movement I know how to do what I do."

"Simone was very mad at me when I joined the government, but to me, it was a way to make changes from the inside. I had always wanted to be a diplomat since I was fourteen years old, and when I was a child, I dreamed of going to East Berlin. So, at that time, to become a diplomat meant it was important to learn Russian, so my parents sent me there to learn it. This is what I wanted, you see? It was a fantasy, you understand." Still, at the age of twenty-nine, Claudine was picked to become a diplomat and do negotiations because she spoke fluent Russian, French, and English.

Claudine is wearing pink. She will always wear pink, different shades of pink. Pink shirt, pink sweater, pink jacket. Perhaps she feels pink provides a softer feminine side, or maybe it's just her favorite color. Our ice cream finished, we walk over to *Poilâne*, a very famous French bakery, for a loaf of bread and apple tarte tatin to bring back for a cozy dinner at her home with her partner, Bernard. Claudine does not cook. Bernard serves us prosciutto, artichoke hearts, and basil pasta, all of it a perfect antidote for the wooziness of jet lag.

Claudine reminds me of my photography professor from Emerson College, Lauren Shaw. They have the same creative, spastic energy, and the same immediate concern for my well being. Lauren would always say, "Follow your obsessions," meaning obsession renders passion. Question why you are obsessed with something *later*; follow it first, so then you can lead. I'm obsessed with finding some answers to the question of what we can do now for women. I'm not sure why. There are the obvious reasons, sure, but for the most part, I'm following my obsession.

To Claudine, I am the young American woman who is interested in the women's movement. Her house has a warm cheerfulness to it, like the color of light sunshine. We sit in the kitchen around a circular table with the very typical Provence-style tablecloth. The apartment is in Montparnasse; from the terrace is a view of the cemetery where Simone and Sartre are buried side by side.

We discuss making the book. She's given me a list of over twenty women to interview. The task is overwhelming. I can barely order a *café crème* without intimidation, let alone call French women and speak entirely in French to request and set up an interview. I am still struggling to remember the days of the week, and I definitely do not pronounce time correctly. *Douze* and *deux* sound like each other when placed in front of *heure*, but mean twelve or two. The solution is to use *quatorze*. Military / European time.

Yes, I have moved to Paris for three months knowing *bonjour* and *s'il vous plaît* but not *je vous en prie* (you're welcome), and also unable to remember right and left, which means I can ask for directions, but not understand where to go. I am also completely confused by the numbers, as the language doesn't have a word for seventy, eighty or ninety; instead, it's *soixante-dix*, sixty ten, *quatre-vingt*, four twenty, and *quatre-vingt-dix*, four twenty ten. It sounds easy, but it's not. I don't admit my intimidation to Claudine, so we go over the names.

The list includes women I've never heard of before but forms a circle of women Claudine either knows through work or through the success of her nine books, seven of them on Simone alone. The first woman is an NGO delegate for several World Conferences on Women, Bernice Dubois. She is an American, and has been living in France for the past fifty years. The next is Marie-Helene Vincent, a French Catholic feminist artist. Also listed: Catherine Zviloff, a lawyer who tried the first case to make female circumcision illegal in France; Nathalie Pilhes, a member of the Protocol for France's then-president, Nicolas Sarkozy; Sheila Malovany-Chevallier, who is just about to release the new English translation of *The Second Sex*; Colette Kreder, the former director of the Ecole Polytechnique Feminine; and Pascale Jeandroz, a conductor and deputy head of the Orchestra Music of Peacekeepers.

It doesn't occur to me at the time, as I haven't met any of them yet, that these are all white women in impressive, high-profile positions. So we'll branch out. But keeping with the theme of all women who consider themselves femme engagée et une féministe active, directly translated to engaged woman and active feminist. As my project progresses, Claudine will introduce me to Hélène Monties, who is awarded the Legion of Honor during my first year in France. Gisèle Bourquin, president of the French Association *Femmes au-dela des Mers* and also a knight of the Legion of Honor who in 2020 is honored with the award for The Senate Delegation of Women's Rights. Daniele Michel-Chich, a journalist and writer who was President of *la Maison des Femmes de Montreuil* for several years after its founder Thérèse Clerc, and who today is President of the association *Femmes Monde* and co-president of FDFA, *Femmes pour le Dire – Femmes pour Agir,* an association specifically for handicap women. Cécile Fara and Julie Marangé, co-founders of Feminists in the City. Eliane Viennot, renowned French historian and writer. Moïra Sauvage, co-chair of a collective of 38 associations, *Ensemble contre le sexisme,* Together against sexism, and Marie-Paul Grossetête, co-president of the CLEF.

Later, I add my own women to the list: feminist artist Judy Chicago and filmmaker Elena Rossini. I'll realize I know some kick-ass women doing incredible things, who are some of my oldest friends: Nicole Brown who in 2019 became the first black woman to run a live-action division at a major film studio. Her extensive career is focused on films that have received both critical and commercial success and she takes great pride in breaking new voices, especially women and people of color. She is on the board of Women in Film, a member of the Academy of Motion Picture Arts & Sciences, and is also a mentor for ReFrame Rise. Shahirah Majumdar, who since 2017 has worked with the Rohingya refugees in Cox's Bazaar, Bangladesh and is currently an editor of the Rohingya Cultural Memory Centre documenting their language and culture before it is lost. Sheila Aminmadani who, with her Master's in International Affairs, teaches public high school in New York primarily for recently arrived immigrants and refugees. Natasha Nixon, an international Theatre Director, who I meet in Paris and goes on to work at The National Theatre in London. In 2020 she becomes Associate for The Women Leaders South West project in collaboration with the WOW Foundation, a global movement which celebrates women and girls. The project is an Arts Council England Transforming Leadership grant with the aim of understanding the barriers women face in becoming leaders in the arts and developing tools to remove some of these obstacles.

In fashion, Tina Tangalakis, who in 2009 created Della, a socially responsible fashion line that provides jobs, education and skills training to women and men of Hohoe, Ghana. Two of my biggest supporters are my dear friends, Rebecca Lerner and her aunt Suzanne

Lerner. Suzanne is President of Michael Stars, activist and philanthropist who in 2015 was awarded "Woman of Vision" Award from the Ms. Foundation for Women, as well as recognition as one of 21 Leaders for the 21st Century by Women's eNews. Suzanne is truly a woman of vision as in 2009, she is one of the only fashion leaders talking about the impact of fast fashion, of sustainability. She says the fashion industry does nothing for human rights, for equality, so she starts doing something. Suzanne and I will talk periodically throughout my writing of my book, she will always keep me informed of her newest projects. She actually talks the talk and goes to Haiti to provide humanitarian aid after the hurricane. With Suzanne's connection, I'll also interview Jodie Evans, the co-founder of CODEPINK and together with Jane Fonda was arrested several times for initiating Fire Drill Fridays at the Capitol.

In Paris, Mariel Chatman will provide unlimited support and resources for navigating learning French and pregnancy in Paris. Emma Tricore, the photographer who is my translator. Barbara Bouyne, our own personal The Holiday story, the photographer who swapped apartments with me. Marilla Destot, who made this all possible by sending out an email to friends.

I'll continuously make calls to my closest friends will keep me grounded, such as my Dutch-American pen pal since we were ten, Laila Contini. Writer and all things comic books extraordinaire, Edie Nugent, who I became friends with instantly when we met on a plane in 2004. While I'm busying writing, my oldest friend since preschool, Evan Schoolnik, creates her own successful business leading food tours in Santa Barbara before food tours are a thing. Michelle Heinz, a fellow writer from Columbia who provides infinite support by reading and rereading and rereading again my manuscript. All these women provide the details of their work life or unique perspectives on feminisms or the actual costs of pregnancies in their respective countries.

The list will also include friends I haven't met yet: Melis Arval from Turkey, Olga Kuzmina from Russia, and Sabrina Casonato from France, which sounds like the start of a joke—an American, a Turk, a Russian, and a French woman walk into the bar...

At the bars, we will pride ourselves on being very international when people ask where we are from and try to place our various accents. Later, it will resonate differently when Putin and that other guy become besties, but for now, we meet in in the blissful Obama years. For now, we think we're on the right path and it's great to be an American in France. The French people I meet love Obama. We are riding high from the Yes We Can movement, #MeToo and #BlackLivesMatter haven't happened yet. But even with that, it won't be until the summer of 2020 that I first hear the phrases "End Racism" and "End Sexism" as actual possibilities. Even beyond possibilities, they're now seen as imperatives that are attainable. Even when Obama won, people were still saying, "Well, it's not like it's going to end racism." But after 2020, it's clear there is a global sea change.

In this moment however, I'm in awe of Claudine's enthusiasm in helping me garner interviews. She is seemingly helping me without asking for anything in return. A cynic would wonder what her agenda is, but I'm not a cynic, and from the start it seems complete altruism. In two years, she will turn sixty-two, the same age Simone was when they met. Because Simone was instrumental in her life, she wants to "transmit the wisdom, strength, and energy for women's rights" that Simone taught her.

Claudine is still surprised she is now old, or what she considered old when she was young. She says that when she found out Simone wanted to meet her, her response was, "She's still alive? She must be so old. Now," she says, "I am the older generation." Her sense of mortality will become more and more apparent as time goes on, just as my sense of gratitude will increase day by day. Three months later, when we are having a very formal lunch right before I leave Paris for the summer, she will tell me I have inspired her, she is honored to have a young person interested in her story, and she finds my perspective interesting. It will be another year before she will tell me she wants to include me in her own book.

At the time, though, I don't imagine she'll ever write about me. I'm thinking that without her, I do not have a project; without Claudine,

there is no book. She says, "Your book should be about three generations of French women. What do you say?"

I agree, just as I agree to the condition that, "Augustine, this is very
important: with all the women you interview, if they ask, you must not
tell them who else you are interviewing, as not all of these women are
friends, and there may be some jealousy between them. They don't all
get along."

"OK, Claudine, no problem." I may not understand French, but I do
understand jealously and territorial nature of women, of humans in
general.

"And also, never use the word *feminism*," Claudine says. "It scares
people away."

Ah, the F-word. It brings to mind *f*ck!*—and, of course, feminism. But
the *f*ck!* is essentially what I felt about feminism when I first arrived in
France. Did we still need feminism anymore? Did we need a new
word? Should we be calling it humanism?

AN EDUCATION

Before leaving New York, there are two events which strengthen my resolve to take off to Paris to write.

I have dinner with a few friends and friends of friends. The restaurant is called *Supper*. It's a favorite among friends for Italian food and the cave-like atmosphere lit by candles.

You end up sitting next to a woman who is perhaps slightly tipsy. Though you've known her for years, she surprises you when she says, "It's a man's world and the men can have it. They've fucked up the world and now they can deal with it and play with their wars. I just want to raise kids and stay home. I don't care." When she says this, it sticks with you.

You're appalled. How could she say this? Feel this? Yet at the same time, maybe women didn't have it all that bad. Stay at home and chill. This is before you have kids, before you realize what a full-time job being a parent is and you're definitely not 'chillin'.' Or maybe you'll chill, but with a baby as a new appendage. Which completely alters your sense independence and immortality.

Still, what's wrong with that? We're all working women at the table, who are all tired of working. It's March in New York. Winter has taken its toll, and we are just waiting around for spring. Everything is gray, depressing, and cold, so you could blame the weather for the apathetic attitude of your friend.

A few days later, still contemplating if it's a man's world and the men can have it, you go uptown to another evening soirée that you've been to on three previous occasions—Columbia University's agent mixers.

They're always held in April, and they're the highlight of the year if you have something to show for the $30,000 a year spent on your education. It is 2009, a week before Paris, and we are mildly prepared with a three-minute, three-sentence dissertation on why what we have to say is of interest to someone other than just the people in this room.

The party is held in a large hall with extremely high ceilings, making me feel small. There is nowhere to sit as the few chairs are pushed to the perimeter and are occupied by our coats. These are the awkward cocktail parties the Writing Department at Columbia University throw in hopes of securing agents for some of their more socially adept and conversational students, of which there are few. Most of us are the clichéd stereotype of a writer with all that entails, which means there is wine, and there will always be wine at this and every other event to lubricate our uneasiness. "Creative types" are known to be heavy drinkers.

Writers at Columbia are a weird juxtaposition of people who know enough to know when they're being pretentious, but at the same time can't help being slightly inclined to one-up each other by sharing how many and which books we've read, meanwhile indulging in the awkwardness of truly talking. Oh yes, we're much better, we assure ourselves, with the "written word." I do not consider myself a typical writer in this way. I enjoy parties, don't usually stand along the wall, and have been known to revel in being the center of attention—I am an only child after all.

However, at these mixers, there is that certain anxiety, like you are about to go on stage. Luckily, the agents can be just as uncomfortable as we are—they're usually writers, too.

We nervously stand around waiting our turn. The ratio of students to agents is seven to one. Some writers, true to another stereotype, come for the free food and drinks, knowing they are not truly ready for a real interaction with anyone, but need to practice their social graces. I'm not a fan of these people. In later years, they'll be advised not to come. Tonight I am not one of these people. Tonight I have come with the mission of talking to as many agents as possible to acquire as many business cards as possible in hopes I will eventually and gracefully step out of just being a writer into becoming an author, a *published* writer. I am in the right circle, and have gone into debt, financial and otherwise, to be here.

Some agents are kindly inclined to my idea of living in France to write about women, but the moment there is mention of Simone de Beauvoir and the F-word, their response becomes the unfortunate answer, "These books are wonderful, but the problem is they never sell."

There is the challenge, should I choose to accept it, which, since you're reading this book, clearly I did: write something about women that is not just for women and, for God's sake, not the Goddesses, doesn't use the F-word in the title, or maybe at all. Can you just write a book about feminism without using the word *feminism*? In fact, don't even use the nomenclature of the F-word, as those books don't sell, either. It appears that, since its inception, the F-word has never been very sexy. Which is not to say only sexy things sell, but sex certainly helps. I say my book will be sexy. I say my book will sell.

I clutch my plastic cup of wine and acquire several precious business cards, or, from the agents who've given all of their cards away, a quickly scrawled email address on a ripped napkin, making it seem like we met in a low-end Lower East Side bar rather than inside the sacred Upper West Side walls of Greek architecture where we are clinging and climbing and clawing our way to the top.

LIKE ANY OTHER -ISM?

I tell this story of the agent party often, because in 2019, 2020, it becomes clear that these feminists books do sell. That's a welcome change. So what is this feminist momentum? What does feminism mean? Looking back from a 2020 lens on Claudine and me that first day we met, it seems apropos we would eat our first meal together at a restaurant called Rousseau's, and that he would be a writer. It would've been more appropriate if we had been dining at a restaurant named after one of Rousseau's contemporaries, Charles Fourier, but there are no restaurants named after him yet.

Fourier is credited with the first documented use of the word "feminism" in 1837. Used to describe women's liberation in a utopian future, feminism, more than just a word, is a movement advocating for women's social, political, legal, and economic rights being made equal to those of men. Of course, even the word for female equality comes from a man! And he's French! When I first arrive in France, I don't have a clear definition of feminism, other than that it's frustrating.

Feminism like any other -ism,—capitalism, communism, socialism, totalitarianism—implies another -ism: elitism. And in 2009 it seemed we were at a point where people didn't want to be aligned with just one -ism, nor any number of -isms for that matter.

Some argue the title is unnecessary, and some argue for another word. Some say we shouldn't even be asking this question anymore, yet it continues to be asked. Prominent artist Marina Abramovic, singer Katy Perry, and actor Susan Sarandon declare they're not feminists, and it still make the news.

While considered one of the most important essayists of feminist thought, Virginia Woolf herself hesitated to associate with the label. From Hermione Lee's Introduction to the 2001 Vintage edition of *A Room of One's Own and Three Guineas:*

> *But to start by calling A Room of One's Own a 'feminist essay' at once draws attention to what a marvelously difficult book this is to categorize. For one thing, Woolf was notoriously edgy about the F-word. She had a horror of propaganda and polemic, increasingly so in the 1930s. Her later, much harsher and fiercer essay on women's exclusion, Three Guineas (1938), would throw out the word 'feminist' in its anxiety not to be read as a propagandist manifesto. It recommends freedom of mind and a critical independence, rather than partisanship or aggression And she was very anxious, when A Room of One's Own was coming out, that she would be 'attacked for a feminist.'*

When you look in the dictionary for the definition of polemic, you find the phrase as an example of a strong verbal or written attack, "a writer of feminist polemic." Even in the most progressive circles, you can mention feminism or women's issues and people's eyes glaze over, but when you mention human rights, people's eyes sparkle.

One of the major criticisms of earlier feminism was that it was only for privileged, white, straight women. It is currently defined in four distinct waves:

First was women's suffrage in the 1920s in the United States and Britain.

Second was the 1960s women's liberation, the invention of the birth control pill and the legalization in some countries, France and United States, of abortion.

Third was the 1990s, when I grew up, which was a backlash against inequality, specifically about the body and reproductive rights. Here again, the pervasive sentiment was that women can do anything. I grew up knowing there was gender discrimination, but I'd convinced myself I'd never experienced it in my daily life. Before I met Claudine, I had horrible sexist radar.

In 1989, when I am nine years old, Kimberlé Crenshaw coins the term "intersectionality," meaning that our identities must be looked at as a whole; being a Black woman cannot be separated into being Black and being a woman, so these two social constructs must be discussed together. Though many feminists or activists I interview will touch on this intersectionality, they won't use the specific term, and Crenshaw's work won't become "mainstream" till the late 2010s. Black feminists like Crenshaw and game-changing writers like bell hooks and Audre Lorde are essential to our understanding of feminism and being a woman. Audre Lorde's quintessential 1984 work *Sister, Outsider* seemed at first like it was not written for me, that it's just for Black women, but this could not be further from the truth. When I do finally read it, I devour it. I'm so dismayed I haven't been taught this before, and that this isn't required reading for everyone.

Similarly, it won't be until I'm thirty-one that I'll read Tony Weschler's *Taking Charge of Your Fertility* and realize that no one every taught me the cycles of my period, and that I could actually predict my most fertile time. How did I go sixteen years not knowing this vital, life-changing information? Why was this never taught in school? This is how I feel about Lorde and hooks and all the women that I have to discover, to dig out, to add to "western history's timeline" that have been systematically omitted.

This timeline of these first three waves of feminism is actually quite problematic. As Claudine will say, "Feminism has existed since time began, as women have always been fighting for equal rights." And the history of American feminism is fraught with omissions. It is only now that we are finally recognizing the contributions of Black and Indigenous feminists.

For instance, Maria Stewart was the first American to speak about equality to what was called at the time a "promiscuous audience," meaning a mixed audience of Black and white, men and women, in 1830. So it was actually Black women like Stewart, Sojourner Truth, Frances Harper, Josephine St. Pierre Ruffin, Anna Julia Cooper, Ida B. Wells, and Mary Church Terrell who pioneered what we call the first wave and who started speaking out for equality and the right to vote before Susan B. Anthony and Elizabeth Cady Stanton came onto the scene in 1851. But Anthony and Stanton are the only ones I learned about in high school. Sure, we learned about Harriet Tubman, but Stewart, Truth, Harper, St. Pierre Ruffin, Cooper, Wells and Terrell I learn from educator and activist, Rachel Cargle's lecture "Unpacking White Feminism." There are so many Black and Indigenous women we should've learned. One woman I wish I would've known is Lozen, the Apache warrior and prophet, called by her brother Vittorio "a shield to her people." Together with her two-spirit love, Dahteste, she fought with Geronimo at his last stand in 1886. Geronimo has persisted in our collective imagination. Lozen and Dahteste have not.

What we did learn in all these waves was that to be a feminist was to be seen as unattractive. For my generation, these feminists conjured up images of militant, bra-burning, man-hating butch lesbians who didn't shave and wore army boots and yelled a lot. Their main source of rage was the objectification of women, and they fought against the psychological and physical damage brought on by the omnipresent airbrushed images of women.

The fourth wave of feminism hadn't started yet when I began writing this book. It's the #MeToo/post-#MeToo movement. Fourth-wave feminism was ushered in by a TED talk from Chimamanda Ngozi Adichie, *We Should All Be Feminists*, which was then sampled by Beyoncé, and by books such as Roxane Gay's *Bad Feminist* and Sheryl Sandburg's *Lean In*. Feminism is now seen as attractive and necessary. This fourth wave is all-inclusive and gender fluid, with a special focus on rape culture, sexual harassment, and violence against women, non cis-men, and marginalized genders. Let us not forget that it was three Black women, Alicia Garza, Patrisse Cullors, and Opal Tometi, who founded Black Lives Matter in July 2013.

Today we say we're staunchly in the fourth wave of feminism, post-#MeToo, but really, we could easily say we're in the hundredth wave of feminism or the thousandth. We will have to contend with artificial intelligence, access to clean water, climate change. There is a direct correlation between the countries that respect the planet and those that respect women. This will become more and more evident as those countries that choose to protect the natural resources of the earth will be those that have the smallest gender gap. Is it because the countries with the smallest gender gap believe in equality and therefore believe in climate change or vice versa?

Ten years ago, I was mildly amused and slightly annoyed that all my male friends happily proclaimed they were feminists because they knew it "helped with the ladies," whereas several of my girlfriends hesitated to claim the label for themselves. Or they would say, "I'm a feminist, but…." A feminist with a disclaimer. Now, there is no but. The fear of being associated with an unattractive attribute such as feminism is no longer a concern now. Feminism has become fashionable.

AN EXPERIENCE

The next day is Sunday. Everything in France is closed, and I'm left to my own devices. I have the freedom to do what I'd like, meaning I have the legendary room of my own, just as Virginia Woolf said I must.

The woman with whom I've apartment-swapped, Barbara, has left me a map of the neighborhood. She's also left me some food in the fridge, and I've taken home half the apple tart from dinner the night before. She's left a sticky note on the map where there is a lovely cafe next to an open-air market, which is open on Sunday and "is fantastic to sit at after shopping," her note says.

The cafe is a living postcard of Paris. It's exactly as I'd imagined it to be. Growing up in Los Angeles, I'm used to the intoxicating feeling like you are in a movie, feeling as if you are somehow dislodged from reality, or as if you've stepped back in time. I sit on the large terrace in the sunshine, order a glass of wine, and indulge in a favorite activity of people watching. There is a three-piece band of musicians: one on the cello, another on the accordion, and a third on the guitar. With the accordion, they make music that is classically French, and it adds to that excitement that I'm really here, and my dream has come true.

The second-story window of the cafe hangs a rainbow flag that says PEACE, a clear indicator I'm among those with similar ideals. I'm reminded of the story that Bruce Anderson, then-President of the Gay Center in New York, where I used to work, tells me of his time in Paris when he found himself amongst the rainbow flags of the Marais. He said to himself, "You are in the right place at the right time."

The bar starts to fill up with people. I'm very much the insecure outsider, though the women seem friendly enough, if hesitant about why I'm there alone. The men are numerous. There is an empty chair in front of me that won't be empty for long. My glass of wine is coming to an end, and it appears the party is just getting started. I discreetly look in my *Lonely Planet* phrasebook to figure out how to order the same thing: *la même chose*. It's a phrase that will come in handy many times.

Giorgio swoops in like a falcon on my empty chair. He is an older gentlemen wearing glasses, his silver hair combed back in a ponytail. He is Italian and insists that I stay for dinner. There have been other men trying to catch my eye, but Giorgio is the one who sits. He speaks French, as well as a few words of English, but his favorite phrase is *la dolce vita*. He repeats this phrase in Felliniesque fashion. The French equivalent, *la vie est belle* is true here, at the cafe, where you assume only locals go, and you're having an experience, a real European experience. Does Giorgio say *la dolce vita* just for my benefit because it's clear that I'm a tourist? No. Here for this moment, life is beautiful and sweet. A man inside the bar is clapping and dancing to the music. The mood is euphoric, everyone around is smiling, laughing, rejoicing. Giorgio orders a bottle of wine and couscous is served to every table. Everyone eats at the same time, and everyone lights cigarettes after they're finished, which means it's time to escape. You try to pay, but Giorgio won't stand for it, so you say your *mercis* and *au revoirs* and leave. Ah, the benefits of being a woman—you could save a lot of money this way.

It won't be until a few weeks later you'll realize couscous is free on Sundays.

BUTTER AND TARTARE

Because I clearly don't speak French, I've signed up for a week-long intensive course at the classic standard of French courses all over the world, the Alliance Française.

Yes, I naively think to myself, *a week will do it*.

In the first week of classes I learn—well, sort of—what it took me three months to learn in a night class at Cooper Union in New York. It's beyond clear I'll have to sign up for a week or two more—yes, this is really what I think to myself—to really get a handle on this French language thing.

The Alliance Française is fantastic in that it is brimming with foreigners from all over the world, not just loud-speaking, smiling Americans like myself. In the very beginner class on the top floor, it is only me and six other women. The ratio of women to men in French classes will always lean towards women. I am paired with a young woman from Japan who nods in agreement any time we attempt to speak to each other. I've heard the intimidation of speaking a new language described as stage fright, which is exactly what it is.

These early French classes are so intimidating, as is the loss of power that goes with being understood. Everything is intimidating, from going to the supermarket to knowing that you need to weigh and price your vegetables before going to the checkout; from knowing that you need to bring a bag with you and you will bag your own groceries to knowing that they're going to ask you if you have exact change when you buy a baguette or croissant. Then there's that expectant look they give you, waiting for an answer when you didn't understand the question while the people behind you in line, any line, sigh, and sigh loudly, as Madame behind the counter repeats the question.

That first day of class is an unusually warm day, one of the few until summer, and from the Alliance Française, I walk towards the Luxembourg Gardens, hoping to find something to eat along the way. On the corner of rue de Fleurs and rue Madame, I find the cafe Bread and Roses. That it's written in English doesn't yet seem out of place as it looks French enough. Inside, behind the glass cases are the most gorgeous-looking deep-dish quiches I've ever seen. They are at least three inches high covered with pine nuts, or goat cheese, or large pieces of broccoli. I buy a slice of the spinach one, which will have the surprise of salmon in it, and continue to the park.

Oh, that first quiche in France! Hands down the best you've ever tasted: the buttery crust, the fluffiness of the eggs enveloping spinach and salmon. It doesn't leave you wanting more but, in its mouthwatering goodness, leaves you satisfied. Like the lure of so many first times, nothing else will ever compare, but you can be content in owning that memory.

You want to write about this moment, the moment of the quiche in the Luxembourg Gardens the second it's finished, you want to capture it quickly, but just as quickly, a day-off security guard who loves techno music descends on you, chatting you up. He'd be more than happy to teach you French if you'd just give him your number–you luckily don't have a French cell phone yet. You'll be wearing a sign for weeks, the sign of *I'm not from here*, which equates to *yes, of course come talk to me* and is legible in French, English, Italian—everyone understands the sign that is a smile. You're wet behind the ears, haven't learned yet how to stare into space to avert the eyes of those trying to make a pass, and you don't complain about it either because it's fun to have a little attention, perhaps a little adventure. Isn't this what you came here for, sort of, to meet people? You may ponder if you're trained to enjoy the flirting, if it's a nature-versus-nurture thing. They're not aggressive— that will come, too, but in the meantime, you're fresh meat, or rather, since we're in France, *boeuf tartare* the hunted, the pursued, an American, *Californienne en plus*, California dreamin'. For them it is a dream, just as for me, the men verge on Pepé Le Pew, and Paris is the dream.

Yes, it's true, the moment there in Paris, it's as if all the clichés you've seen in movies become real. The fantasy takes the reality, but the reality stays fantastic. People really are wearing the blue-and-white-striped mariner shirt. People really do carry baguettes on the street. People really do say *Voilà! Voilà quoi* is the motto, the confirmation what you've just said is evident, obvious, and final. They say it with a singsong splendor that the mastery of French language allows.

Ah, and the beauty, the incredible beauty! The way the light sparkles on the Seine at dusk, and the streetlights shine rose at precisely the instant of twilight and go to white gradually in accordance with the setting of the sun. And just there, while standing on a bridge you spy the Eiffel Tower and its seemingly ephemeral sparkling. *Voilà quoi.* No matter how many times you see it, even out of the corner of your eye, it can still bring a joy, that yes, you are here in Paris. Paris, where you don't have to do much to be romantic.

And the buildings, those glorious buildings! Wrought iron, black intricate designs, and sooty cream stone that appears immaculate topped with metal slate. Green broadleaved trees that reach just to the height of those buildings lining the long Haussmanian streets. Perspectives growing long out of the horizon; the florescent flashing green Pharmacie cross on every corner, the red neon sign of the tabac. (Don't say the 'c'—it's *taba*, not *taback*.)

Each window surrounded by unique designs in stone, carved faces everywhere. Randomly, a statue of a lion over a doorway. A crest of arms, stone-faced women under the windowsills staring out near the Gare St. Lazare. Women, like the profiles of coins, and the devilish looking men on each corner of the buildings. Bright red explosions of petals in the planters lining the windows, those geraniums you hear are rumored to grow particularly well in Paris pollution. And then the wind changes, the trees start moving, the clouds cover the sky, rays of sunlight shine through, and you know it's about to rain.

Paris in the springtime is a myth, like many of the great myths of Paris and the French. It is incredibly cold in the springtime, raining more often than not. Raining all the time, gray and raining. My Nana says over the telephone, "The rain washes all the bad stuff away." I've come to Paris with enough "bad stuff" baggage, most but not all of it self-imposed, and now I imagine I'll be clean.

You can smell the rain coming, as Paris, more than anything, is a city of smells. It's true the streets can smell like butter, and often do when you walk by the *boulangeries* that are usually only a few feet away from each other. The particles of smell invade a ten-foot radius around every bakery: freshly baked bread, *pain au chocolat, croissant aux amandes,* seducing you with the possibility of eating to indulgence, with giving little to no consideration of the consequences of freshly baked croissants.

Ah, butter. As a kid, I ate butter– would sneak into the fridge on my own and scoop morsels of butter from the plate where the unsalted Land of Lakes butter chilled on its own, uncovered, delicate droplets of condensation its only protection from my tiny fingers. Raw hamburger meat —*tartare*—was another favorite of mine, perhaps because there was something forbidden about it, so I could never get enough. Or perhaps it's that I already had some French in me.

My parents took me to Paris when I was four and again when I was six. What I remember from the trips are memories created from photographs that I'm in. I remember a giant tower of butter, the size of my small round head, set in front of me to butter bread. I remember thinking the butter was just for me, my dinner.

When you finally figure out the size of two hundred grams, you go to the open-air markets and cheese shops, and there they'll have this freshly made, immensely misshapen block of butter and will slice off your request with a wire string.

Why come to Paris if you're not going to eat?

CAMARADERIE

I n America, you could call me a foodie.

In France, there is a difference between being a *gourmet* and a *gourmand*. I'd never heard of a *gourmand* before. A *gourmet* is a person who likes those exquisite small dishes one finds in fancy restaurants. Like art on a plate, where every dot of sauce counts, indicating a very refined palate.

A *gourmand*, on the other hand, is someone who loves good food and a lot of it. This is not to say you overeat or over-indulge, but that the plates are *copieux*, meaning plentiful and generous. I'm more on the *gourmand* side, and I'll learn that for dessert, you can order a *cafe gourmand*, which is an espresso accompanied by four or five mini-desserts from the menu. A great alternative if you're like me and want to try everything!

Like any major city, Paris is a place where it's not considered odd to eat alone.

Feeling the pressure to live each day like it's my last, which is what everyone tells you to do when you're traveling, I'll go out to eat with myself. While I don't mind going solo, it's lovely when I make a friend.

Her name is Carolina, Carol for short. She is a Brazilian who is fortu-
nately here for a month, as that's what Brazilians—like the French, and
like several other nationalities—do: take a month off for vacation.
Carol's ex-boyfriend lived in Paris for five years and has marked up
her guidebook with some of the best spots. It's through her that I will
go to *Chez Janou*, the über-touristy yet classic French restaurant near
Bastille, which serves chocolate mousse out of a giant bowl made fresh
that day and where you are allowed—encouraged, even—to put as
many large, heaping spoonfuls as you want on your plate. They just
give you the bowl as well as leave the rum for the Baba au Rum.

Through Carol, I'll discover *Bistrot Vivienne*, which serves delicious
escargot and a filet mignon topped with seared foie gras and
surrounded by a decadent mushroom sauce, as if that was the deca-
dence. This, of course, finished off with a molten chocolate soufflé lava
cake called a *molleux au chocolat,* which means it oozes deep dark
brown chocolate once the tongs of the fork have had their way with it.
This precious warm chateau of chocolate is surrounded by a moat of
pistachio cream edging all the way to the perimeter of the plate.

She'll also teach me about *Favela Chic*, the supposedly Brazilian night-
club that is really just a bar / restaurant / small sweaty dance club where
all hipsters who listen to Radio Nova go. When we walk in, though,
they're playing the Beatles and *Jailhouse Rock* by Elvis. It'll quickly
jump to *Jump Around* by House of Pain, which is typical. Everyone
loves an excuse to jump.

Carol has long brown hair and a tan, and together, we speak a combination of broken English and French. She is heartbroken like me, and
we get along quite nicely. She calls me "my friend," and she holds her
nose in the metro, fighting off the smells of urine from seemingly out
of nowhere.

We'll try to get behind the velvet ropes of Le Baron, the chichi club on
avenue Georges V, but we've come either too early or too late, and the
bouncer won't let us in. We're most likely not wearing the right outfits;
we're most likely not French enough; we're most likely only going to
be able to afford one drink, if that. After standing around in the cold,

pissed off and wondering what else to do, depressed we're just not cool enough to be glitterati, we walk past other clubs that look equally hard and expensive to get into, and we curse the system. We say that we hate velvet ropes, anyway, and we pretend to be Groucho Marx saying, "I'd never want to belong to any club that'd have me as a member."

We return home.

WORK IT

Y ou may be wondering by now how it was I had the money to come to France and embark on this endeavor.

I worked. After I graduated from Columbia University in 2006 with my Master's in Creative Writing, I worked in New York City for three years as an event planner for some of New York's most VIP art events. This was the time before the crash, when opulence was the key word and no one gave a thought to the 1%, except to say they wanted to be part of it.

One of the cooler events was The American Patrons of the Tate, where for fifty-thousand dollars a table, you could sit next to your favorite artist. The event was photographed by Annie Lebowitz and appeared in *Vanity Fair*. Many of the greats were there: Cindy Sherman, Chuck Close, Robert Rauschenberg. Among other awesome events we did were the annual gala of The Studio Museum in Harlem, and all the opening events for the New Museum, Dia and Dia Beacon, and Art in General. All of the museums were run by women, from the formidable Thelma Golden, director of the Studio Museum, to the indomitable Lisa Phillips, director of the New Museum. My boss was a woman, and almost everyone we worked with was a woman, except for the sound guys and security.

This meant that these women were sometimes considered bitches, or at the very least were considered scary by us underlings. I was impressed by all of them. I'll never forget when we were in the throes of the week-long events of the New Museum's grand opening and needed to get approval to put up a tent on the Bowery. We had to call the police commissioner, and just like that, the other Lisa, the CFO, picked up the phone and called him. *What a badass,* I thought. *What agency! This is how you do it, just pick up the phone and call right now.*

I worked two jobs all through my undergraduate studies at Emerson College in Boston, one at a high-end restaurant guide called *Where To Eat,* run by a twenty-eight-year-old woman named Jill Epstein. To me, she was what an adult was. She was a role model.

And then I had help from my family. My mother, who won her seven-year claim against Fen-Phen (the 90s diet drug that killed thousands of women and left her with five heart attacks, a pacemaker, and countless medications she will have to take for the rest of her life), helped finance my education. She sent me to Columbia.

Like Virginia Woolf, I inherited money from my Aunt Barbara. And while the money won't keep me in food, housing, and clothing for the rest of my life, it did allow me some security to be able to travel to France. With the money I should've spent on a house or stocks, or should've maybe hidden away for that eventual rainy day, I went to France instead.

My mother is the youngest of three girls, raised in the 50s and 60s. Barbara was the first, and like the simultaneous invention of the Barbie doll in 1959, she was raised like a Barbie. Key importance was placed on her looks, her hair was done up just so, and she wasn't trained to do anything with her life other than look beautiful and marry rich. This is not to say that she didn't work: her first job was at Sloane's, a department store, where she was an elevator operator. Nana has said that after that first job, Barbara became morose, most likely from boredom, and she married Nana's hairdresser by the time she was nineteen.

Relissa, the middle child, arrived at the intersection of the women's movement independence and the underlying belief that the goal was still to get married. And not just married, but married to someone who would support you.

Karen, my mother, was born in 1949, the same year as Claudine, the same year *The Second Sex* was published. She got the full dose of hippiedom and followed her heart. Still trained to marry rich, she went against the rules, as was perhaps the new set standard for women in the 60s.

The exception to this my Nana's sister, Pearl's children, Delene and Jory. Delene escaped Los Angeles and got her degree from Berkeley in the 60s and all that entails. She went on to work for the government for years, as did her younger brother Jory who went to Cal State Northridge and worked for the city of Santa Monica.

Delene, an ardent feminist, always questioned what we would now call the "narrative of my Nana," that my father was a broke artist, or that he was the one who was supposed to be making the money. Whenever my mother would complain my dad didn't make enough, she'd turn it on its head: "You can make more money than him! You can support him!"

Why should your father make more money? Why can't it be your mother who makes more money? This astute and very feminist thought is one I've never had before, but once she says it, it's that aha moment of epiphany! Yes, why can't you be the one to make more money instead of complaining your partner doesn't make enough. My parents will still fall into this trap, asking me why my partners can't make more money. To which I'll say, "Don't worry about him, stay in your lane. I'm the one who's going to make the money." But it will take me years to come up with that answer.

Still, the effect of the 1950s epoch is obvious when comparing how my grandmother's daughters were raised to how her youngest sister's children, three boys, were raised. The boys were told to get jobs, and moreso to get a career. Glenn, the oldest, became a lawyer. Kurt, the middle, became an antique jewelry dealer. Russ, the youngest, after a stint in Berkley Business School and a major in Philosophy, became CEO of the company founded by my great-grandfather.

Delene and Glenn will both have their degrees from Berkley. While my mom and Aunt Relissa did both receive their Associate's degrees, of the women in my immediate family, I'm the first one to be have the opportunity to go on to my Master's. It is Glenn who is the first one to tell me when visiting me in Paris over falafel that my great grand-mother was illiterate. "She was a master of the kitchen," he says, "but never wrote any recipe down. How could she? She never learned to read or write." I'm thirty-three years old, and no one in my family has ever mentioned this before.

FINANCIALLY INDEPENDENT WOMAN

I n my first week of class, I learn how to define myself by learning how to pronounce "I'm a writer" in French.

So as not to sound like a complete idiot, take note not to use a determiner in French for a profession. *Je suis ecrivaine,* not *je suis une ecrivaine.* Directly translated, it means *I am writer,* not *I am a writer,* "a" being the determiner. When I asked why, *"C'est comme ça"* was the response. It's like that. This will be the response for many French grammatical rules that don't make sense to me.

What is entirely logical, though, is that I would come to Paris to write. I love the way everyone says, *"Ah oui, c'est logique! Pour l'inspiration!"*

I'll learn how to say that I'm American, *"Je suis américaine,"* again with no qualifier. The crucial pronunciation is with the final *e,* indicating feminine. If I was a man it would be Ameri-can, as in *yes, we can!* But with the e, it's more like Ameri-Ken. Yes, I'm an American. Born and raised in Los Angeles, CA, and true to this American mythology, I'm immigrant, settler, and native.

My name, Augustine Frances Blaisdell, is after my father's mother, who died tragically when my father was nine. Her name was Frances

Augusta, and she was an artist, a painter. A woman of exquisite grace who, according to my father, was always singing.

I am Irish, Welch, Dutch, English, Russian-Jew from the Ukraine, and Native American Wampanoag. The story goes that those Irish, Welch, Dutch, and English ancestors on my father's side came over on the Mayflower in 1620, jumped ship, and made friends with the Wampanoags, "made friends" being a euphemism for "making babies" or for having sex, but could also be construed as rape. I don't really know. I don't really know if any of this is true. My dad says we're related to Brewster and Turner, who indeed were on the Mayflower, but Turner died within the first months of arriving, and though Brewster did go on to have children, it's unclear where the story goes from there.

Things being what they were, the women and men who might have been from the Wampanoag and other Native American tribes were left out of our family tree, or perhaps included without last names. One day, I'd like to trace my roots—not quite like Alex Haley, but he's the author who comes to mind when embarking on such an endeavor. The proof might even be simply in my father's steamer trunk, but since both his parents were killed by a train hitting their car on the tracks and all that's left is in the trunk, we don't often go in there. Still, this is the story I've been told all my life, and I have always been proud that some part of me is Indigenous—a "real" American or an original "American"—without understanding what that really means. If this story is true, I'm part of a culture that decimated another by disease and deception.

How these stories have been fictionalized, how they have coincided with the romanticized version of major events, makes me wonder if it's just the pervasive narrative that convinced my family they were part of this larger history. It wasn't until the nineteenth century that Thanksgiving entered the American imagination. There were only about one hundred people on the Mayflower, and it won't be until 400 years later, in 2020 for its anniversary, that we'll finally get the real story about the Wampanoag and the reason they were able to help the pilgrims: Tisquantum or Squanto, who had been sold into slavery twice, negotiated his freedom by becoming a translator. When he returned to his village, it'd been destroyed by plague, and he went on to teach the struggling Mayflowerians how to plant corn, hunt, and fish. We accept this story that the nice Native Americans taught the explorers how to survive, but we don't typically question how were they able to communicate. Squanto had learned English because he'd been captured. So it's also about the questions we think to ask.

Nana tells me the story of her father coming to America, but in 2011, I don't think to ask about her mother's story. I don't even learn that her mother was illiterate until after Nana is gone.

On my mother's side, my Nana's father, Jakey Kubernick, originally named Yonkel, came to America from Ukraine through Ellis Island in 1905 when he was just nine years old. Jakey was welcomed by the Statue of Liberty, a gift from the French, the representation of freedom and liberty. A Ukranian Jew with an American Dream, who had saved enough money by the time he was eleven years old to send for his sister.

Nana loves to tell this story: "Jakey's mother and father died very young at the ages of 24 and 27, only months apart from each other from tuberculosis in Russia. At the time, everyone died of tuberculosis. After that, he came to America when he was nine years old and stayed with Aunt Sussy, whose name was Sophie. He worked as a Sears box boy. In those days, there was no law against children working. He made eleven dollars a week and paid Aunt Sussy $1.50 for room and board. That was how he was able to save up to send for his sister.

"His story is unusual—no really, he was a fruit peddler, and he used to go door to door selling fruit. Then he had an accident. He broke his hip with the cart because the horse or donkey got scared. And this is incredible, because it turned out that George's uncle was the partner of Jakey. I think that's just incredible." George was my grandfather, Nana's husband. In Chicago, he had the foresight to recognize that lithograph printing was the next big thing, and he moved to Los Angeles in the 40s not only for the health benefits of sunshine, but also to start a lithograph printing company. I'd work for that same company straight out of college, sixty years later as a "rite of passage." Everyone in my family does.

Jakey was smart and bought properties in downtown Los Angeles, houses in the small cul-de-sac-filled neighborhood of Cheviot Hills. Nana remembers one street near Westwood Blvd lined with track housing that, in the 1940s, you could buy for $5,000. In 1945, $5,000 would be worth about $68,000 today. Now, most of those houses are worth more than a million. No one at the time could have imagined them being worth more.

Nana grew up in the Depression. Born in 1917, she remembers the bread lines, Apple Annie, and barely having enough to eat. Depression-era thinking informs her every decision about money. She cuts coupons, and she negotiates prices. "When I was a little girl, Jakey had a little grocery store, and I used to hide in the back and eat all the profits."

"We used to go to the movies for ten cents," she recalls, "and for ten cents you could go to the nickel theater and still have enough money for a hot dog and a soda. Three cents for the hot dog," she pauses, "with all the toppings. He used to put all the buns on the length of his forearms and fill them up with the dogs and mustard and relish and sauerkraut, you know. And he had these big sweaty arms holding the buns, but we didn't care."

Nana is like any Jewish grandmother, though not like any other because she is my Nana. She speaks fluent Yiddish but thinks keeping kosher plates is ridiculous. Her mother did that and kept plastic on the couches. It was a different time.

I've come to France with a dream of my own and a few concepts in mind. One is Beauvoir's catchphrase: "One is not born, but rather becomes, a woman." The other is Virginia Woolf's equally famous adage, "A woman must have money and a room of her own if she is to write fiction" from *A Room of One's Own*. Those two doctrines informed my decision to come to France. I want to know: what the f*ck does it mean to "become a woman"?

Born in London in 1882, ninety-eight years before me, Woolf's insight is the ambition of most writers. It was specific to women because of the gradual acceptance women could have money of their own. But not necessarily for all women, and this is still being contested, of course, as there are still countries where women can't open a bank account on their own accord. Even the idea of women being able to work isn't universally accepted, as Black, Indigenous, and POC women were doing unpaid work for centuries. This idea Americans have of women entering the workforce in the 1950s and 60s means essentially white women entering the workforce, because Black women were always there, and then they started also taking care of white women's families so white women could go to work. What is considered "work?" What should we be paid to do?

I am not a financially independent woman. I'm independent in other ways, though what this means is challenged constantly. This is one of the several ironies in coming to France in search of Simone, of what we can do for women's rights and for feminism. The point of Beauvoir's *The Second Sex* was not only to prove discrimination, but was also a call for women to be financially independent. Independence would follow once women had money of their own.

I am not a financially independent woman. I do not rely on a husband, but on my Nana, and there is something more comforting and less confining about not being completely reliant on the man with whom I live. There was a time when I was financially independent. I've worked almost all of my adult life, and I've always been extremely cautious and concerned about money. I grew up under the impression we were always broke.

"Broke" means different things to different people. There are different categories of broke. My broke was to know money was always an issue. It didn't mean we went hungry, but it meant we lived an hour away from my high school because that was the house we could afford. It meant my parents didn't own a couch until after they had been married for twenty years because that was when they could finally afford to buy one. It meant I didn't get a computer when everyone else had one and had to do my homework at Kinko's for all of my freshman and sophomore years of high school. It meant I did get a brand new car because my mother had never had a brand new car and she wanted to give me something she never had. It means my mother will still claim to have counted pennies all her life because she married an artist.

~

I am an artist's daughter.

My father, at four years old, would draw underneath the kitchen table. He didn't want to stay in the lines, but to draw his own lines. All he wanted to do was paint, like his mother. Born in 1942, a teenager in the 50s, he had an admiration for James Dean and non-conformity that eventually led him to become a bohemian. Not a hippie—there is an important distinction, as he is quick to remind me. A hippie was after his generation. I think in his mind, a bohemian was more literary as it sprang from the Beat poets. They were more intellectual than the hippies who embarked on free love and acid as an experiment.

After a bout in New York City at Pratt Institute, and following Kerouac's example from *On The Road*, he hitchhiked across the country a total of thirteen times, ultimately settling in a tree in Griffith Park in Hollywood and then, more comfortably, in a bungalow in Manhattan Beach, where he met my mother at a dance club called Cisco's.

It's a story I've heard many times, a favorite. He was stoned, it was 1966. He walked into the club, saw a beautiful girl with straight hair sitting directly under a spotlight, and said to his friend, "You see that girl? I'm going to marry her." His friend said he hadn't a chance. He asked her, "Would you care to dance?"

This is the part of the story where my mom always interrupts, "I had never heard such a gentleman—it sounded so formal." The use of the word "care" impressed her. My mother, who is shy, and was nervous to be in the club illegally as she was only seventeen, said she would be right back, and hurried away to the bathroom. Obviously, they found each other again and danced, and eventually he asked her back to his apartment "to see his sketches." My mother's two sisters thought this was such a line, but they let her go anyway, back to his bungalow near the beach, where they talked until sunrise. It turned out he did just want to show her his sketches. After she left, my father, ever the broke artist, with the last four paint colors he possessed on the last canvas he had, painted her picture.

The portrait of her reclining on the couch in her miniskirt and knee-high boots, long brown hair, eyes bright, a Mona Lisa-esque smile on her face, hangs in a gold frame in their dining room to this day.

You might be thinking, *But wait, where is your mother in this story? Is this just from the perspective of your father, a.k.a. the "artist," the "male gaze"?* Nope. My mother went back to his apartment building looking for him, but she thought his name was Don Lazer, not Blaisdell—hey, the club was loud—and he thought her name was Maria, from the popular musical at the time, *West Side Story:* "Maria, I just met a girl named Maria." Somehow, they found each other. Just like somehow, my ancestors made it here, the circumstances unclear.

There is beauty in never having to question love. They've been married fifty years, and while it hasn't always been easy, they remain each other's best friend.

This is what I grew up with—my mother, much to the chagrin of her family, married for love. My parents instilled in me a belief in love, in never doubting "true love," and that being an artist is not an easy path, which usually means having to struggle with—or, rather, without—money one's entire life. In truth, I should've known better. I should've perhaps followed a different career path. I realize I grew up operating on two quintessential ideas:

1. If you want to be an Artist with a capital A, you believe that means being an Artist with life (i.e., the art of figuring out how to make money doing what you love), so you look for "free" money in the form of grants, sponsorship, or, like the rest of us, work at a 9-5 or like I did 10-6 job.

2. Typical of my generation, I was feeling overwhelmed and apathetic but had been trained to believe I was supposed to do something with all that education that had been given to me. I was supposed to somehow change the world.

A BREAKTHROUGH

In 2009, the year I came to France, the love locks weren't yet on the *Pont des Arts,* and it was hard to find a *bio* (organic) market. Now, organic markets, like Trader Joes or Whole Foods but not as expensive, are as abundant as the *boulangeries,* and eternal love weighs down the bridge.

I came to Paris to write about the simple, undaunting subject of women. Women! They were so trendy then, and are even more so now, though the subject is always pretty popular. Still, most books about women start the same way: enough about women already! (I'm a woman, so obviously I use exclamation points!) It's so, so, so, so annoying. Especially for women. The subject is complex, and there is nothing new to say.

That's how Simone de Beauvoir started her book, *The Second Sex,* which became the foundation for modern feminism. Her first sentences:

> *I hesitated a long time before writing a book on women. The subject is irritating, especially for women; and it is not new. Enough ink has flowed over the quarrel about feminism; it is now almost over; let's not talk about it any more. Yet it is still being talked about.*

It was over sixty years ago that even Simone de Beauvoir felt that this whole "women's issue" was already exhausted. And I feel the same, after pondering women's "condition." The word "sisterhood" still makes me cringe, except when used by the Liberian Nobel Peace prize winner Leymah Gbowee.

Why, when she says it, do I not—as I normally would—think of a ya ya divine secret rainbow traveling pants kind of thing? Is it because she's awesome? Is it because she's Black? Is it because she's tough and has fought for her right to say whatever she pleases? All of that, yes, and also the way she adds a sense of humor to adversity. I see her on *The Daily Show with Jon Stewart*, and she is joyous. By threatening to take off her clothes in front of the governmental building where she and her other sisters protested, Leymah Gbowee ended a war.

The word *Sisterhood* just sounds right coming from her. I believe it when she says it—her women really do have her back. Otherwise, is mine a socially conditioned aversion to the use of *"sisterhood"*? Yes, but an aversion nonetheless. Just as I can be as easily dismissive of goddesses because they've been appropriated by New Age influencers. And just as "New Age" has been appropriated from Indigenous and people of color's cultures. Layla Saad addresses this issue eloquently in her book, *Me and White Supremacy*, when she discusses how the centuries-old practice of yoga now calls to mind white women in yoga pants saying "Namaste." This is appropriation.

I have to face my own prejudice, which is not easy to do when it's been turned into a joke. I have wonderful women friends who I believe are my sisters, so I know it's possible. Roxane Gay discusses this concept of sisterhood in the end of her quintessential book, *Bad Feminist*: "I'm not even sure what the sisterhood is, but the idea of a sisterhood menaces me, quietly, reminding me of how bad a feminist I am. Good feminists don't fear the sisterhood because they know they are comporting themselves in sisterhood-approved ways."

I feel, like Gay, that somehow sisterhood has been appropriated, and I'm not sure I fit in. How do we disrupt our social conditioning? I suspect it's not just social conditioning, but also the residual guilt that I betrayed the sisterhood by sleeping with my best friend's boyfriend. To be fair, they were on a break at the time, which sounds more like something out of an episode of *Friends* than real life. Melis will call me her sister, and though I won't realize it, this will help me heal. It won't be the sleeping together that will be the betrayal, but the honesty.

My girlfriend Edie tells me in 2005 I've been branded as Jezebel, which is the first time I'd hear the name. Two year later, the website Jezebel launched, and writers like Roxane Gay, Jia Tolentino, Ijeoma Oluo, and Lindy West started making their mark. I devoured everything they wrote. Gbowee wins the Nobel Peace Prize in 2011 with Tawakkul Karman, Yemeni journalist and activist, and the president of Liberia at the time, Ellen Johnson Sirleaf.

Can I move beyond what's been ingrained in me?

Yes, yes, I can, and it's through reading Beauvoir and Woolf, Gbowee and Gay, hooks and Lorde, and meeting Judy Chicago and working with Claudine. And though Beauvoir thought the subject of women was exhausted sixty years ago, we were, in fact, just getting started.

When we're talking about women, what we're really talking about is autonomous women, independent women, women who are on their own, who live by their own rules, who are making the rules. These are the women we are told to be, but what does it really mean to be an independent woman? And why are independent women so *à la mode*? In interviewing specialists in the field of women's rights, I quickly realized "financially independent" was what was really implied. Can you be a strong, independent woman but not be monetarily self-reliant?

And if so, is it beneficial to believe there is no doubt of discrimination against women? The women who succeed have an automatic obstacle to overcome: they're women. Their stories, therefore, become more interesting, and they become immediate heroines/(s)heroes since they were able to do anything in the first place.

Or is it more beneficial to believe women throughout the ages have had power and influence, and that inequality was just a ruse, a cultural tactic? Perhaps they were not the targets of discrimination, but instead subversive strategists, like master puppeteers controlling the strings all along, because that was what they had to do to feel more empowered and not victimized. If that's the case, do I want to be the one to blow their cover? Or is women's cover already blown?

Finally, could these two ideas coexist?

Let's be perfectly clear: this is not a battle of the sexes, but a balance of the sexes. It is not men versus women, but the debate of archaic customs rooted in cultural ideology versus the present and the future. Which is a fancy way of saying: *It's not a man's world, it's our world.*

But "being a woman in a man's world" is the narrative. That's the myth. That's what makes women heroines, I mean heroes, I mean sheroes. They had to overcome something or there is no story, and it's the stories we believe.

Though I don't really understand it at the time, I'm writing my own story so I can believe in myself. This is a feminist act, which is indeed an act of sisterhood.

THE TORCH IS YOU: BODY AS POWER

Leymah Gbowee's successful technique of using her own body, or the threat of her nudity, as a weapon is a tactic that will always work. Over the past decade, there have been several women activists who have created our understanding of a new fourth wave of feminism. We begin with the Russian music group Pussy Riot, who gained global fame when five members of the group staged a performance inside Moscow's Cathedral of Christ the Savior on February 21, 2012.

A few months later in September, the activist group FEMEN moves to France. FEMEN is known worldwide for their topless protests. Co-founder Inna Shevchenko, says that a woman's body is sexual by definition in France, and FEMEN members get arrested for sexual exhibitionism, just for going topless, for using their body as their voice. She says during a 2020 webinar hosted by Cécile Fara and Julie Marangé, co-founders of Feminists in the City, that the question to ask ourselves is not "Are women offensive?" but "Why is our society offensive to women?"

In 2011, Egyptian activist Aliaa Elmahdy posts a nude picture of herself on her blog. She stands defiant wearing red shoes with a red flower in her hair. The blog goes viral, getting two million views, and Elmahdy receives so many death threats she flees to Sweden in 2012. She has been living there in exile ever since. She joins FEMEN on several protests.

In October 2012, Malala Yousafzai had already started to make waves for the right to girls' education. Two years later, she wins the Nobel Peace Prize.

The Nobel Peace Prize is a barometer of our global culture. In 2018 Nadia Murad, an Iraqi Yazidi survivor is awarded with a co-winner, Denis Mukwege "for their efforts to end the use of sexual violence as a weapon of war and armed conflict." Murad is the first Iraqi and Yazidi to be awarded a Nobel prize.

Starting with Marie Curie who is awarded the prize in physics in 1903, the Nobel Prize has awarded fifty-one women in its history. And in case you were wondering about the ratio of women to men, this is from their website:

Between 1901 and 2018, the Nobel Prizes and the Prize in Economic Sciences were awarded 590 times to 935 people and organizations. With some receiving the Nobel Prize more than once, this makes a total of 904 individuals and 24 organizations.

What exactly is the Nobel Prize? It started with millionaire Alfred Nobel, the man known for inventing dynamite and the holder of 355 patents. Nobel left his roughly two hundred million dollar fortune to establish the Norwegian committee to give five categories of Nobel prizes to people who benefit mankind, I mean humanity.

The Nobel Committee understand the importance of highlighting these fifty-one women who have won. Fifty-one women out of 904 winners. What they may not highlight as much is the only sixteen Black people who have won, with Toni Morrison being the first Black Woman to win in 1993. It's clear racial and gender discrimination existed these last one-hundred-plus years. The Nobel Prize in all its forms is a reflection of the times and a vision of the future. The Peace Prize was not awarded, for instance, during World War I and World War II. How could it be if the world was at war?

It's also important to note that the Nobel prizes are given from Sweden and the Peace Prize from Norway. These two countries are the leaders in world peace. So it's very important that Stacey Abrams, the American politician who increased voter turn out to change the state of Georgia democratic blue and the Black Lives Matter movement, are both nominated for the Peace Prize in 2021.

Momentum for the word "feminist" continues to build, but the major sea change from unattractive label to attractive proclamation is thanks to Beyoncé. In 2014 at the Video Music Awards, she ends her performance of *Flawless* with the word emblazoned in large letters behind her as the writer Chimamanda Ngozi Adichie defines the word from her TED talk, "We Should All Be Feminists."

In 2010, The International Herald Tribune with *The New York Times* creates a section entitled "The Female Factor." Their tagline states, "Articles in this series examine the most recent shifts in women's power, prominence, and impact on societies around the world, and try to measure the influence of women on early 21st century development." The Female Factor seems to dwindle out in 2017 when Hillary Clinton doesn't become President of the United States, and eventually the section shifts to "In Her Words."

That year, TED, "A nonprofit devoted to Ideas Worth Spreading," which "started out (in 1984) as a conference bringing together people from three worlds: Technology, Entertainment, Design," joined the bandwagon of talking about women and held their first conference, TEDWomen, "focusing on how women and girls are reshaping the future."

Again in 2010, Newsweek launched its own foundation, "Women in The World," which in 2012 featured a conference of major power players of women's rights, women such as Leymah Gbowee, and Christine Lagarde, Head of International Monetary Fund.

Lagarde, the French business woman who replaced the acquitted alleged rapist DSK in 2011.

THE BRAVERY OF BECOMING KNOWN

I n an interview in *The New York Times* in 2010, author of the bestselling biography, *Cleopatra*, Stacey Schiff touches on an important factor of why women are included in the history books.

Deborah Solomon: Did you read biographies in your childhood?
Stacey Schiff: A few. I notice in retrospect that biographies for kids seemed to be about women who are famous for their disabilities, delusions or sensational deaths. The big three were Helen Keller, Joan of Arc and Isadora Duncan.
Solomon: It's true that we wouldn't be talking about Isadora if she hadn't been strangled by her scarf.
Schiff: I fear that sudden demises always help. Think Lady Di or Amelia Earhart or Sylvia Plath.

It is not just disabilities, delusions, sensational deaths or sudden demise that makes women of the past famous but also for surviving something horrific. Think Malala, Nadia Murad, Chanel Miller (the woman who was filmed while being raped while unconscious behind a dumpster at Stanford University in 2015) who went on to write the best selling book, *Know My Name*. This bravery of becoming known, of giving up one's anonymity for the greater good is well known for women throughout history. And sometimes even the tragedy does not prohibit erasure, as their talents and achievements are overshadowed by what's happened to them. Still they have the courage to make beauty out of atrocity. This has been happening for centuries.

Artemisia Gentileschi, the Italian renaissance painter is one such talented woman. Raped by another artist who was supposed to be her mentor in 1611, she came forward and placed charges against him. Her father believed her, which was exceptional at the time. Apparently what was not exceptional was tourturing the survivor to make sure they were telling the truth. As Gentileschi was tourtured with thumb-screws during the trial to prove she wasn't lying. So women are very rarely believed, but we know that already. Gentileschi will go on to have a very successful career and though her masterpieces are not well known for centuries, in 2020 The National Gallery in London features a solo exhibition on her magnificent work.

There is the matter of safety in speaking out, in being known. My dear friend and fellow writer from Columbia University, Shahirah Majum-dar, speaks to this when she talks about the security for the women who were raped by Myanmarese soldiers. Shahirah has been working in the Rohingya migrant camps in Cox's Bazaar, Bangladesh since the genocide in Myanmar in 2017. She is a part of the preservation project of Rohingya culture. We need these stories, but they come at a cost. In the camps the women will carry a social stigma for speaking publicly of their violation. So not only were they at risk before, they are more at risk for speaking out.

And yet, they speak anyway, and we must speak anyway, because visibility changes cultural attitudes. And we must amplify their voices by using our voice.

WHAT IS WOMEN À LA MODE?

What is *Women À La Mode*? It's a bit tongue in cheek. In French, *à la mode* means "in fashion," and in the States, *à la mode* means "with a side of ice cream." For my purposes, it's both.

Women succeed when they are in fashion, and by succeed I mean gain equal representation in fields that were once denied to them. In addition, to be a feminist is to eat well. In Woolf's book, she goes to a lovely dinner party at a men's club. There is wine and delicious food. I'm not sure if there is ice cream, but there is definitely dessert, and she leaves with a warm feeling of being well fed and well taken care of. The next evening, she goes to a dinner at a women's club. Here, there are no candles, no wine, and the food leaves much to be desired. Perhaps there is even no dessert. She leaves hungry and tired and in terrible spirits, and she thinks, *How can we make advances and do good work if we are not well fed?*

This is a simple idea, and yet it speaks volumes. This is what Simone always told Claudine, and it is what Claudine always tells me: we must be well nourished, we must be well fed. Ice cream is a symbol of luxury, of necessity. It is a symbol of self-care. This is what the French are very good at, self-care. They understand—innately, it seems—that in order to take care of others, we must take care of ourselves. Ice cream is taking care of yourself, and in moderation, there is no guilt associated with it. In France, you get to enjoy all the pleasure with none of the guilt.

Dessert is included in the menu prix fixe on lunch menus: appetizer, main dish, and dessert. Claudine always takes ice cream, two scoops— chocolate and vanilla or coffee and vanilla. Many of our most progressive discussions about feminism are over a cold glass dish of ice cream. There is always room for dessert. There is always room for self-care. If there isn't, we can't get very far.

For me, Woolf and Beauvoir and Lorde and Monteil are the literary titans of feminism. They represent what an intelligent women can be. A woman with freedom to education and financial resources.

THE WEIGHT OF EATING AND PRAYING AND LOVING

Under the weight of *Eat, Pray, Love* and *Under the Tuscan Sun,* *Sex and the City* and *Bridget Jones Diary,* I begin writing, hoping my book won't be regulated to chick lit, which is another way of saying it won't be taken seriously.

It will take me ten years to realize I have no control of how my work will be seen. It's not my responsibility. This should be self-evident, but it isn't.

When I started writing these were my touchstones—Elizabeth Gilbert, Francis Mayes, Candace Bushnell, and Helen Fielding. To be clear, I didn't read their work at Columbia, as though these books sold and sold well, they weren't considered "literary" enough. Gilbert and Mayes's books are memoirs, and *Sex and the City* and *Bridget Jones* are novels. *Bridget Jones* gets misaligned with chick lit as it is actually a satire of chick lit, though this has been debated. Rereading *Sex and the City* now, I might even call it satire as well, or a perfect time capsule of living in New York at a very particular moment.

Sex and the City came out in 1997, the television show in 1998. The British equivalent with more social commentary, *Bridget Jones,* began as a newspaper column in 1995 and was published in 1996. The film came out in 2001. *Under the Tuscan Sun* was published in 1996 as well, setting the stage for *Eat, Pray, Love* to stay on the bestseller list for one hundred and eighty-seven weeks in 2006. With the exception of *Eat, Pray, Love,* I hadn't yet read these books, seen the films/television shows, sure, but their effect was palpable.

I've grouped the four books together because of their profound cultural impact in creating a vision of an independent, empowered woman. Also they're about some of my favorite things: sex, travel, and writing. Going on a solo journey. It is also worth noting that Mayes does not go alone to Tuscany in the book; she is with her partner. In the film version, Diane Lane travels alone.

Somewhere in my mind, I've learned women writers have been and continue to be dismissed as just that—women writers writing about women's stuff. From Jane Austen to Grace Paley and still today, women writers are not as present in the literary canon as men. When women write domestic drama, especially if it's humorous, it isn't considered literary. Writing about women is a way for my work to be taken seriously.

In 2020, the statistics of Black and POC representation in the publishing industry are unbelievable, averaging just four to five percent of authors, literary agents, marketers, and reviewers in each of their respective fields. There hasn't yet been a Black *Eat, Pray, Love.* But most literary agent websites advise against comparing your work to *Eat, Pray, Love.*

The generalization was that these main protagonists represented the modern independent woman. The film or television show of these books perpetuated a feminist fairytale: once you love yourself, you'll find love.

Still, chick lit books sell. Why? Could it be that they are well written? Could it be that they appeal to an unconscious or very conscious female desire to live a more happy and fulfilled life? These women, in their own style, are trying to figure out what it means to be an "independent" woman, and the media, in turn, respond: "None of these books, and subsequently films are 'serious,' and they are made only for women (which is a bad thing). There is no gravity to the situations they address, and to read the books and see the films is to participate in cultural phenomena of lightness."

Women have to become independent, while men are inherently so. This sounds like something Simone might say, with her famous line, "One is not born, but rather becomes, a woman." Is this what she meant?

The irony with all of these books or films is that the true main goal is first to love oneself, and in doing so to find a man, to still find true love. A fairytale with one important step added. Perhaps the earlier princesses didn't need to learn how to love themselves to begin with, and we trust they are wise enough to know that Prince Charming doesn't exist, but it wouldn't hurt to have a knight in shining armor. The fairytale ending is the same, even though the journey may appear more empowered.

The narrator may not admit it to themselves or us, but all of them end up with a fairytale ending, all while proclaiming that we are all too intelligent, too independent, too financially savvy to believe in fairytales. The obstacle our modern heroines need to go through first is to figure themselves out, but the end result is love. And why not? And now I'm writing one myself. Spoiler alert: I have the fairytale ending, too. I fall in love and move to France and get married and have two kids, too.

But I don't know that yet. When I first come to Paris, my husband is quick to remind me that I'm highly suspicious of marriage, will go so far as to tell him I don't believe in it and don't think I'll get married. But don't get me wrong, that could've been just as easily a fairytale ending.

While there can be different endings, one commonality these princesses and the women in these books have going for them is visibility.

"Independence" is now equated to happiness, and happiness has come to mean the state of constantly "being in love" and satisfied with "the One."

First you must be alone, and from that aloneness you are sure to find the comfort of yourself, security, and the confidence in being self-sufficient like all the good feminists told us to do. After you've done that, next will come a balanced dependence on a man, where since you love yourself first and foremost, you can begin to love a man equally, and he will love you the way you are supposed to be loved. That is the promise these books propagate, and it's not a bad promise. I'm inclined to believe it myself. It's happened to me, which is why my own book risks becoming another one of those chick lit books. It's a risk I'm willing to take.

APOLOGIES FOR VERSAILLES

Claudine and Bernard take me "biking" in Versailles. I say "biking" because I've actually never learned how to ride a bike. When I ask my parents what happened, their excuse is I was stubborn. I didn't like it, and when I didn't like something, I didn't do it.

I don't remember this about myself.

What I remember is living on a hill, and though my parents bought me a pink and purple bike with a picture of a koala in between the handle bars, I never got around to riding it. Was I busy doing other things? What were my parents doing at the time? It's unclear. I want to say Dad was napping and Mom was at Jazzercise, but it doesn't seem fair. They did teach me so many other things, but biking definitely wasn't one of them. I apologize to Claudine when she sees me wobbling on the bike, unable to balance, and putting my foot down every few seconds.

She quickly decides biking is out of the question, so she rents us a golf cart to tour the immense grounds of the castle. The golf cart speaks to us in French and plays classical music while Claudine apologizes for her driving skills. I forget the fact that, true to a Parisian, she doesn't really drive all that often. "I've never done this before, Augustine, you understand. I'm sorry." It strikes me then how many times she apologizes, and even years later, when she reads one of the first drafts of the book, she'll comment on the pages about women's tendency to apologize, writing a resounding "YES!" in the comments and "Remind me when I do this!"

Claudine also apologizes for the weather. It's freezing in Versailles, so she lets me wear her puffy hot pink vest over my sweatshirt.

Over the years, there have been many friends, lovers, and boyfriends who have sincerely offered to teach me how to ride a bike, but no one ever has. Secretly, I've always said to myself that the man who finally teaches me how to ride is the man I'm going to marry. Something about the selflessness of the act and the taking-care-of-business attitude. This is a thing that, for whatever reason, I feel I can't teach myself.

You need someone to hold the bike. You need someone to let go.

A RENDEZVOUS

When Americans hear the word *rendezvous*, we think of a sexy liaison, scandalous in nature, but in France, a rendezvous is everything, from the most banal to the most enticing.

You have a rendezvous with your doctor, your dentist, your friend, your lover—it's all the same word. There can be something extremely sexy about it, or nothing sexy at all. Still, whenever I say the word to make a rendezvous, there is the possibility something tempting, intriguing, or mysterious may be going on. It gives me a thrill just to use the word, and as I make more friends in Paris, I incorporate *rendezvous* into all text messages and commonplace talk in place of the plain average word *meet*.

I make a rendezvous with Mariel; her French boyfriend, Thibaut; and his single friend Vladimir. They pick a very chichi place called Klong, an Asian-fusion restaurant, on the top floor of a building with a glass ceiling. I see it as an extended metaphor for Women in Business and Hillary Clinton. I came to write about feminism after all, but here the glass ceiling means it lends itself to a spectacular view of the Seine and the Eiffel Tower.

Later, I re-watch *Sex and the City* when Carrie goes to Paris and discover that this is the restaurant she goes to when she meets the Russian's ex-wife. In the scene, they smoke, but now, in 2009, there is no more smoking. Carrie Bradshaw couldn't hack it in Paris, but then, she moved here for a man.

The restaurant has very hip Philippe Starck Louis XIV ghost armchairs. You've seen them. They're clear hard plastic, very designed. They were always expensive to rent, but every event I ever organized in New York City had to have them, if they could afford it.

The food, as you would expect, is served in minuscule portions that are not very good, and the drinks are, again as you would expect, extremely expensive. Mariel is an old friend of my good friend Becca. Mariel is also from California, Berkeley, but for the past year has been working as a lawyer at a major law firm in London. In London, Mariel met Thibaut at a Halloween party when tasked with carving pumpkins, and now they're in love. Ten years later, they're married with two daughters, and she is an American diplomat for the foreign service.

Despite the loud music and small portions, we have a lovely dinner of primarily wine. By the time we leave, we're quite fully intoxicated, and I believe I'm speaking French. After dinner we meet Eric, Mariel's ex-boyfriend, at some Irish pub.

I do know I'm trying to speak French in an Irish pub and the bartender says it's unnecessary with mild scorn in her voice. I do know we order white Russians, a drink I grew to love in high school from watching *The Big Lebowski* too many times. We used to go to the same bowling alley, Hollywood Star Lanes, from the movie in high school. Like many awesome historical buildings in Los Angeles, it's since been torn down.

I'm surprised when Eric speaks French fluently, and the bartender seems to like him better. He sounds perfectly French when he speaks French, but then perfectly American when he speaks English, using words like *hella* and *wicked*. He's wearing his glasses because it's nighttime, something I'll learn about later.

I tell Eric and the girl who is with him, some friend of Mariel's from London, about the difficulty of having a yeast infection in a foreign country and not knowing the word for yeast in Greek, and discovering it's *fungus*, and using hand gestures to indicate where the fungus is. Pretty charming stuff.

Surely, this seductive and totally non-gross conversation is endearing. I'm sure I regale them with stories of my Albanian boyfriend from Greece who came to New York, and how by the time he got there, I was in love with someone else.

Somehow, Eric found it fascinating the way I told the story, as he'll tell me two weeks later when we're on his balcony smoking a cigarette. Not tonight, though. Tonight, in my tipsy stupor, I put him in my phone as *Eric Mariel Friend*. He will stay that way long after the possibility of forgetting who he is, is gone.

A week later, on a Saturday, I have nothing to do and no friends to go out with. Tonight is *Nuit Blanche*, loosely translated as all-night party, the one night of the year when every museum in Paris is free. So I make a decision: I text *Eric Mariel Friend* and ask if he'd like to go with me to the Louvre. He texts back, "Sure, can we stop at my friend's show first? I'm at A Dumas." He means the metro station *Alexander Dumas* on line 2. I learn we're both born in 1980 and he just moved here in February because he found himself becoming a workaholic. He had a successful career as a sound engineer back in San Francisco, but always wanted to live in France. He grew up in South San Francisco, went to French American school and Berkeley too and his mother is French.

On the metro sitting next to each other, I notice his hands, his nails long on his right hand and short on his left. I ask if he plays guitar. "You noticed," he says. I think this scores me cool points.

The band is loud, and then the Louvre is crowded. We "hit up" the *Mona Lisa*, now an inside joke as we hear some Americans say that, and have vodka tonics at a cafe across the street just before it is starting to rain. He invites me to his apartment next Monday as his roommate is having a dinner party. There will be a feminist poet there.

Monday afternoon, we speak on the phone, and Eric says it's best we meet up before and have a drink and maybe some food. Again, I'm surprised when he says his roommate, Rasul, is a 60-year-old trumpet player from Chicago who always eats late. My assumption is that his roommate is our age. "No. Yeah that's why it'll be better if we meet up before, as usually by the time Rasul has finished cooking it's eleven o'clock at night. Musicians."

I suggest a place I've read about in a tongue-in-cheek guidebook, *An American In Paris*. I got it for free at some event I did in New York. It's called The China Club near Bastille. Made famous by the battle of Bastille, the prison that was attacked by the people during the French Revolution, the area now has a great statue and a gigantic roundabout going off in several directions. We meet at the exit of rue de la Roquette.

Even writing it now, I'm filled with that same anxiety I had in the beginning. How quickly I fell for this man. How immediately comfortable I felt around him, like he was someone I'd known all my life.

We order absinthe sours, a few dumplings, and coconut curry mussel soup. We're sitting on a leather couch looking at the bar, the lights glow red, the floor is black and white checkered. The China Club feels like the movie set of the opening scene out of the movie *Indiana Jones and the Temple of Doom*. Being from LA, I might have that movie syndrome, where you turn everything into your own movie—is this a thing? Still, the low lighting, black-and-white-checkered floor and red velvet curtains of The China Club makes me feel sexy and it remains one of the best places in Paris to get a good cocktail. For some reason, good cocktails are not the *forté* of the French.

When we leave, we walk past the Promenade Plantée, the former elevated railway line that has now been converted to a park. And it's there on the corner that we kiss. He says, "Is that all right? I felt like I was getting the vibe, but I wasn't totally sure."

"Yes," I say and smile, "there definitely is a vibe." We hold hands and head back to his place near the metro Alexandre Dumas and the Père Lachaise cemetery, I always called it Pierre Lachaise, where Jim Morrison, Edith Piaf and Oscar Wilde are buried. The party is in full swing when we get there, and I decide it's too late to take the metro home.

I sleep over, and we don't have sex. Later, Eric will say he wanted us to wait. I'm pretty sure I didn't.

On our third date, we meet at the very *bobo area* of rue Oberkampf and Avenue Parmentier in the 11th arrondissement. *Bobo*: a combination of bourgeois and bohemian, at the time basically the French word for hipster.

In France, lingerie is everywhere. Before our date I buy lace-topped thigh-high stockings, just in case I get lucky. We have dinner at a Thai restaurant, and I discover Eric is more gourmet than I realized.

"You've been to French Laundry?" I say. Now he's the one with super cool points, and I'm the one who's super impressed. French Laundry, chef Thomas Keller's Napa Valley flagship, is a restaurant I've known about since 2000, before foodies were even called foodies. It's where my old boss for the restaurant magazine I worked for in Boston went to specifically on her honeymoon.

"Actually, I've been twice."

"Twice, what? How?"

"Both times for free."

French Laundry is upwards of $400 for the ridiculously delicious (Eric tells me) seven-course meal. One of their signature dishes is Oysters and Pearls (caviar). Eric doesn't even like oysters, but liked them then. The actual food we're eating doesn't leave as strong an impression as our conversation.

When we leave, we walk along the canal St. Martin, a place I've never been to before and didn't even know existed in Paris. The lights reflect on the canal, and it really can't get any better than this. We have an easy rapport. We're getting to know each other. He tells me, "I was a late bloomer."

I was not.

Still, he takes me to the very cool Point Éphémère, an artsy bar right on the canal, so-called because it is right next to the fire station. *Éphémère*, the French word for ephemeral, transitory, fleeting. And just like that, he earns cool points again.

"I knew you'd like this place," he says with a smile. Eric is tall with salt and pepper hair already, which I find sexy. When I came to Paris, I was secretly looking for a younger version of Anthony Bourdain, and it seems I found him. He's smart, well traveled, adventurous. He also lived in Italy and speaks some Italian, is clearly into food, and is thoughtful. Plus, I think my Nana will like him.

Before he decided to move to Paris, he came for a few months last year to make sure he liked it and had a lot of musician friends who had told him about the bar. And it *is* my type of place—seemingly on the fringe, underground, and very unique. We get two beers and sit on the edge of the canal. We watch the elevated metro pass by. From here, we can easily take the metro back to my place, which is what we do.

When we exit the metro, Eric says, "Where are we?" Montreuil, a suburb on the outskirts of Paris, is different from Paris in its architecture and style. It's dark, but I can tell from his expression it's now me taking him somewhere he's never been before. Cool points on my side now. And the stockings? The stockings will keep me cool for years to come.

Maybe I can be the sexy Parisienne I came here thinking I wanted to be.

BECOMING PARISIENNE

OR HOW TO EMBRACE YOUR INNER AMERICAN

U nder the same principle as "sexy things sell" and "don't put *feminism* in the title or it won't sell," if you put anything having to do with the French or Paris in the title, it's almost guaranteed to sell.

Why do Americans admire the French so much? What is it about them that entices us so? Is it that we believe the French really know how to live—meaning it is in their culture to enjoy wine, eat cheese, and dessert? It almost certainly has something to do with weight and appearance, and how to wear your scarf in a French way. The French are masters at adding intangible value. For example, champagne has to come from the Champagne region of France. Otherwise, it's not champagne. Together, Eric and I develop this thesis; anything French— perfume, wine, chocolate, bags—has added value because it comes from France.

The proof of the enviable French lifestyle is in the success of books like *French Women Don't Get Fat,* by Mireille Guiliano; *French Women Don't Sleep Alone,* by Jamie Cat Callan; *All You Need To Be Impossibly French,* by Helena Frith Powell; *Entre Nous: A Woman's Guide To Finding Her Inner French Girl,* by Debra Ollivier; *La Seduction: How the French Play the Game of Life,* by Elaine Sciolino; and finally, after all these methods work, *Bringing Up Bebe: One American Mother Discovers the Wisdom of French Parenting*, by Pamela Druckerman.

Is it that the French have five weeks' paid vacation and numerous holidays throughout the year? Most Americans barely believe that to be true. Conversely, all French people I meet want to live in California or New York, until I tell them that Americans only have two weeks' vacation, and then they don't believe me but think twice.

But French women are the most admired and envied women on the planet. I don't have a statistic for this, so you'll have to take my word for it. They exude confidence, sexiness, and independence, a testament to their own freedom. I'd be lying if I said that somewhere, some part of me didn't dream of becoming this sexy Parisian who spoke perfect French and made an art form of being provocative. As Meg Ryan's character in the movie *French Kiss* says to Kevin Kline, "I'm supposed to be this pouty little girl who says yes when she means no and no when she means yes, and I can't do it. Happy, smile. Sad, frown. Use the corresponding face for the corresponding emotion." We're taught no means no and this is important, but where does seduction come in to all of this?

We hear a lot about how American women want to be French women. French women are known as incredibly sexy. If French women don't get fat, Americans get fat easily, though not necessarily gracefully. We would do well to learn not only how to embrace our inner French woman, but also how to embrace our inner American, the French way.

When French women are asked about American women, they say that American women are perfect. American women are always perfectly put together. Every hair in its place, nails always impeccably done. Is there something more desirable than just immaculate fingertips? The cheap manicure is indeed a legend in Paris, but surely there is an attitude that accompanies it. In the classroom at Alliance Française, we're struggling with the alphabet for hours, I is pronounced as E, and E sounds like Uh. It's very confusing. We ask our teacher, how long does it take to speak French fluently? She says, "Three years." Ugh, I think to myself, I'll never be here that long.

Three years later, still living in Paris, I write: it occurs to me that I don't want to become the sexy Parisienne I thought I wanted to be. I don't want to dress up to go to the market. I don't wear lingerie all the time or wear sexy dresses where the point is "to have them take it off you" all the time. I don't want to not smile.

There is a bumper sticker one sees sometimes of vespas and motor-bikes, "Je suis Parisian, J'aime Rien," which means, "I'm Parisien, I love nothing." I am truly a California girl at heart, and as the winter starts to transcend on Paris and it becomes frigid cold and gray, there is something to be said about the constant sunshine that lulls one into contentment.

I love the seasons. I love the food that comes with the changing of fall to winter. When I first moved to New York in 2004, I believed that working in the winter would make me more productive because I'd be forced to be inside working, struggling away with words like they were oysters just waiting to be opened with the right tool. Now, however, the idea of a tan, of working in the sunshine, makes the ideas of being miserable and struggling in the cold seem immature at best.

I will never be the sexy Parisienne. My American accent will always give me away. But French men love American women. While we read books in America about being more French, once we get here, they are happy to hear our American accents, happy to see us smile, and speak in English to us, because they want to practice and sound more American.

French women don't get fat? What a load of hogwash. Everyone gets fat when they are eating buttery croissants, cheese, and charcuterie. Still it's surprising how many ads there are for weight-loss programs, spas that give thinning massages, and Special K. Even Jenny Craig has made it across the Atlantic and is coincidentally across from the Pizza Hut. It is not just that America's obsession with weight has come over to France; they have their own obsession, too.

Our American belief that French women are naturally skinny (a.k.a. they don't think about weight issues or eating like we do) would be completely false. The difference is they are not guilty about it. And it has to do with an acceptance and pursuit of pleasure. After I've been in Paris for a while, I buy an excellent book, *Naughty in Paris* by Heather Stimmler-Hall. She sums it up perfectly when she says:

> *The pursuit of pleasure permeates every aspect of Parisian culture, so that even the cuisine, the fashion, and the language are elevated to sensual experiences. It's no wonder that so many women are drawn to the City of Light. Its unspoken promise of sexual (re) discovery speaks to our feminine sensibilities and inspires us to embrace our hidden desires. Paris, we feel intuitively, is a place where women are truly liberated.*

She goes on to say, "Though the same vices could be found in cities around the world, Paris began to set itself apart from other European capitals with its unabashed view of sexuality." I would amend this to include every American city. "Unhampered by secrecy, the French revealed – and still do, to a certain extent – in flaunting their liberal beliefs and hedonistic activities as evidence of their lack of Puritanical prudery."

Puritanical prudery: that's America to a T. Puritans were one the major influences on American history. As the name suggests, they were not the most accepting of hedonistic pursuits. We can even again return to our Declaration of Independence of 1776: "life, liberty, and the pursuit of happiness." It's happiness Americans are seeking, not pleasure. There is a difference. And it's the pursuit even more than the attainment! Can't sit and enjoy like the French if one must constantly be chasing happiness. That's not to say the French aren't pursuing something and don't like the chase. Though similar, France's motto, "*Liberté, égalité, fraternité*" (or death, which was eventually deleted) "Freedom, Equality, and Brotherhood" is written on every postage stamp and official government correspondence as the rights of the French. Notice it's not *sororité*, sisterhood, despite always being shown with Marianne, the personification of France. We're just supposed to accept fraternity includes us. When I talk with co-founders of Feminists in the City, Cécile Fara and Julie Marangé they say when doing a survey on Instagram that a lot of their followers suggest the French word, *adelphité*, meaning "sibling hood" in place of *fraternité*.

In France, the "inalienable rights" that weren't granted to women in its Declaration are liberty, property, safety, and resistance against oppression. It's time we change both of these precious documents. Cross out the word men, and replace it with people, human beings, humans, so that it reads: "All human beings are created equal." For the French version: "Humans are born and remain free and equal in rights." It makes such a difference. Even seeing the word *human* makes me feel more free.

TALKIN' BOUT MY GENERATION

Gertrude Stein called Hemingway's generation, "The Lost Generation." If they were lost, we're unclaimed.

We're the generation with no name. Like Holly Golightly's cat in *Breakfast at Tiffany's,* we don't belong to anyone and no one belongs to us. We're the generation between Generation X or Y and the dreaded, highly publicized millennials. We may be hipsters, but we definitely don't want to be millennials—unless you're reading this and you are one, then you're super cool. But you knew that already.

No, we're the urban naturalists, the environmentalists, the cultural curators, the anti-materialistic constant consumers of content created by our underpaid counterparts. We're the over-achieving, technology-addicted tastemakers shamelessly engaged in selfie promotion.

We're the instant gratifiers obsessed with sharing—sharing our likes, our apartments, our cars, our experience, our lives. We're uncensored, upscaled, and up-cycled. We act globally, but buy locally.

For all we can say about American culture and the influence it has upon the world, America is good at image-making, and this will be a key to the success of women, all women, trans women, non-binary and genderqueer.

GETTING OVER HEARTBREAK

Back on the metro, anonymous, listening to music, I allow myself to reminisce about New York and my ex. They've become one and the same. I came to France heartbroken, imagining my heart shattered like the *Rolling Stones* song of the same name, dangerous and sharp, tiny little pieces like a puzzle I had to put back together again. Super melodramatic, I know, but when you're brokenhearted, you take what you can get, which means you succumb to the gravitas of the situation and listen to the song *The Things We Did and Didn't Do* by the Magnetic Fields over and over and over and over again.

Breaking up is about the things you had planned to do that, now, you won't do, and about the things you wish you hadn't said. It's a four-minute song that sums up five years of your life perfectly. At the time, I remember all the details: the things we wanted to do, the things I said, and the things he said, but by the time that Gotye song, *Somebody That I Used to Know* featuring Kimbra comes out in 2012, my ex has become somebody that I used to know.

He used to joke that I moved six thousand miles to get away from him. I didn't have to say it to give him the satisfaction of knowing he was right. He took pride in that fact. I had sacrificed so much to be with him. I had sacrificed what I had thought was my most valuable posses-sion, my best girlfriend, my identity, because my identity had existed in relation to her. I broke my own heart. I couldn't let him go because I wanted to insist it had been worth it—losing her over a man, if we were still together, would have meant it wasn't all for naught. What it really meant was I just didn't want to let go of either of them.

But in the end, you have to, and write it off as some crazy sh*t you did in your twenties. It was all very *Beverly Hills, 90210.* (The show epony-mously named after a zip code which ennobled teenage drama and exalted the rich, was created by pioneer Darren Star who would go on to create the other highly influential television show, *Sex and the City.* I told you I grew up in Los Angeles, didn't I?) Which is not to say it was trite. I was devastated, so much so that even four and a half years later, I was still getting over it. (Kelly stole Dylan from Brenda, didn't she?) Just as I, by default of location, he and I were both in NY, she in LA, "stole" him. If we had all been in LA, I'm not sure whom he would've "chosen." Love triangles, like the following phrase, are the oldest in the book.

My ex used to say, "May the bridges I burn light my way." It's not a sustainable philosophy. All these years I thought it was from Julius Caesar and I, like Brutus, had betrayed my friend, betrayed the sister-hood. But a quick internet search reveals the quote is actually from Dylan in *90210,* and it brings it all back home.

The heartbreak of losing her, which was really losing myself in ways I didn't expect, meant that he and I had sacrificed our friendship, too. But in this moment, on the metro, I know my heart is on its way, still a little bruised and with the residue of scars not yet faded, but not shat-tered anymore. I know I've done the journey all these books about women for women expect of their readers: to love themselves and put themselves first and live an independent life without a man. To stop looking for men, be happy with themselves. Once that happens, men appear.

It doesn't occur to me until I meet her that what I'm looking for isn't a man at all. I'm actually looking for a girlfriend.

TURKISH AND FRENCH ALLIANCES

"I met a girl from Turkey in my class at school who already speaks really good French and has an excellent sense of style. She is from the same town I visited when I went to Turkey, and her face lit up when I said I had been to her town. I hope that we can be friends."

I write this the day I meet Melis at the Alliance Française in May. She is by far the most attractive woman in the class, and she is wearing the same ankle-length boots I just bought. Cute little black boots with two useless buttons on the side. She looks like Christina Ricci from the film *Buffalo 66*, and perhaps this is part of the attraction. She's brunette, same round face and same bow-tie lips. In line at the cafeteria, she is talking with some tall, mildly attractive Brit, and she mentions she is from Turkey.

I want us to be friends, and so I say, "I've been to Turkey, Izmir near Selchek."

"Really?" She says, "That's amazing, that's where I'm from! Not many people have been there. What were you doing there?"

I'm excited because I've impressed her. "I was doing a study abroad in Greece, and we went there for a week to see Ephesus." Ephesus, assumed to be the final resting place of the Virgin Mary. The Temple of

Artemis: goddess of the hunt, and among other things, the forest and the trees, fertility, virginity, and, of course, childbirth.

"Oh, of course! But still that's incredible. It's very rare people stop in Selchek. She's been to my hometown!" Melis says to the tall blonde Brit.

"Yeah, great." He can see I override him for her interest.

After class we exchange numbers in the courtyard.

"Augustine, it's difficult here cause, you know, it can get lonely."

"Yes, I know, Melis. We'll hang out."

We become friends, slowly at first. We have in common our love of drinking whisky and wine, eating good food, and going out. We also share our loneliness, as we know so few people in Paris, except for men who don't respond to text messages in a timely manner. Men are easy to find, hard to keep interested. Women are much harder to find, but easy to keep interested. Because of this, we understand the fundamental need for girlfriends, if only to talk about what he meant when he did finally respond.

I hate to tell Melis I didn't like Turkey, but then, I don't have to because she doesn't like Turkey, either, and for the same reasons I felt uncomfortable there. Turkish men were everywhere in groups with seemingly nothing to do but stare and flip prayer beads. Melis knows them more intimately and is over them.

She is very open-minded, like how I believe myself to be, but she is doubtful of love. In my conversations with her, it becomes clear love has become something like God: something to question the existence of; something you do not take for granted exists; and you are now allowed to not believe in it. Together, we create a new religion of not only believers in no God, but nonbelievers in love.

Is there a word for an atheist/agnostic but for love?

COURAGE

Emma becomes another friend and nonbeliever in love. She is a photographer who will also act as my translator, as I realize very quickly I need help to do my other interviews with women.

Emma is a hip girl. She lived in New York for three months doing a personal photo project, the likes of which look like the intimate photographs of Nan Goldin. We meet at Place de la République in front of Habitat, an Ikea-type housewares store which begs for couple disagreements upon entering. République, like Bastille, is a historic roundabout with a statue of the personification of France, Marianne, in the center. This is one thing among many the United States and France have in common: their countries are represented by women. It's no accident that it was the French who gave the United States Lady Liberty at the same time as the sculpture of Marianne was dedicated. In one hand she holds an olive branch, and in the other, the Rights of Man and Citizen. Ironic now that she would hold those rights when they didn't apply to her at the time.

Emma has short brown hair with bangs, an authentic smile with a slight dimple in her cheeks.

She leads me to a quiet street with very cool cafes under big trees. It will take years for me to find this street again. We sit outside and I order a coffee, she gets a Coke. She's brought the book she had made of her photographs of New York. It's clear she found a different world than the one I inhabited. She wears a three-fingered gold ring that says "Miss Fat Booty" in cursive. It connects her index, middle, and ring finger like brass knuckles. Her images of New York are either lonely scenes with no one in them, filled with long shadows and bright colors of the urban landscape, or they are very intimate black-and-white portraits of men with muscles, people on subways, women with big earrings.

She agrees to help me, and we agree on a price. Our first rendezvous is on a Sunday at the home of Jaqueline Pasquier and Hélène de Monferrand. Jacqueline is the Editor in Chief of *Lesbia* Magazine, and her partner, Helene, is a writer who received the Goncourt prize for a first novel in 1990 for *Les amies d'Héloïse.*

They live in the 9th arrondissement on rue Henri Monnier. It is a lovely part of town. Later, it will become the street that has the really good sushi restaurant where I will take Eric before I go back to the States for the summer. Emma and I meet at the St. Georges metro. After we are in the apartment and settled, the beginning is very awkward. The uncomfortable silence, my own nervous laugh and ridiculous attempt at French. When I can't say what I want to say, I'll revert to English, so Emma will translate. But it's slow going.

When Emma asks my question, "Qui sont vos héroïnes?" our conversation finally gets interesting.

"Louise Michel and Olympe de Gouges."

I take my notebook out and have Emma write down the names. I've never heard of them before, but I'm not the only one. Later, after we've done several interviews together, Emma recognizes all of the women we meet have mentioned Olympe de Gouges as a heroine, though Emma says she never learned about this woman in school. I've never heard her mentioned before until I come to France.

In comparison to the States, France starts improving the visibility of women. When I move to Montmartre, the Square in front of the Sacré-Coeur is called the Square Louise Michel, which is again ironic because it was Louise Michel who led the Paris commune that went against the French government and set up their own utopian society, which sadly only lasted ten days and became the reason the Sacré-Coeur was built in the first place—to atone for the sins of the Parisians 125 years ago.

Unlike the United States, France does not have a Women's History Month, which began in 1988, or a Black History Month, which began in 1970. The only other countries who celebrate Black History Month are the United Kingdom, Canada, and Ireland. Women's History Month is celebrated in the US, the UK, and Australia in March, and in October in Canada. Emma is about the same age as me, so we can only hope kids are learning about them now.

Together, we learn that Olympe de Gouges was born May 7, 1748. She wrote her *Declaration of the Rights of Woman and the Female Citizen* in 1791 in response to the French Constitution, which did not give women the right to vote, own property, or divorce. The French Revolution sparked the idea of liberty, equality, and fraternity, France's kindling catchphrase, but this "equality" excluded women.

It was Olympe de Gouges who used the method of writing an exact parallel copy of the same document of the *Declaration of the Rights of Man and of the Citizen*, only changing or adding women to the mix. She attempted to appeal to men in power, by asking questions to change the minds of her male readers based on their common sense—logically, women should have the same rights. It didn't succeed. She was convicted of treason in 1793 and immediately beheaded by guillotine at the age of 45 at what is now the Place de Concorde in Paris.

The guillotine, it sounds so archaic, so ancient, from olden times, but we can't allow ourselves to be mistaken. The last woman to be executed in France was as recently as 1945 during the Vichy regime of German occupation. The woman—Marie-Louise Giraud. Her crime—performing twenty-seven illegal abortions, which became a capital crime punishable by death under the Nazis. Giraud was a woman's right activist, a mother with two children married to a sailor, who came from a poor family, cleaned houses, and, during the war, rented rooms to the sex workers. Not far from where we're sitting in the courtyard of the rue de la Roquette prison, she was beheaded at thirty-nine years old. So we're lucky, we're not going to be beheaded for performing or having an abortion in France anymore at least.

Lest you think France is barbaric? The United States is the only western country which retains the capital punishment.

After the interview, they serve us whiskey. French women like whiskey. I fit right in with this, and it does what whiskey does best– lubricate the mood. The conversation becomes smooth, as if suddenly we've become old friends, laughing at how awkward that all was. Jacqueline says, "We must have courage!" The incantation in the way she says it is so definite, so inspiring, so French. *Cour-rage.* Pronounced more like coeur, the word for heart and raje, not rage, as we would say. (When you look as if you're about to give birth at any moment, strangers on the street will tell you, *Bon Courage!*) They have fought their battles, and now, like most women I have met, they say it is our turn.

When Emma and I leave, Emma turns to me and says, "This project is good. I mean good for your life to meet such women, good for you to be a strong woman."

At the time I agree, but we don't really need courage, I think. There is nothing yet to be courageous about, or so I think at the time. There is no sense of urgency.

Emma points out that they address each other using vous. She finds this very odd, as this comes from a different generation. It is the formal way to address your lover. Just like in the song, *"Voulez vous coucher avec moi ce soir?"* Typically, it is a very polite way to ask someone to sleep with you.

We wonder if sex workers back in the day addressed the men they were about to sleep with in the vous form, or alternatively if they addressed the women in the brothels in the vous form.

In my imagination, it would seem the Madame of the house would of course be in the vous form, but not necessarily the sex workers.

Emma comes with me to several interviews, and after every interview, we have coffee, an espresso for her and a cafe creme for me. Once the coffee is finished, she puts her cup upside down for the coffee grains to dry. We try to tell our fortunes in the remains.

"What do you see?" I ask her. It almost always relates somehow to men. After our very independent feminist talk, we'll return to being, for the abundance of a dismissive nomenclature, "just girls."

WOOLF'S SENTENCE CONTINUES

I imagine one needs much of the same to write nonfiction.

Woolf inherits five hundred pounds a year from her aunt, and though five hundred pounds a year doesn't mean too much anymore and wouldn't be sufficient to live in a major city like London, the point is that you have to have money. Money affords her the freedom of the mind.

Woolf's sentence continues: "and that, as you will see, leaves the true nature of women and the true nature of fiction unresolved." Obviously this is what she goes on to discuss in her essay, imaging if Shakespeare had had a sister, how she would have fared, (badly), wondering why women's mothers and grandmothers had not left them such nice libraries and schools as men had, and citing that of women's right to vote passed in England in 1928 and the money she receives from an aunt who passed away, the money is infinitely more important.

No force in the world can take me from my five hundred pounds. Food, housing, and clothing are mine forever. Therefore, not merely do effort and labor cease, but also hatred and bitterness. I need not hate any man; he cannot hurt me. I need not flatter any man; he has nothing to give me. So imperceptibly I found myself adopting a new attitude towards the other half of the human race. It was absurd to blame any class or any sex, as a whole. Great bodies of people are never responsible for what they do. They are driven by instincts which are not within their control...Moreover, in a hundred years, I thought, reaching my own doorstep, women will have ceased to be the protected sex. Logically they will take part in all the activities and exertions that were once denied them. The nursemaid will heave coal. The shopwoman will drive an engine...Anything may happen when womanhood has ceased to be a protected occupation.

Twenty years later, Beauvoir continues Woolf's declaration by promoting self-sufficiency and independence. When Simone was writing, the word "gender" as we know it wasn't even invented. There were no gender studies in school, no discussion on where women may have been erased from history books. They simply weren't there because supposedly they literally hadn't done anything to affect the course of the world. There was no attempt to find them.

Now it seems we don't need to prove sexism exists. It's obvious now. So I'm not going to waste my time proving it. Beauvoir's book proved that discrimination against women prevails, and as Claudine says, "The thesis of Simone's book was that women needed to be financially independent to have freedom. That was the key—not to rely on anyone else for money." We can congratulate ourselves that this has come to pass. Most women do indeed have their own money. But let us not forget that nearly half of the world's population, roughly three billion people, live on less than $2.50 a day.

It's touted as a recent discovery that *if you educate a woman, you educate a nation.* Women are the key to our survival. Initially, this African proverb was attributed to the Ghanaian scholar Dr. James Emmanuel Kwegyir-Aggrey (1875-1927). Now several websites use it as a proverb catchphrase for different women's organizations.

Why did I think French women might know the answer to...well, what was the question? Women are not yet where they should be? Where do we think they should be now?

They should have equal parity in governments throughout the world. Rwanda and Andorra are the only two countries that have this, though Cuba and Sweden are close.

They should have equal pay, but on average, women earn 17% less than men worldwide.

They should not be bought and sold, but approximately 40.3 million people are enslaved. This figure comprises the twenty-five million humans in forced labor (4.8 million in sexual exploitation of which ninety-nine percent are women) and includes fifteen million girls in forced marriages.

They should be educated, but two thirds of the world's 796 million illiterate adults are women. This is really just a few simple demands, but that's a good start.

If you are a working woman, or are dating a working woman who has her own bank account, can vote, can hold property, has access to contraceptives, menstrual products and can have an abortion, then you are a feminist, because you are participating in the pleasures, rights, and freedoms allotted to you thanks to feminism.

If you're reading this book, you are what a feminist looks like.

WE ARE A MINERAL RESOURCE

WE ARE RARE EARTHS

Though Claudine and I meet for several lunches during my time in Paris, it's already some time in June when I come to her house to officially interview her. What she says completely surprises me, and everything turns out to be true.

I set up the video camera so that it looks upon the portrait of Simone done by her sister, Hélène de Beauvoir. Yes, Hélène was an artist, an incredible one, and in 2018 the Würth Museum in Strasbourg organized a retrospective of Hélène de Beauvoir's work. Her canvases filled the two-story museum, and the portrait of Simone we're sitting under was featured. We don't know this will happen. For now, we sit in the two pink and cream flowered upholstered 18th century chairs inherited from the Beauvoirs, an old aristocratic family. The chairs have been casually clawed up by Hélène and now Claudine's cats.

Claudine begins, "It's great to see you, the young generation!" And she takes hold of my hand.

"It's so great to see you, too," I say as I squeeze tightly back. "When did you know this is what you wanted to do for women's rights?"

"In 1968, I was not aware of it, when the revolution happened. But my mother had been fighting to obtain her career and her jobs in academia. She was a scientist, which was very difficult because she had an accident, a badly wounded hand. And she was always staring at men scientists, coming to the house and saying, 'This man does not like women, this man is antifeminist,' and I would be five years old and she would tell me that in such a dramatic tone.

"And these men were usually scientists. So even though I was only five years old, I knew I wanted to be respected. I knew I wanted to work and have a career, but I knew I did not want to live and go through what she had gone through. It is thanks to May 1968, the student riots, which was only directed by young men, who had less experience than I had, as I had been behind the Berlin wall. So at the time I did have some concrete experience, at a time where people did not travel as much. I had been in the US, also in high school as a student in the USSR and I was from a very political family.

"Nevertheless we as women were only allowed to shut up. So when the Women's Movement started, I was very excited. But I heard they were terrible, horrible, hysterical women. I entered Simone's room, which was in Montparnasse, nearby the cafes of La Couple and La Rotonde, where she and Helen were born upstairs. My life changed that day. And I became one of those women who were horrible…"

"Do you think we need a new word for a feminist?"

"You have to understand. A feminist has been considered negative since the word was born. Feminism is probably the most obscene word in the world. Men and women are afraid of being called feminists. Women are afraid because they are afraid men won't talk to them anymore. I have many friends who say, 'Though I am not a feminist, I think there is a problem with women rights.'"

"Ridiculous, which is saying the same thing," I say.

"Let me just say, a feminist is a person, a human being who simply wants human rights and equality to be observed and considered. It's nothing more and it's nothing less. But even that is considered not possible, and considered as very scary.

"We don't say it anymore as it's not the fashion in the 21st century, but I will use it. I think the worst racism in the world is sexism. Sexism is racism against women. I am against any kind of racism. The problem with sexism is that you have the word sex in it, and I think people immediately and unconsciously think of other matters."

Sexism isn't supposed to be sexy, I think to myself. In France, race and sex are both considered social constructs. I don't know this at the time, as I'm still contemplating if people's minds really go to sex when they hear the word sexism. I am not aware yet of the concept of intersectionality, though whenever there is a question of sexism, I discover if we put the discriminatory act in question in terms of racism, it instantly becomes clear certain behaviors would not be acceptable. And likewise, when racism is considered through a sexism lens, white women in particular are more likely to understand it.

This is what Rachel Cargle writes in 2018 in an essay in *Harper's Bazaar*, "When Feminism is White Supremacy in Heels."

"I've learned through my work that white women seem to only digest race issues when it is reframed in the light of (white) feminism. So I often have to lay it out this way:
• When you try to exclude yourself from the conversation of race by saying things like "I don't see color," or "I married a black man and have brown kids," that's just as irrational as a man saying there is no way he could be sexist or misogynistic because he has a daughter.
• When you seek to not be lumped into the conversation about oppressive systems against marginalized people, because you view yourself as woke, you are essentially screaming "not all men."
• When you try to rationalize police brutality by saying "but black people also

kill black people," you're coming in with the same argument that men have
when they say "she shouldn't have worn that skirt, she deserves to be raped."

In 2011, a Hasidic newspaper the Hasidic newspaper *Di Tzeitung*, erases Hillary Clinton and Audrey Tomason from a photo of the situation room the moment they got the news Osama Bin Laden had been killed because in accordance with Rabbinical board, they are not allowed to publish picture of women because of modesty. If for a moment we say that instead of being women Hillary Clinton and Audrey Tomason were Jewish, and some newspaper decided to erase them, or instead President Obama was deleted because he is Black, we would never stand for it.

Later in 2015, *Elle UK* magazine will run a campaign, #MoreWomen, where they will photoshop the men out of pictures to prove how few women there are in influential places and how much space there is. The pictures work only if you see the before and after.

What I think Claudine means when she says this or how I interpret it, is that sexism isn't taken seriously, not as seriously as racism. This is why Crenshaw's work is so important.

"What do you think is the greatest danger facing women today?" I ask.

"The greatest dangers for women are very simple: it's overpopulation and mineral resources. Overpopulation means we're not going to be able to feed everyone, and already over one billion people are not being fed. I'm not saying we could not feed them; we could, but what I'm saying is we are in a global economic war for access to mineral resources, and also for oil, for access to oil, and I always say the more expensive oil gets, the more in danger women's rights will get. Because the countries where there is oil are not the best—and that's an understatement, of course—are not the best in terms of women's rights in the world. So governments don't care about women rights.

"They need, when they negotiate, to have something that they can accept in exchange for getting oil or mineral resources and so they are going to, just slowly in a very subtle way that you young generation will not see like we can see it, because you have not been raised in the same kind of atmosphere and environment. So you are going to have to be careful, and fight. What I mean by fight, I don't mean to fight against men. I mean to show every minute that you want your rights to be preserved and respected, because otherwise, very subtly, you are going to lose them, and you're going to wake up one morning having lost part of your women's rights, and you will not even realize it. And when you will realize it, it will be too late."

At the time, I don't truly believe her. But, of course, this ends up being true.

"Overpopulation means we're not going to be able to feed everyone. We're not going to give access to water, to food, to minerals. Also mineral resources are not in the most democratic countries, usually. So that's why I think solar energy and environmental energies are very important because it may help your generation. They are the energies that will help women to keep their rights. At the same time, the biggest danger for your generation as young women is the religious situation."

"How so, Claudine?"

"Communism has died. And what was the importance of communism? The importance of it was that it was giving, even if it was a horrible dictatorship and it killed millions of people. So I'm not praising communism. What I'm saying is that in terms of strategy in people's mind, communism gave hope for justice to the poor people in the third world and for the poor in wealthy countries, a sense of self-respect and justice. I'm not saying that I'm defending it, but it was a value of hope for poor people.

"Now communism has shown what it really was, horrible dictatorships. I spent some time in the Soviet Union. Now that it's gone, religion has taken its place. Poor people need to have hope. Starving people need to have hope. At the same time, there are a lot of countries where religious people have lots of money from mineral resources, so the result is they can provide health care; they can provide education. So they are doing the work that communism has done, which is to assert that every human being in life is hungry for dignity. Not only hungry for food but for dignity, and this religious thing is giving a sense of dignity to every human being, including the very poor. It's giving a sense dignity and a sense of self-identity. And every human being needs to be acknowledged as a human being, as a citizen of the world. So this dignity that governments are not capable of giving, well"—her voice raises—"the religious people, even if they are the most totalitarians of people, are giving it. This is why overpopulation and religion are the two worst dangers for women in the world.

"And because of the climate change you're going to have huge immigration. Bangladesh is going to be one day totally covered by water. Bangladesh at the beginning of the 20th century was one million people and now it's ninety million people. You're going to have a lot of little wars, and the people who will lose are the women, on all these matters."

It's the first time I'm hearing this, so it's a lot to take in. We take a deep breath together.

"So what do we do?"

"I know I sound pretty terrible. But there is one optimism: that you young women are much stronger than we were. You are much stronger in the sense that you have less self-doubt because you've been raised by parents who were mostly more respectful of women than our generation.

"I was lucky to have parents who respected women. My father respected my mother and was very supportive, and wanted her to achieve what she wanted, but that was exceptional in their generation after World War II. My generation was put down all the time by young men. It was terrible. We had to fight against the self-doubt; we had to create the Women's Liberation Movement to free ourselves. You don't need that.

"You've been raised in the feeling of that generation. So you are stronger in the sense that you are not wondering all the time if you can do things like men. You're a human being before being a woman, of course you're a woman, and enjoy it.

"So the minute you decide to fight, and what I mean by fighting is not taking a gun, what I mean is so that the minute you're going to decide you don't want your rights to be attacked, you're going to be stronger than a lot of people think."

I think of this moment whenever I read depressing news and I believe, like so many of the things Claudine has said over the years, and in this interview, she is right. We are stronger. We will be stronger than people think.

"So how do we get involved?" I ask.

"There is one thing which is really important, which is the internet, which is a fantastic opportunity. But I would like to say something as a souvenir [*souvenir* being the French word for memory]. When we changed the world in France by making abortion legal. We were less than thirty women, and I would say with Simone and around Simone de Beauvoir, we were about ten women. So this is to say, there is always hope. You can change a world. Thirty people can change a country.

"For years, there were people who would not talk to me, or they would insult me. For the first five years from 1970 to 1975, we were 'horrible, sexually frustrated.' I mean, how could people talk to us? And then after five years, we were becoming fashionable. Well, if you become fashionable, it means that your ideas are starting to consciously spread into people's minds."

"So I think what you're going to have to do, which is going to be necessary when you realize you are in danger, you're going to have to unite. Now, the internet is very useful, because you can unite within a few minutes.

"You also have to put pressure on the government, on the economy. And to have other women's images. Like in America, you have Women's History Month. And I think this is a fantastic idea. I have tried to suggest to the French government, and it didn't happen because it's intolerable that women can be put ahead on the scene, in the light, where men want all the light. You're going to have to unite the idea: you should be more political than you think you are.

"What I mean is, the strength of the French Liberation's movement is the fact that we were extremely politicized young women, which means that we consider that everything is political…a very subtle political way. You have to be politically concerned about the conflicts in the world to survive. Access to food, water, and energy, because these are going to have consequences.

"You are going to have to be alert enough on what is happening, economically, politically, to speak up! Since Simone de Beauvoir died in 1986, there has been no woman that has been allowed to speak publicly, and I always say this is on purpose. This is because they don't want a woman to have women who speaks up and says things."

"Well, that brings me to next question. Who are your heroines?"

"The first, of course, to me is Simone de Beauvoir, who published *The Second Sex* in 1949, who changed my mother's life and with whom I became friends.

"I will say two more who are not being treated well enough in the rest of the world these days, and I'm very angry about it. Eleanor Roosevelt. I'm not saying this because you're American. When Simone de Beauvoir was writing *The Second Sex,* she wrote it during 1947-1948, she wrote it in two and a half years, just a few thousand pages.

"Oh, you know, no problem, Claudine, just a few thousand pages." We both laugh, knowing how hard just a few thousand pages can be to write, and knowing how complex *The Second Sex* is just to read.

"At the same time, Eleanor Roosevelt was negotiating, was chairing the committee to write the Universal Declaration of Human Rights. This document is one of the reasons that you have equality. So you have to read it, and when you read it, you are going to see. I've read about in the archives. They wanted to write, 'All men are created equal.'"

∿

A brief interlude here on the Universal Declaration of Human Rights: the thirty articles that comprise the document were written in response to World War II, when it was determined that there needed to be international laws guaranteeing the rights of human beings. As Article 1 states, "All human beings are born free and equal in dignity and rights. They are endowed with reason and conscience and should act towards one another in a spirit of brotherhood." They still kept brotherhood in there, but hey, at least they used "human beings," which is start.

"And there is my third, Hansa Mehta. She was the leading lady for the liberation of India, and she was representing India in the committee of eighteen people. There were two women, and she said, "I cannot go back to India, my country, because Indian men are going to take for granted that it's only men who are equal. And it took them a year to come up with the word 'human beings' and to accept it. Our French constitution is all men. But, you see, your generation could ask for that to include women or change it to 'human beings.' I know it's very difficult to change your constitution. It's like the Bible."

"I think one thing that is really nice about your generation, is the fact that the relationships between young men and young women in the Western world is very casual. We were put down very rapidly, we were hardly able to express our thoughts on serious matters. The notion of equality in a love relationship was a lot harder. Also, we were not allowed to live with a man without being married."

According to Melis, this is still the way in Turkey. Even as a forty-year-old woman, she still lives with her mother because it would not be acceptable for her to live alone.

"The ideal world would be if men and women could stay at home with their children if they want to stay at home. Why not? I think it's really important that your generation looks at the Nordic states, like Sweden and Norway, because they are ahead of us. Because you're going to need them. What I mean is that I understand some young women want to stay at home. Because they've seen their mothers working hard, and they don't want to do both. What I'm saying is be careful: real independence starts with economic independence, and usually men like younger women. You're not going to be young all your life.

"I think your generation is going to have to rebuild what we have destroyed. We have destroyed the planet in a century. I mean there are things which are too late. You're going to have to rebuild again, and also give again a sense of value. Money is not the value. I don't care whether I have a big house. I prefer to be in a comfortable house. But I think the hope of your generation is that you have to give values back. The planet is so wasted that you are going to give values again.

"Human trafficking is worth billions of dollars around the world, and it's going to happen more and more because there are no borders anymore. It's much easier to organize human trafficking and pros-titution.

"And because of the globalization, let's get values back, and that your generation can do. And I think there is hope because your generation sees how the world has been destroyed. So there is hope."

"It's overwhelming, we don't know where to begin…"

"You start with a small thing, but you start, even if it is local, but it's a start. Even a small thing is useful, and that gives you an idea to become national and then international. The problem is also your generation is raised with television, and TV has the positive aspect and negative aspects. The positive is that you see what's happening around the world, the negative is that you are very passive."

We take a beat.

"Well, I know we've been talking about this the entire time, but what is your message to young women and men?"

"Enjoy life, because life goes very fast. When Simone de Beauvoir was saying this to me, I thought it was so long when I was young. It is true that it goes very fast. Make your century beautiful. You can make your century beautiful. The century will be what you will it to be. Don't ask anyone else to do it for you. Do it!

"Love, a man, a woman, whoever you want, have a partner, enjoy it, be happy, be respected. Don't ever let anyone put you down. Eleanor Roosevelt always said, 'No one can make you feel inferior unless you accept it.' Even with love, be careful, stand up, and be active and don't complain with how the world is. Start changing it tomorrow. Today is even better, but it's a little too late tonight."

We laugh together.

"Yes, Claudine, we must have dinner!"

"Yes, of course Augustine, we have to eat! A good feminist is a feminist who eats well. That's what Simone de Beauvoir always said.

"And I want to say now, in conclusion, I understand now how she could be happy to meet young people. So I want to say that you are a sunshine. You are the present and the future of this planet. It is my duty to transmit, but it will not only be your duty, it will be your pleasure, as it is my pleasure. Take good care because women need you and the world needs you. I'm getting too old. I can still do a few things, but you are going to have care of yourself."

TIENS AU COURANT?

eanwhile, I make more friends. We don't know at the time
that our time together in Paris intersects with this magical
time in our lives. That thanks to that and social media we
will stay in touch even after we're no longer in Paris.

I meet Suzanne and Sander, a Dutch couple who become dear friends.
They introduce me to Gosia, a polish woman who owns her own business. I meet Jarbas, another Brazilian like Carol who has taken a
month-long vacation. Together, we practice our French so much so that
when I speak French, people will question if I'm from Brazil. Together
we go to the gay bars of Pigalle, and he's the first one that I have a
picnic on the Seine with. I'm so happy that I finally have a friend like
all the rest of the Parisians. He humors me with interpreting text
messages from Eric, and one in particular when Eric is supposed to
meet us but can't. He sends, *"Tiens moi au courant."*

We spend a good hour contemplating what this could mean. We both
have simple cell phones, so we can't just look it up. Jarbas suggests
something very romantic, like "he'll keep you in his heart," derived
from the word *coeur,* meaning heart. What it actually means is simply,
"Keep me posted." Which is a phrase that comes in handy as well.

My parents come to France, and we spend one week in Paris staying in Barbara's apartment and one week in the South of France. I invite Eric to come with us, but he's in the Pays Basque with his godmother, Marie Antoinette. That's her actual name. But most people call her Marinette or Marie. When we come back from the South, we spend two or three extra days in Paris, and my parents finally meet this man I've been talking about our entire trip.

My parents and I want to do something very special for Claudine, so I find the perfect place. We take her and Bernard to Hélène Darroze's flagship restaurant in the 6th. Knowing Claudine now, I know she's embarrassed. Darroze is one of the thirty-three female chefs in France with Michelin stars. In 2015, she becomes an integral part of the French television show *Top Chef*.

In France, *Top Chef* is three hours long on Monday nights. It's like watching *Lord of the Rings* every Monday. There are only two commercial interruptions, and like most shows in France, it starts at 8:40pm and lasts until just before midnight. In France, it's assumed that everyone is on a similar schedule and that by 8:40 the kids have most likely been put to bed, dinner has been eaten, and now it is the adults' time.

On the show, the contestants cook for three hours. They have none of the drama that the American show has, for the most part they are all compatriots. They are usually nice to each other. Part of a team.

On our last lunch together before I leave for the States, Claudine reveals she's been writing a book all this time, and she wants me to be in it. A rush of jealously surges through me. It's the same feeling I get over the years when someone publishes a new feminist book, of which there will be plenty. But feminism is my thing! Similarly, someone will tell me they want to be a writer, and I'll think, *But writing is* my *thing!*

This sense of possession from what we now call a scarcity mindset is how capitalism functions. Or this fear that someone is going to "steal" your idea, but we have to reinforce the idea that no one can do it the way you do.

I'm now very suspicious of why we tell artists they can't make any money.

But seriously, how has she written a book while working more than full time as a Minister of Foreign Affairs while I haven't been doing anything else but writing and feel nowhere near done?

"During my lunch break," she says.

We say goodbye. Will this be the last time I see her? It's the reminder of our mortality, the way continual leaving will do. Each time you get on a plane or have to say goodbye, you have to recognize you don't know if you will see each other again.

On my last morning in Paris, I leave a suitcase at Eric's house with the promise to return. He's offered to keep it for me, and I've taken it as a good sign. In a fury the morning we're leaving Paris, on the hotel computer because I'm a nervous wreck about leaving Paris and not be able to come back, my mom says, "Just make the appointment. Do it now."

I schedule my visa appointment at the consulate in Los Angeles. I don't have all my paperwork together yet, but I do it anyway as by the time my appointment comes, I will. *Just one more year*, I tell myself. I have to come back.

PART II

THIS IS WHERE SIMONE DIED

I return to Paris after a summer in New York and Los Angeles, and I start right where I left off: seeing Eric again, having lunches with Claudine, and taking classes at the Alliance Française.

I am back in the same apartment for now, but I spend the month frantically searching for a new one. I visit some awful places and am reminded of searching for my apartment in New York, which ended with a super almost beating up the realtor I was with in the stairway of a shabby building in the Lower East Side. The realtor was trying to be shady and show me an apartment that was still under construction, and the super wasn't having it. This is not nearly as bad. Luckily, I meet Laetitia Lafayette, a charming French woman who likes me (most likely because I'm from New York, sort of), and who designed the apartment that will become my home. It's literally steps away from the Sacré-Coeur, in the 18th arrondissement, in the cobblestoned streets of Montmartre.

Metro Chateau Rouge, line 4. The second most packed metro in all of Paris, the first one being Barbes-Roucharart, the stop before. This area is what the French call *quartier populaire*, which means the working-class neighborhood. Beware of *populaire*, by the way: this is one of those *faux amis*, meaning fake friends. It's a word that sounds the same in French and English, but doesn't mean what you think it means. In French, *populaire* doesn't mean popular; that's *bien connu,* or well known. The underlying meaning of *populaire* is vibrant, lively, and immigrant.

The metro line 4 cuts straight through the city from North to South, from the train stations of Gare du Nord to Gare Montparnasse. To step out of the metro at Chateau Rouge is to be overwhelmed by people. Immediately, I step into an open-air market that sells specialty items not found in every market quite yet, like plantains, sweet potatoes, dried black beans, passion fruit, cilantro, and copious amounts of fresh mint that tickles the nose. There are a few other neighborhoods you could find these items, like the 13th and the 20th, but the open-air market always provokes this feeling of adventure, of the foreign and unknown.

Paris is foreign already, but it's also familiar because of all the movies I've seen. This isn't usually what you see in the movies. This is what one would deem "exotic," though that's a loaded word. It's exotic and exciting to me but it's also welcoming because it is diverse—a real *mélange,* as Montmartre is known for of people. Walking up rue Poulet to the apartment, I see that the only shops on this street are hair-braiding places, with pictures of all the different hair styles in the windows. And it's quite a family-friendly scene. On Friday and Saturday nights, this street is bumping, with everyone getting their hair done for the weekend. On early Sunday mornings, it is quiet—the only things left are hair tumbleweeds at your feet.

If you take the metro and follow the stops on line 4, you'll traverse the former central market called Les Halles, which was closed in the 70s due to a rat infestation so is now a shopping mall. Next is Cité, the island in the middle of the Seine and of Paris. Above are the police department and Notre Dame, which then leads to the St. Michel fountain in the 5th arrondissement, home of the Latin Quarter—it's overrun these days with tourists and gyro shops, but it used to be the home of intellectuals and students from the Sorbonne. The students are still there, as well as the bookstores, for now. The most famous bookstore is

Shakespeare and Company, where James Joyce and Hemingway hung out with Sylvia Beach.

The next stop is Odeon and Saint-Germain des-Pres. Odeon is still a good meeting spot, and Le Comptoir, a hole-in-the wall tapas place with standing room only, makes a delicious crepe with sun-dried tomatoes and foie gras brochettes. It's where Anthony Bourdain goes in the first episode of his show *No Reservations,* entitled "France, Why The French Don't Suck." I'm obsessed with this show and Anthony Bourdain when I arrive in Paris and have printed out all his recommendations of places to go.

On to Saint-Germain-des-Pres and the expensive cafes of Deux Magots and Cafe des Flores, where it's rumored that the servers make over two hundred thousand euros per year and the most inexpensive food item on the menu is the onion soup for nine euros.

It didn't always used to be this way. These cafes used to be for the working class, the proletariat, the people fighting for a cause, like Simone and Sartre who met there every day at the same hour to write on the second floor. There is a plaque bearing their names, and the square in front of these cafes and the Louis Vuitton store is called the Simone de Beauvoir and Jean Paul Sartre Square. They made these cafes what they are. Those who know why they go want to sit in the same place they once sat and think big about being an intellectual.

Next is St. Sulpice, where I discover the amazingness of Pierre Herme macarons. There is a debate between who has better macarons, Pierre Herme or Ladurée. Founded in 1862, those who are more classic will like Ladurée, and those who like more inventive flavors will prefer Pierre Herme. Who thinks to use olive oil and mandarin orange in a macaroon? Don't be fooled, Pierre Herme is by far superior. After that distraction comes St. Placide, where I first met Claudine and where the Alliance Française is, followed by Gare Montparnasse, the modern train station and only skyscraper in all of Paris, and then Vavin. And this is where I wait for Claudine on a still-warm September day with my rental contract in hand.

I wait on the street for her for a long time, looking in the shop windows. It's an expensive street. I've returned to Paris on a student visa for a year and the night before have found an apartment, the apartment that will be my apartment. Claudine is at an appointment with her doctor, and when she finally meets me, she says, "My doctor wants me to go to the hospital because she believes I am about to have a heart attack, but I don't have time for a heart attack right now. I have too much to do."

"Wait, Claudine, what did the doctor say?"

"She made me sign a release waiver that I was taking my life into my own hands by leaving and not going to the hospital. Augustine, if we go to the hospital we are going to have to wait around forever."

"If you tell them that you are having heart problems, they will see you right away.

"Augustine, let's just go eat lunch. I'm sure I will be fine. It's much too important of a week. I can't die right now. I have too much to do."

This week, Claudine will host a party at her house for her friend Hélène Monties, who has just been awarded the *Légion d'honneur*, the highest French honor, by then-President Sarkozy.

So what do we do? We find a pizza place on the corner and sit down. We order a pizza to share.

Claudine, like many people in my life, can be very dramatic. Ever since I was a child, my father believed he was going to die. His parents both died tragically when he was nine and so perhaps for that reason, he thought he would die at arbitrary ages, twenty, twenty seven, thirty-five. When that didn't happen, he thought he would die at forty-two, like his father. When that didn't happen, he thought it would be when he was fifty. When again he still hadn't died, like the spirit voices told him he would, every year thereafter seemed like borrowed living. And every year brought in the idea that this was the year.

"I'll be dead soon," is something he can be heard saying often enough that it has lost its dramatic edge. A drinker and smoker for years, he used to hike the Santa Monica Mountains at least once a week to take his students painting.

The therapist once told me that my parents are always operating on an emergency level of life or death. They live in a constant state of knowing how fast life can change, but this state of emergency can be paralyzing when trying to make rational decisions. It hinders clear thought to worry that I or someone I love might die at any moment. While this may be true, logic doesn't apply when everything feels like life or death. I find myself continuously grappling for control in something which is beyond my control. I'm not sure if my parents always operated this way or not. That's a lie; I can pretty much grantee they were always like this.

If Romeo and Juliet had lived, they would've ended up like my parents. (They did get married to the theme of *Romeo and Juliet* after all, the entire wedding party decked out in handmade Elizabethan costumes.)

I've been in a lot of hospitals in my life—never as a patient, always as a caregiver. First up was my mom, and I remember the surreal feeling of being young and seeing my mother connected to all sorts of tubes. Next was my Aunt Barbara when she got the big C, as she liked to call it. We went to every hospital in the Los Angeles area looking for a cure, a better doctor, better answers, a way she could live.

Even though Claudine might be dying, she still asks to look at what feels like my now-frivolous rental contract. I'm scheduled to bring the first month's rent plus half a security deposit in cash to Laetitia's apartment tonight. But if something happens to Claudine, what would be the point in staying?

Our pizza on the table, we eat a slice in silence, but it's too difficult to eat and our anxiety mounts. Claudine says her heart is racing and she's starting to have "vertigos."

"We should go Augustine. I think we're going to have to go."

We wave for the check. The situation quickly becomes life or death. We need to go, and we need to go NOW. Adrenaline kicks in, and we both start shaking a little. What if somethings happens to Claudine on my watch? We find a cab. I start praying in my head, *Please God, let Claudine be okay,* over and over and over again.

And this physical feeling of stress courses though my blood. And it's all too familiar. Like I'm praying for my mom again.

Claudine has to direct the cab driver, and he is not being very nice and does not drop us off where we should be dropped off. It's in French, so I don't understand his rudeness or Claudine's response.

When we arrive at the hospital, the first thing Claudine says is, "This is where Simone died."

"Oh, great, Claudine."

"Well, Augustine, it's true."

In the hospital, a genuinely concerned doctor offers to help us find the emergency wing. I do not understand all of their conversation, but I do understand he has said, "Would you like me to walk you there?"

Claudine says no, I know this much, so I immediately chime in "Oui, Oui, Oui."

Without missing a beat, Claudine says, "Je vous présente mon amie américaine." A very un-French thing to do, perhaps—or, rather. a very American thing to say, "Yes, yes, yes, we would very much like your help."

And so it is that the very attractive man helps us. Sometimes, there is a kind man who wants to help just when you need him.

Claudine is still talking to the doctor in French. I'm not sure if she is telling him about her condition or remembering the time she was here when Simone died.

"Claudine, it will be okay."

"Well, Augustine, we'll see. All we can do is pray to God. Not that I believe in God. I'm an atheist, as you know." Such is Claudine's continued humor as we enter the ICU.

We check in. Claudine gives them all her cards. It is the same in France as it is in the States. If you say it's your heart, they take you right away.

We enter a hospital room. There is really no one else around. Claudine sits on the bed and takes off her shirt, "I'm sorry Augustine, I don't have time to be modest. You understand."

Her breasts surprise me as she is so petite. They are the same shape and size as my Aunt Barbara's, and I have a flashback of being with my aunt and all the hospitals and tests I took her to. In that moment our relationship changes, and we really become like family.

The nurse arrives with the machine to monitor heart rate, and because I am not really family, I am asked to leave. I sit in the hallway outside the door freaking out, focusing my energy on positive thoughts. *She'll be okay, please let her be okay,* and remembering.

"Your mother has an arrhythmia," the intern behind the desk at the ER had said. "Her heart is no longer functioning properly. Follow my hands." He held up his fists to explain, "The beats are off-sync." One hand pumped, indicating one side of the heart, while the other hand opened and closed at the wrong moment.

"We need to put in a pacemaker to put the beats back in sync." This was how it was explained to me, and I hung on his every word. The memory is as clear as if I am standing in front of him again.

The nurse comes out of the room, "*Vous pouvez entrer,*" she says.

"Hi Claudine, how are you feeling?"

"I'm feeling better, Augustine, now that we're here."

"What do they say?"

"Well, we wait for the doctor. But they think it is a bad reaction to the medication I take for my blood pressure. It was a good thing we came, Augustine. They need to monitor me."

"Did you call Bernard?"

"Yes, but he is out of town at a conference. He will head back now, but he may not make it till later tonight. Hopefully they will let him in as he's not my husband, and it will be past visiting hours, you understand."

"Hopefully, he'll make it back as soon as possible. I'm so glad you're feeling better."

"We'll see what the doctor says. Either way, it looks like I will be staying here overnight. I wonder, Augustine, if you could go to my apartment to get me a few things?"

"Yes, of course. Are you sure you'll be okay? I can wait."

"No, no, if you can go now you can take a few things back for me." It seems the state of emergency has subsided, normalcy returned. The nurses sit around the table in their break room, casually talking and smiling between each other at my attempts to speak French and thank them.

I have a list, with the door code written on it and Claudine's keys. I'm still trying to calm down even though it seems Claudine will be OK. I still want to get her things as quickly as possible.

When I get back to the hospital, I stay with Claudine awhile, holding her hand, saying everything will be OK. I believe it will be. It's not Claudine's time to go. But you never know. Things can happen so fast. And though it took my Aunt Barbara two years to die, death is only a second. Here, and then gone. I wasn't there for Barbara's death. I'd already moved to New York. I came to see her a week before when she was in the hospital, clearly dying, and even at that point, my family still wouldn't admit I was there to see her.

She was still lucid and asked me, "Do you have anything to say?"

"No, do you?"

"Me neither."

We looked at each other, deep into each other's eyes, and it was true. There was nothing left to say. We didn't need to say any more. I want to say I told her I love her and that she told me. Years later, I often wonder if I should've said something more comforting, but I comfort myself knowing the honest approach was the way she would've wanted it. But the truth is, I'll never know.

Ten awful days in intensive care found my mother alive with the help of a pacemaker. It would be another month or two before she was out of the hospital. But she'll never solve her issue with what put her in the hospital in the first place. She'll never solve her issue with food. The fear of being fat will always outweigh everything else.

Why am I writing this book? Because my mother almost died from taking diet pills, and this, more often than not, seems uniquely a woman's problem. Because I want to be a free independent woman, and I'm not sure what that really means or how to get there, and I want to help other women. Because it appears we're profiting from another's demise. We've created anorexia, bulimia, obesity—obsessions from the same disease of the unattainable beauty standard of airbrushed magazines. Going to high school in Los Angeles, I had lots of girlfriends who experimented with laxatives to lose weight, or tried throwing up just to see if it worked.

Being comfortable in one's own skin is not a skill we teach, though perhaps this is changing now. It is something we must learn at a high cost, and sometimes it isn't just the anticipated cost of life or death, but freedom.

GROWING UP HOLLYWOOD

I lost my virginity last century.

As if virginity was something I'd misplaced and might still find again. Better to say I gave it away because it was mine to give, and it wasn't taken from me. I'm very lucky in that respect. Better still to say I shared it with someone, and he shared his with me. We were in love, sixteen, and had tried unsuccessfully to consummate such love a few times.

Back in those days, we didn't have cell phones, but pagers, and we made mix tapes of radio songs because music wasn't on computers yet. Music has advanced, but virginity is still analog.

I was already on the pill by then under the pretense that it helped with menstrual pain, which meant I wouldn't know what my body was really like until sixteen years later when I went off the pill and discovered that all those years and hormones aggravated my face, my chin red with spots that I wouldn't have had otherwise. All for the 99% reassurance I would never get pregnant, never have to have an abortion, but still be worried about any unprotected sex because I came of age in the age of AIDS.

My best girlfriend at the time had, like me, just started taking birth control pills, initially under the presumption it would help with period pain. It was a handy disguise as we were about to have sex. I remember being super excited to have sex.

We didn't have many girlfriends. We'd lost them more unwillingly than we'd "lost" our virginity. We'd lost them once we got steady boyfriends. We understood each other while we ate donuts, drank coffee, and smoked cigarettes during our second-period Journalism class that allowed us to go off campus. Eating donuts is something I doubt either of us would do with such abandon now. We'd read the fine print of side effects in the miniature brochure that came with those little pink and blue pills. The box warned that smoking greatly increased your risk of heart disease, especially in women over 35, but we were nowhere near thirty-five, so what did we have to worry about?

Still, those minuscule side effects were not minuscule. They were the first steps toward becoming adults. That things could happen to you was a calculated risk we had to be willing to take.

This was back when everyone we knew got an SUV or Jeep Cherokee for their 16th birthday, and the parking lot of our private Mar Vista high school looked more like a car dealership than a school full of teenagers. Everyone with their Toyota 4x4s, and no one thought anything about the environment. It just wasn't even a consideration. Los Angeles is a car city—that's one of the major problems with it, if not the main one. In the vast spread-out spaces connected by highways like some sort of racing track, it could take twenty minutes to go from the valley, where I lived, to Playa del Rey, where my girlfriend lived, going 75mph at two o'clock in the morning, or it could take an hour and a half in traffic.

Nana was always saying that was the biggest mistake Los Angeles made. "They could have put in an elevated system like Chicago," she would say, accentuating every syllable. "I remember in the 1940s when they were discussing it, but instead they decided to build freeways, never imagining traffic might be an issue. That was their big mistake."

Five days a week for twelve years, I spent more than two hours a day in traffic. Cocooned in my car bubble, no one could reach me. The most they could do was page me, but I would have to wait to get home to call whoever wanted me. I realize now my children will never know that freedom. By the time they are old enough to be on their own, they will most likely have a phone.

Sitting in traffic, I had a lot of time to read bumper stickers: "If you're not pissed off, you're not paying attention." What happened to the rage of a generation? Now, we're sedated by a wash of dance music and Facebook. Before it was grunge, and our national anthem was *Smells Like Teen Spirit* by Nirvana. "Here we are now, entertain us." And, really, we weren't going to do anything but be entertained.

We were the generation of the anti-protest, we wanted a Movement. Movement with a capital M, because we'd seen the protests of our parents and what had it really done? The hippies turned to yuppies, driving around in Volvos and saying if you remember the 60s then you weren't really there. Protesting seemed like a waste of time. It didn't really change anything. We don't feel that way now.

We wanted to be in the 60s because we wanted to do the drugs and practice free love and listen to the music. In some ways, we did just that. But after September 11, we got dealt a different hand. We moved back in with our parents. We watched Bush steal the election not once, but twice. Our youth passed by with too many movements to join. Facebook was invented, and we turned the cameras on ourselves. We turned inward and just struggled to move out, to make something of ourselves. We went to grad school, and the risk-averse went to law school. Men still became doctors. The women I know didn't; they still married the doctors, as my mother had been taught.

The values surrounding women's education had changed by the time I was sixteen, but the values around sex had not. My parents lied to me about sex. They told me they waited to have sex until they were married. It wasn't until I found their Beatles *White Album* in their record collection that I said, "Oh, what a shame I drew all over it when

I was a child." There were crayon drawings of rainbows and hearts, so I just assumed it was me who had drawn them.

But no. My father informed me, "That was us. One time, we were really stoned and your mother and I were just lying in bed naked for three days when the *White Album* came out. We didn't move for three days, I'm not kidding you."

Wait a second—it was clear now they clearly hadn't waited. I don't think they really expected me to wait, either. But they wanted me to be in love. They wanted it to be special. I had found a wonderful man, a boy, a boy becoming a man, with whom I was madly in love, a poet. He would write me poems upon poems declaring his love. One in particular I remember ended with the line, "There's just one promise I'd like to make, I'll be here when you awake." This was before we had sex—obviously—it was a rhyming poem. His reassurance was sweet, and unnecessary, I wasn't at all worried he wouldn't be there in the metaphorical morning. A real morning nonexistent as we weren't allowed yet to sleep over at each other's houses.

Still, my parents taught me I was the keeper of my sexuality. I was the one in charge, and what this meant was that I was the one in charge of saying no. Or rather, it was my job to say no. I was the one who decided it was time. Women were supposed to be the goalies, only letting the good ones in.

Sometimes you're not clear what you want, because you've been taught to deny first. I remember hearing a quote from Sinead O'Connor saying she knew her daughter would be all right because her first word was no. No meant no. But then I recall John Lennon meeting Yoko Ono at her art exhibit where she had created a piece where you climbed a ladder, and at the top there was a door you opened that just said *yes.* John Lennon admired her then and there as it was such a positive message.

Before I fell in love, I wasn't taught to say an enthusiastic yes, either. The default was that you were supposed to say no whether you wanted to or not. You were always supposed to say no, to deny, to wait, so when you did finally agree with yourself because it was super clear this was really what you wanted, you still felt this pang of guilt, were you doing the right thing? Because the culture put such high priority on waiting. And this might make all the difference in the world. Instead of being encouraged to say *no*, what if we are taught to say *yes*? The yes is much more exciting to say. What if boys are taught they have a choice to say an enthusiastic *yes*, too?

Later, after love, came the question: could you be in love and be independent? The two seemed mutually exclusive. Somewhere along the way, I learned you couldn't be one while being the other. "In love" was not freedom, and "freedom" was not love. But it should be. At least, this is one thing I learned when I was sixteen.

CODE BLUE

t sixteen, I learn what Code Blue means.

I don't know as I stand against the wall in St. Johns Hospital, what is happening to my mom. That my dad is able to make light of the situation by asking the security guard, "Why can't they just say what's happening? Why do they have to use code?" Code Blue has been announced over the PA system, but without emotional urgency.

"Man, don't you watch ER?" It's the 90s and the guard has a grave look on his face because he knows what Code Blue means, and he knows it is something happening to us because it is happening to her, whereas we assumed it is happening to someone else.

What is happening is that Mom is having five heart attacks, flatlining twice, and coming back to life twice.

It's July 3, 1997, the day before Independence Day. I'm supposed to leave for Paris for a summer abroad program in two days. I don't go. I don't care. Nothing else matters to me but for my mom to live. My mom is my best friend, she can't die, and she doesn't, because she is strong. All those Jazzercise classes she takes every day after work? Well, they worked. We believe they're the reason her heart pulls though. We have to believe in something.

We drive back to the house, and we feel Topanga Canyon is safer than the freeway in our exhausted state. Driving along the Pacific Ocean and through the windy road of the mountains, we allow ourselves to breathe for a moment before unconsciously holding our breath again. We collect all the pills she's been taking and bring them back to the hospital so they can figure out what went wrong. It's Fen-Phen, the diet drug. We don't know. Few people knew what it could and would do. Two months later they'll take it off the market. Seven years later, my mom, along with fifty-thousand others in one of the largest cases of product liability in the US, will win their case against Wyeth.

We don't know the way things will change—that my mom, who is so joyful, so healthy, and so independent will lose all of that. We don't know she wouldn't be the same. It might've occurred to us, but keeping her alive is the priority. We don't worry she might not be able to work again. That comes later. We don't consider she'd go on disability; that she'll suffer from blackouts and major depression and won't be able to take care of herself anymore. That her autonomy, my dad's, as well as my own, would be forfeit. That the mom of my youth would not be the mom of my young adulthood.

So when I arrive in Paris twelve years later in 2009, a grown woman, recently heartbroken, unemployed but carefree, having enough money saved up yet still deeply in school debt, having gone through the loss of my best girlfriend from my own indiscretions with her ex-boyfriend/boyfriend, and having extracted myself from three successive "co-dependent" relationships, what do I know about being an independent woman?

I know more about the consequences of not being one. I know about the consequences of weight, of beauty, of obsession with perfection, of just ten more pounds. "All my life" Mom says, "I've battled with cellulite." It's a pointless battle, but for all my mother's obsession with it, I grew up without that. She told me I was beautiful, and I was lucky I had high metabolism and could eat whatever I wanted and not gain weight. When I was a kid, the other kids would make fun of my skinny legs, and she just said, "You wait and see. You'll be so lucky. You'll never have to worry about your weight." And she knew what a blessing that was.

My Nana gave contradictory advice on food—always saying to eat more and then reprimanding when you ate too much. Mom didn't give me that baggage.

Other baggage I escaped was to marry rich and Jewish. This is not to say that marrying a nice, wealthy Jewish boy would have been shunned—on the contrary—but it wasn't required, even though the first question my Nana and my mother ever asked when I started dating someone new was, "Is he Jewish?" or "What does he do?"

It doesn't matter if I make good money, I never will. My money isn't part of the equation yet. But it won't be enough and neither will his, whoever he is. So I get subsidized, but am still taught to work hard and feel guilty for accepting the money they would never let me refuse anyway. And it will be years before I realize I grew up privileged but not entitled, and there is a difference. Entitled people rarely seem to have guilt. My mother grew up the same way.

THE SOCIAL CURRENCY OF INFLUENCE

Claudine stays in the hospital for three days. I bring the cash to Laetitia's apartment and sign the lease for a year.

She says we'll meet at the apartment the next day to go over everything in the apartment and make sure everything is working. I've been taught to be so weary of craigslist scams, but everything looks legit. She gives me the keys and the door code, and even invites me to a cocktail party she is having on Saturday night.

On the metro on the way to the party, I have a flash of inspiration. I pull out my notebook.

It makes sense that with the rise of feminism and women's rights that the assault on women's weight would begin. Long gone are the days of Marilyn-Bettie Page, of curvaceous women, a.k.a., healthy women. In their place, anorexic-waifish women. The image of the curvaceous woman won't come back till J. Lo and Beyonce. Just like putting women in heels so they can't run away and a corset so they can't breathe. Are there any parallels to contraptions that we have put men in? Powdered wigs? Pointy shoes? Circumcision? A necktie?

Are any modern-day fashion accessories as detrimental to men's health as corsets, or that even make men as uncomfortable as a burka or stiletto heels? Some could say men's suits are uncomfortable in their conformity.

The history of high heels, corsets, foot binding, burkas, and women's fashion has always been connected to women's rights and are also issues that intersect with race. Take the 2019 controversy of women in Japan being banned from wearing eyeglasses at work because eyeglasses are unfeminine, or being forced to wear high heels at work as part of a mandatory dress code.

Women's clothes signify her oppression or liberation—from the long skirts of the suffragettes to short skirts of flappers, from Yves St. Laurent's tuxedo to the pant suits of Hillary Clinton, from Maria Grazia Chiuri's design for Dior's haute couture, "We Should All Be Feminists" t-shirt to the hand-knitted pink pussy hats of the Women's March in 2017.

Clothes are symbolic. Advertisers know this best, though we also know it internally. To me, there is nothing sexier, in term of shoes, than the red-soled Christian Louboutin's Pigalle Follies shoes. Invented by Christian Louboutin in 1993, and currently costing around 800 euros (and up to 6000!), they've become an example of a classic status symbol. When two of my girlfriends buy a brand new pair themselves with their own money and know that they can afford it, it's a sign that they've made it. As I can't yet afford a brand new pair, I can't help but look in the windows of the *Depot Vente,* the vintage stores in France, to see if there is a pair in the window. Though I don't even wear high heels, there is something so sexy about that red lacquered shoe.

Thinking about the history of high heels, I discover it was King Louis XIV in 1673 who wore red-soled heels and restricted those who wore them to the nobles. And, surprise surprise, high heels were initially for men. Invented in 15th century Persia to help keep soldiers' feet in the horses' stirrups. Like the cowboy boots of today, the creation was a practical one. Eventually, and particularly for Louis XIV, who was very short, heels made one seem taller and more intimidating.

Ultimately women start imitating men in an attempt to have more power, but by the Enlightenment, where the shoes were considered impractical and not logical, everyone stopped wearing them. They returned around World War II with the popularity of the pin-ups, all of whom wore high heels. It's worth noting that, initially, heels were a sign that you were so rich you didn't have to work, which is also how foot binding in China began as well. I mention foot binding not to reinforce the stereotype of the Chinese but because it became a common practice in 970 AD, coincidentally, shortly after the Chinese invented the printing press in 923 AD. At the same moment that literacy rates began to soar, so did the oppression of women according to Shlain in his timeline for *The Alphabet versus The Goddess*. This factoid always stuck with me. Proof that the patriarchy is in the printing of books.

In 2010, back when *The New York Times* was focusing on The Female Factor, a section on the changing influence of women in the world, the British-Ghanaian cultural theorist, Kwame Anthony Appiah published an article entitled "The Art of Social Change," which discusses how the campaign against foot binding succeeded.

The American political scientist Gerry Mackie, an expert on social norms, gives the example of a large group of families in a rural area south of Beijing, in which 99 percent of women born before 1890 had bound feet, and none of the women born after 1919 had bound feet. The campaign against foot-binding didn't work immediately. But when it took hold, that thousand-year-old practice essentially vanished in a single generation.

The wisest campaigners began by insisting on their respect for China's civilization. A second essential reason for the campaign's success was that it created institutions; it didn't content itself with rhetoric. In particular, it created organizations whose members publicly pledged two things: not to bind their daughters' feet, and not to allow their sons to marry women whose feet were bound. The genius of this strategy was that it created both unbound women and men who would marry them. To reform tradition, you had to change the shared commitments of a community. If Chinese families bound their daughters' feet because that was the normal thing to do, you had to change what was normal.

First, begin with a dialogue of mutual respect, free of self-congratulation. Second, when you have a core of converts, organize a program of public commitment to new practices, which takes into account the traditions of the

community. To end one practice, as the anti-foot-binding campaigners
grasped, you need to start another.

Time and time again, I come back to this article, and not only because I love the phrase, 'unbound women and the men who would marry them,' but because it illustrates so succinctly how we can make real change. As we've witnessed with the #MeToo movement and the success and failures of climate change action, we must come at it from a place of mutual respect.

Not to be self-congratulatory, but the first title of my book was going to be *Mutual Admiration*. As after all my research, I come to the same conclusion that respect and admiration are the first step to change, but even before that you need awareness. Like the awakening parties of women in the 1970s, an awareness of our complacency in our own oppression is necessary. This awareness has already taken place with diamonds and fur and is currently happening with high fashion and fast fashion, where consumers are demanding more eco-friendly options to clothes.

Did Marilyn Monroe unwittingly manufacture our desires for diamonds?
And later Madonna, who emulated Monroe in her 80s video Material World?
It's highly unlikely. Women and men were wearing jewelry from our earliest
archeological digs. The Mayans, the Incas, the Egyptians all loved gold and
jewels.

It was a DeBeers campaign that invented the diamond engagement ring. From the start, though, it was actually for the protection of women: if their soon-to-be husband took off with another woman before their marriage, she had some insurance, or some compensation.

Diamonds are a girl's best friend works out for my purposes because it underlines the power of influence on a global business, and this is where women can use their power. The hope is that the social change is swift. As Appiah observes in his article, within a single generation, a thousand-year-old practice ceased to be cool, and a new normal was created. If the success of new inclusive feminisms are any indicator, we are in that new generation.

Like that 1960s television show *The Outer Limits*, "We will control the horizontal. We will control the vertical. We can roll the image, make it flutter. We can change the focus to a soft blur, or sharpen it to crystal clarity."

USEFUL PHRASES IN FRENCH

A ll French nouns are denoted as either masculine or feminine. For example, my current teacher Stephanie loves to correct students when saying, *J'ai un problème*, masculine, even though it ends with an e, typically reserved for feminine words, and there is *une solution*, feminine. Masculine problem, feminine solution. It pleases Stephanie to correct this mistake. She takes pride in the simple fact that if her language is sexist, at least there are some things that seemed justified or correct in this way.

A list of some other phrases will come in handy when at a very ridiculously French dinner party:

Tu viens d'où? Where are you from?

Ça te plaît? It pleases you? (Usually in reference to living in Paris)

I will not be seduced by your charms: *Je ne serai pas séduite par tes charmes.*

Are you single?: *Tu es célibataire?* Not to be confused with the English word, celibate, as clearly single people are not necessarily celibate. But it's a helpful mnemonic device. You should ask this early in the evening. Most likely, the response will lead you to the next question.

How long have you two been together?: *Depuis combien de temps vous êtes ensemble?*

At the party, someone may inevitably say to you, *Montre-moi ton tatouage.* Show me your tattoo. This means, of course, that *il te drague*, he's flirting with you. It's easy to remember this word because it sounds like dragging, like caveman-style flirting of just hitting you over the head with a club and dragging you back to his cave. Hopefully, though, he is no *lâche*; same word for men and women meaning coward. If things do get out of hand, you can say, *lâche-moi*, meaning "let me go" or "leave me alone." Sometimes, this technique is used as an element of seduction.

Shut up: *Ta gueule*, but which is very familiar, as *gueule* is a feminine noun meaning face of an animal. You do not use the word for humans unless you are trying to be insulting. And just in case you are wondering, the word for a human face is *le visage.* Another usage of the word *gueule,* which they love to teach you in French school, is *gueule de bois.* Directly translated, it means "face of wood" but in this case, it is the French word for hangover. After the French party, you will be able to say you drank too much wine and now have a *gueule de bois.* When you're in a foreign country, and can't express yourself, you suddenly realize what phrases you use when you don't know what else to say.

On verra, we'll see.

Followed up with, *on ne sait jamais,* we never know.

La vérité est plus étrange que la fiction, the truth is stranger than fiction.

Il n'y a pas assez temps, there is not enough time.

But the two of the more important phrases are:

Ce sera tout? Will that be all? Typically asked by any store owner, and if you don't know what they are asking usually makes you feel like an idiot, as you stand there, with everyone else behind you in line waiting to buy their roasted chicken.

The other phrase is, *Comment voulez-vous fait cuire?:* How would you like it cooked? Clearly, this is only useful if you order meat in a restaurant; however, the French will ask you how you would like everything cooked, even things which should be cooked to a certain temperature such as duck and pork. The responses are equally important as the French undercook everything. *A point* seems to be a safe bet, without pronouncing the T; it's just there to confuse you.

A point means to a point, which is apropos if you don't want your meat literally just seared for a second on each side and otherwise totally and completely rare. Which is called *saignant*, again no pronouncing the T, meaning bloody. Or you could say, *bien cuit*, but only Americans order meat that way. Besides if it's overcooked and you asked for it that way, there is no way you can send it back to the kitchen.

Actually, forget sending anything back, as it is rarely done. And never take home leftovers.

I come from a family that always takes home leftovers, even the bread from the bread basket, and Nana always asked for the bread to be warm when it came to the table. Maybe when you get to be ninety-four, you don't have time anymore for cold bread.

It's rare that French restaurants have the accoutrements to pack up food. They pride themselves on having the correct portion size. And most restaurants always serve a three-course meal. Entree (appetizers), plat (main course), and dessert. They do always eat dessert. Claudine and I always get dessert.

Dessert, two "s's" in French make the sound ssss like a snake, or in French a *serpent*. This is important to remember, especially when using what has become a naughty word, *baiser*. It used to mean to kiss, but has now come to mean to fuck. *Baiser* is not to be confused with *baisser*, which means to lower, or to bring down. One "S" makes a Z, two "S's" make SSSS, serpent, snake. Most French women end conversation with their close girlfriends by saying *Bisous,* pronounced bizou, which means, affectionately, kisses. However, if you want to say I kiss you, which is incredibly common saying as well instead of using the word baiser, you use the phrase *Je t'embrasse.* Which always reminds me of the English word, *embrace,* as if the words are this warm welcoming hug, *I embrace you.* It's not something we Americans say—we just go in for the hug—but these words of affection make the action in my mind. You can add in the tres fort, very strongly. *Je t'embrasse très fort.*

Later, my new friend Sabrina teaches me that when the men selling roses come up to the table, it can be commonly crass to say, *"Non merci, on a déjà baisé!"* Which means, no thank you, we've already fucked. Therefore, flowers are no longer necessary.

BRUNCH AT MARIAGE FRÈRES

W hen Claudine is feeling better, we meet for Sunday brunch at *Mariage Feres*, the most famous tea spot in Paris on the Grand Augustins.

Today Claudine tells me a story of her going to Helene de Beauvoir's gallery near the tea place when she was seventeen. The owner asked her in a very commanding tone, *"Qu'est-ce que vous voulez, mademoiselle?"*

She responded just *to regard*, regard being the word the French use instead of *voir*, which is the verb to see, Americans look, the French regard the paintings. She was seventeen, drenched from the rain, and very shy. She had been hoping to meet Helene and at that moment she thought she would never meet her. Years later Helene would give her a poster from that gallery show saying something like, "The moment we met but didn't know it yet." We are walking in the rain, as it is always raining in Paris. I say, "Everyone should have their dreams realized," and Claudine agrees.

Another brunch with Claudine at *Mariage Fères*. Afterwards, I'll sit in the small park near Shakespeare and Co and try to write down everything that we have talked about. Overwhelmed from all the things that we just spoke of and she says that I must not lose the flavor, that I must incorporate the historical perspective. "History is adventure." She says. We sit in the café upstairs, the room is all yellow and she has so much energy, more than I.

She says, "When I was a child, my father was getting death threats for support of the Algerian war for independence. For two years no one could stay over, and my mother would check the front door for a package every morning."

She tells me I must put emotion, humor, historical significance, all of this in my book, and again I'm sitting here worried because maybe I've lost all the details already. She knows, like I do, that I need to organize my interviews and get to work before I get too overwhelmed.

I eat foie gras and she gets scrambled eggs in a cup with salmon and shrimp and brioche toast. We both get *tarte tartin*, and dessert, of course. We don't share, we each get our own. The piece of cheesecake is never as large as it is in America. In France it is a mere suggestion of dessert.

IL M'AIME, UN PEU, BEAUCOUP...

...PASSIONNEMENT, À LA FOLIE, PAS DU TOUT!

I was giddy like, well, a schoolgirl. I wasn't writing my first name with his last name, Augustine Frison, a thousand times in a notebook, with squiggly lines and hearts, but I might as well have.

It was as if I was electrified, wired, energized. I was on a natural high. Was it Paris? Was it Eric? I called friends for reinforcements. They didn't recognize me. "What's happened to you?" they said. "You sound like yourself, but you are not yourself, you're crazy."

And I was. A momentary madness. People who fall for it know what I'm talking about. All you want to do is be with that person. You go through withdrawal otherwise. And the endless questions: *Does he feel the same way I do? What will happen when I leave? Will he wait for me?*

Eric played it cool throughout, as I pretended to do. Perhaps I succeeded.

Meanwhile, on the phone with my friend Laila in Australia, whom I've known since I was ten, after spending most of the time wondering these questions and recounting all the romantic and thoughtful signs that would lead to all answers being yes, she said, "Well, the next time we speak, we'll have to talk about this feminist project you've been working on." Feminism, sheminism. Did he like me or not? Could he love me or not?

I joke. It was a joke. I knew how ridiculous I was being, and at the same time was still very much entrenched in feminism and being an independent woman, et cetera, et cetera, et cetera…

In the States, when you're a child, you pluck a daisy to decide whether or not your crush loves you. *He loves me, he loves me not.* In France, there is a more nuanced approach. They don't have simply he loves me, he loves me not. Instead they have, *Il m'aime un peu, beaucoup, passionnément, à la folie, pas du tout!* He loves me, a little, a lot, passionately, like crazy, not at all!

In French class, we learn that obviously the childhood game comes from the French and is called *effeuiller une marguerite, effeuiller,* to pluck (coincidentally if you use the verb as reflexive, *s'effeuiller,* it means to strip) and *marguerite,* a daisy. And granted I wasn't pulling apart daisies–yet–but instead reading coffee grinds with Emma, which clearly might as well be the same thing.

I call my father from the Tuileries on a warm day sitting in the park (there did happen to be daisies there) and asked him if I should call Eric and see what he's up to. My dad says, "What would you do if he was just your friend?"

"I'd call him," I say.

"So then go ahead and call him," he says.

I call my therapist in LA, whom I speak to on occasion, and ask her what she thinks of the matter at hand: *Did he really like me as much as I liked him? Was this even possible?* I was so smitten, I literally did not know what to do with myself.

She says, "We're quick to make large brush strokes on a blank canvas and want to paint the whole picture, when really you only have enough information for one small corner of the painting."

This was a metaphor that stuck with me, a metaphor I could understand. So I tried not to be in a rush to paint the whole picture and realized what an impatient girl—I mean woman, obviously woman—I am. I never considered myself impatient. It wasn't until I met Eric that I couldn't wait for anything.

AT THE PLACE DES 'VOYAGES'

I n the late afternoon at the Place des Vosges, you sit at a cafe and
write—

*You want to start with Eve, because that seems like the most obvious
place to start–the first woman, according to Western Civilization, so you've
been taught. But then you want to start with Lilith instead, as she perhaps
was the first true woman, the one who got kicked out of the Garden of Eden for
not being submissive to Adam. Or so the story goes...*

You're not quite sure. You don't have your smartphone, just a simple
prepaid purple Nokia. Later you look up the history: according to
Jewish folklore, she was created from the same earth as Adam but
didn't just want to do missionary style—because they were equal—so
she left him. It's worth noting she's found in the *Alphabet of Sirach,* a
satirical text of medieval times.

Three doors down from where you sit is Victor Hugo's house, and it's
just started to rain. No one seems to mind, as it's only a light drizzle.
His house is in the south-east corner of the Places des Vosges in the
Marais, the Jewish neighborhood of Paris, which to you is one of the
most beautiful spots in Paris. You look around at the square and the
rain and start writing again.

But when you think of Lilith though, you think of the successful concert tour of the 90s, "Lilith Fair" founded by singer Sarah McLachlan, which featured only female artists and bands, such as Tracey Chapman, Bonnie Rait, Indigo Girls, Lauren Hill, Queen Latifah, Erykah Badu, Sheryl Crow, all influential women to you, even though you didn't go to the concert. You remember it. As if you were there.

It's a perfect square. Built in the 1600s, it's the oldest square in Paris. It's a place you will go to often for a glass of wine at the end of the day, or coffee in the afternoon. At this particular moment, it is even more beautiful and inspiring because of the rain. It is 5pm. Huge thunder rocks the sky. You're relaxed, with no umbrella, just waiting for the rain to pass. So with your journal, you keep writing what you think could become the beginning of your book.

After Lilith and Eve, you're inclined to mention the poet prostitutes who wrote lovely sexy erotic verses in Sanskrit. And following the line of writers, we have Sappho, the Greek poet from seventh century BC. Though not much of her poetry survives, her reputation precludes her disappearance. Next you think of all of the Goddesses from India, Greece and Rome. Women like Athena, the warrior goddess who gets appropriated in masculine terms as she is born from Zeus's head. The goddesses used to be pretty sweet. Now they've become dismissed as New Age annoyances, disregarded the same way astrology is considered unscientific, together with Wicca and witchcraft, a feminine spirituality that's been discounted because it was in the female world.

Just then you're interrupted by a text message: *Bonjour, qu'est ce que tu fais ce soir? Tu veux venir chez moi?*

Interesting. Your heart skips the proverbial beat.

How long do you wait before responding? You start writing again.

Each generation chooses a new heroine from the list to admire and focus their common struggles. In the 90s, it was Lilith, who exemplified how women were feeling at the time. They felt strength and power, and particularly the idea they were no longer going to be ignored. The musicians/singers such as Gwen

Stefani, Ani DiFranco, and Tori Amos embodied this vibe, the prequels to the "girl power" of the Spice Girls and Britney Spears.

You write back: *Peut-être.* Maybe.

Tu es déjà Parisienne? Tu es coquine. You're already Parisian, he's said. *You're being coquine,* meaning naughty, coy, coquettish even.

Hmm, you think. *Yes, it's good to be flirtatious. I've played your cards right so far.* Back to writing.

What if the modern day question is not just about empowering women (is this same as women having equal power?), but also to show where women were always empowered (have always and continue to have equal power)? Is it not more empowering to show how and where we as women were in control? (Subversively, of course. No one would ever believe that they were really in power all along, would they?)

You're making a joke here as you don't mean to imply men were puppets on strings controlled by women's desires—well, maybe you do—but there is a certain frightening truth to the metaphor. If you were to look back on history and be raised with the knowledge women did indeed have power, (even if it seemed otherwise) this is where an internal shift would take place. We are in control of our stories.

Text received: *Où es-tu?*

You write back quickly now, *Place des Voyages.* Though a lovely metaphorical meaning, it's not *Place des Voyages,* but *Place des Vosges.* Still you think of it as voyaging somewhere magical. This magical moment in the rainstorm, just waiting for the rain to pass. The *Place des Vosges* is almost empty now. It's all yours. The four fountains in each corner, the perfectly manicured trees. Victor Hugo was right to live here. I might be mildly getting wet but I don't care. I've fallen in love with this cafe, sitting here in the pouring rain. Another bout of thunder roars and it starts to hail.

It's hailing!

I write in my journal now. The raindrops splatter the blue ink. My simple purple phone hums.

Et alors? And so? Are you coming or not? To go to his apartment, you'd take the same metro line, Ligne 1 as your own, from *St. Paul* to *Nation* and then instead of changing to line 9 you'd take the line 2. Simple. It'd take the same amount of time.

You text back: *Oui, je viens.* Yes, I'm coming. Knowing he most likely will understand the double entendre. Even though the actual phrase *double entendre* doesn't exist in French. They don't have double entendres. They have *jeux des mots*–word play–which is not exactly the same thing.

If we accept women are equally responsible for the situation we as humans find ourselves in, women cannot just blame men (or other women as we're wont to do) by continuing to say it's a man's world. When we do exactly that, we as women negate responsibility and return to the status of a child.

Just as you have an aversion to websites that focus solely on women, because you know' their audience is primarily women and this is what irks you, "Women's issues" are actually "Men's issues" too, so where are the men? What are you talking about you may say, men are everywhere!

Message received: ;-)

One in particular, who is waiting for me.

FEMALE EQUIVALENTS

Many journeys for women start out basically the same, looking for women they can admire and then realizing they learned only about men. Hopefully this will change, is changing, but women still aren't enfolded into the cannon the way men are.

But there are female equivalents for each and every one of these men. Women who were influential in their time. Women who made discoveries.

In interviewing Judy Chicago about the current plight of women, I learn that she still says the same thing she said in the 70s: we are not taught about women in high school, so we are destined to keep repeating what women have done before us, thinking that it is new.

In our interview, she references the quote by Gerda Lerner, which begins the book version of her feminist masterpiece, *The Dinner Party:* "Men develop ideas and systems of explanation by absorbing past knowledge and critiquing and superseding it. Women, ignorant of their own history, (do) not know what women before them had thought and taught. So generation after generation, they (struggle) for insights others had already had before them, (resulting in) the constant reinventing the wheel."

Asked to list women who have changed the course of history, many people can think of only a few names, usually women who have had one or several movies made out of their lives. Most likely it's Cleopatra, Eve of Eden, Marie Curie, Jeanne of Arc, Sacajawea, Sojourner Truth, Harriet Tubman, Margaret Thatcher, Susan B. Anthony, Eleanor Roosevelt, Amelia Earhart, hopefully Simone de Beauvoir, and more recently Kamala Harris, Alexandra Octavio Cortez, Golda Meir, Angela Merkel, Hillary Clinton, Ruth Bader Ginsberg, Beyoncé, Oprah, and Madonna. It ends up being a short list. After all, what other women are we supposed to know? How about Sappho, Trotula, Hypatia, Christiane de Pizan, Margery Kempe, Olympe de Gouges, Maria Stewart, Frances Harper, Juana Inés de la Cruz, Hansa Mehta, Louise Michel, and so many others who weren't at all obscure in their time?

We must look at what the women were doing while the important men we've learned about in history class were changing the world. There were female equivalents to the men whose names we so readily know. We have to start with the major men whose actions and writings still affect the way we think today.

One of the first mind-blowing misconceptions to acknowledge is that women were most likely the first artists. In 2013 in an article for National Geographic, "Were the First Artists Mostly Women?" Virginia Hughes writes, "The Archaeologist Dean Snow of Pennsylvania State University analyzed hand stencils found in eight cave sites in France and Spain. By comparing the relative lengths of certain fingers, Snow determined that three-quarters of the handprints were female." We're raised on this vision of cavemen, drawing bison for good luck for the kill, but it was most likely women who were doing those drawings. Hughes continues, "The question Snow gets most often, though, is why these ancient artists, whoever they were, left handprints at all. "I have no idea, but a pretty good hypothesis is that this is somebody saying, 'This is mine, I did this,'" he said." Women have been making their mark since the beginning of time, contrary to what we've been taught otherwise.

So when someone says Plato, Aristotle, Socrates, (when not referencing the film *The Princess Bride*) you can say Sappho, Hypatia, and Trotula.

Sappho, the fifth century B.C. lyric poet who we get the words sapphic and lesbian from, who wrote over 10,000 lines though only about 650 survive. Hypatia, the forth century A.D. Alexandrian philosopher, astronomer, and mathematician who was well-known and highly influential in her time. So much so that she was dismembered by a Christian mob for having too much influence on the pagan leader. Trota of Salerno, the twelfth century woman or three women who were one of the firsts to write a treatise on women's health and childbirth known as the Trotula.

And when someone says Darwin, you can say Lynn Margulis and know who you're talking about. Her theory of symbiogenesis collaboration and not competition as the major driving force of evolution is the kind of thinking we need right now. What if Darwin was wrong? Or not completely wrong. From her interview with Dick Teresi in *Discover Magazine* on June 17, 2011:

Most scientists would say there is no controversy over evolution. Why do you disagree?
All scientists agree that evolution has occurred—that all life comes from a common ancestry, that there has been extinction, and that new taxa, new biological groups, have arisen. The question is, is natural selection enough to explain evolution? Is it the driver of evolution?
And you don't believe that natural selection is the answer?
This is the issue I have with neo-Darwinists: They teach that what is generating novelty is the accumulation of random mutations in DNA, in a direction set by natural selection. If you want bigger eggs, you keep selecting the hens that are laying the biggest eggs, and you get bigger and bigger eggs. But you also get hens with defective feathers and wobbly legs. Natural selection eliminates and maybe maintains, but it doesn't create.

Why is this mind-blowing and what does it mean for us? It means that collaboration is key to success rather than competition. If we remove the idea that philosophical thought of the "capitalistic, competitive, cost-benefit interpretation of Darwin and change it to in collaboration we thrive, in harmony, in symbiosis is how we actually evolve.

When someone says Nietzsche or Freud, you can respond with Sabina Spierlrein and Karen Horney. And when someone says Einstein, you can say Emmy Noether. Or Kepler and Newton you can counterpoint with Wang Zhenyi.

Haven't heard of these women? That's okay. I hadn't, either. But we must learn them. And we must learn them in relation to their historical context. They must be incorporated into the cannon of the so-called creators of Western civilization. Spierlein, a Russian doctor and the first female psychoanalyst in the early twentieth century. Horney, the German pioneer in female psychiatry who wrote the first "self-help" book in 1945. Noether, also of German descent and one of the most important mathematicians of all time whose work influenced Einstein. Zhenyi, the eighteenth century Chinese astronomer who was the first to explain a lunar eclipse.

Beauvoir states in the chapter on women's history that Christine de Pizan's book, *Épître au Dieu d'Amour, Letter to the God of Love* is the first time a woman writes in defense of her sex. Pizan publishes that book in 1399. Her best-known works, *The Book of the City of Ladies* and *The Treasure of the City of Ladies,* were published in 1405. She wrote them because she noticed women were being systematically erased from history books. This was 1405 so that tells you something right there. She focuses on the "community" of women. They are the first manuscripts of their kind to have sole female characters, be told from a female point of view. She creates an allegorical city of ladies and argues women's success comes from reading and writing. She was certainly a genius for her time. A precursor to Shakespeare who published forty-one poems and prose in her lifetime and whose books stayed in print until the 15th century.

Who could we use as a counterpoint for Shakespeare and Picasso? It's not just that they are *National Geographic*'s definition of genius, as evidenced by their docu-series of the same name but also that their output was immense. Women were typically not afforded the right to be so prolific.

Well-Behaved Women Seldom Make History, the historian Laurel Thatcher Ulrich tells us. And we want to make history!

We may also consider Cleopatra, Catherine de Medici, and Queen Elizabeth. We retell the stories based on our own ideals now, based on our own purposes. Leonardo, Shakespeare: with men like that, does there need to be a woman equivalent? Yes. Do we see women as geniuses? Yes. Is there any woman we study for her philosophical and political acumen? The first woman warrior we know Fu Hao—the twelve hundred BC Shang Dynasty general, or the seventeenth century West African Queen Njinga who fought off the Portuguese slave trade in Angola or one of the leading figures in the Indian Rebellion of the nineteenth century Lakshmi Bai. These names should become our common knowledge.

Which women should every woman know? A complete herstory, instead of history. Perhaps an idea for the title of this book is the *Complete Herstory of Modern Women.* I'm already dismissive of this title, but we do need more "herstories" readily in our minds, more images of heroines.

The word *herstory* annoys me so much. It's not herstory—it's history, coming from the ancient Greek, *historia.* Granted, that meant "from a wise man." Regardless, it is completely unrelated to the possessive pronoun "his." I understand the impulse, the opportunity to right the wrongs, but history is always being rewritten.

HER STORY

Women were always in power in some way.

I'm wrong, of course, but this is a discovery that I can't quite pinpoint, that I circle around for ten years, trying to write about. Trying to understand why is it that we're not equal yet? What the fuck were women (and men) doing all this time? Beauvoir explains it this way, that women who were in higher positions of power did not want to lose what little power they had by associating with a different, lower class. In this way, the class system and women's status as second-class citizens continued. In one of my earlier versions of my manuscript, I write:

I will not propagate the myth that women are victims; this has been done several times and to no great advantage for women. It is not serving us. It is true that women and men are still victims, victims of cultural and religious rules that no longer make sense, victims of themselves, of government, of whatever; however, to truly take the position of a victim is not only to relinquish responsibility for yourself but also to live from a perspective of inferiority and inability to change; to be powerless. This is not the case. It is true women lacked the right to vote, were seen as property and therefore could own no property themselves, that it was unacceptable for women to learn how to

read, to open a bank account, or get birth control without a man's approval,
but these are rights, privileges, cultural mores not power.

But it is power, Claudine writes in the margins of my manuscript. It is a strong metaphor to let ourselves believe that it's a man's world; or a highly enlightened deceptive strategy to tiptoe around men and women's egos by saying *it's still a man's world.*

There is a reason we still tell each other this; whether it is true doesn't matter. In fact, it will never be "true" as it will always remain, like the existence of God (or love), a matter of belief. Those who believe in something will clearly state subjective ideas as fact, which is why there must be a reason we continue to propagate the myth of a man's world. But the question isn't whether it's a man's world; the question is how is that thought serving you?

The major women who continue to hold our imagination today are seen as temptresses and seductresses who used their "charms" to succeed; after all, there were only so few ways women could achieve power, either by blood, charm, or deception. There were obvious benefits to being seen as the "second sex," and primarily it was the condition of pregnancy which made women take a back seat to politics, but were they controlling from the bedroom? Obviously.

When we talk of equality, we instantly turn to power, to control, to these inalienable rights. And this is where the confusion begins. We have a unique opportunity to alter our belief to the idea that women have always been in control, if not equally so. Together we can investigate women and men's choices. We can suspend disbelief, and admit there was some balance of power when the roles of men and women were clearly defined, and this created a successful society.

History has not been written this way or with this perspective. History has been written that men, and primarily white men, are always the victor, the dominating force. As we begin to question if it is really possible to believe, to know, that women have always been in control, there is just as instantly the counter argument and a trillion examples disproving this fact. Let us instead say of women that, clearly, they are not equally represented in government, in the film industry, in the top 500 most powerful companies. But what aspects of society and culture are women controlling? Who are the women (and men) inclined toward equality, and do they have power over anything?

Yes, we do, and this is what I'm trying to say.

TWO STEPS BACK

A fter being in Paris for eleven days, which basically consists of purposely wandering around the city–the French have a word for it. It's called *flâneur,* to stroll as an activity.

I'll add drinking wine in different locations in the afternoons, (turns out trying to change the world is a lot of pressure and makes one thirsty) wishing I had some friends, (Carol has gone back to Brazil) but feeling exhilarated by rambling on in a Moleskine journal, like all good writers should do who come to Paris, I have my first interview on May 1st–Labor Day in France. I go to meet Madame Dubois, (but I will call her Bernice) in her apartment in the 6th on rue des Rennes.

Labor Day is celebrated like most holidays in France–with the day off. I'll remember the day by the beautiful fragrance of the white flowers *le muguet*—in English, lily of the valley, also called *fleur à clochettes* because they look like little bells which are sold everywhere to be given to those who work. The flowers are eight euros and define the word pungent. She is so pleased when she opens the door. "I love these!" she says and inhales deeply.

Her house, the pastel yellow and green paint colors, the 60s ornate style of the furniture, the curtains, which are drawn but allow the sunny day to come in that diffused way, her short black hair done up in a very traditional bouffant way with giant glasses—everything about her reminds me instantly of my Nana. Bernice is an eighty-five-year-old woman who has the energy of someone forty years younger. She is an American but has lived in France for over sixty years. As we're talking, I'm setting up a tripod and video camera. I'm shaking a little from being nervous and wanting to get it set up as quickly as possible.

She moved here with her husband, who she says was "the exception of French men," meaning he was kind, considerate, and faithful, the last being a key trait according to reputation, many French men (and women, and if the success of the extra-martial affair website is any indicator) have.

She wishes he were still alive as they were not done having fun together.

"No, seriously, I mean that," she says. I haven't pressed record yet, so I don't capture it, but I make a note to remember it. It's the way she says it with such sincerity and sadness, I instantly feel just how much she loved him, and I wish it was on tape. But the video recording of this interview leaves much to be desired as I don't have any professional lighting, so Bernice will be backlit giving the impression of deep throat, or that character on the television show *The X-files* based on the informant in Watergate. And what she has to say is no less controversial.

We sit down with tea and little cookies, I press record and begin.

Bernice was the General Secretary of the French Coordination for the European Women's Lobby (C.L.E.E) from 1992 to 1998, and again from 2000 to 2006. She was also an NGO delegate to world conferences on Women in Copenhagen, Nairobi, and Beijing. A brave and outspoken woman, she was a History major at Sarah Lawrence College, and loves to question rules. She has my list of questions in front of her, I've come up with these questions, as they are things I generally really want to know.

- Do you consider yourself a feminist?

- How do you define that word?
- What are some of the greatest dangers for women in the 21st Century?
- Who are your heroines, both real and mythical?
- What are some ideas you have in order to make real change in this country and around the world?

ONE STEP FORWARD

Bernice looks back down at my paper of questions. "Yes, of course I consider myself a feminist.

"How do I define it? To me, that is not a problem; to me, feminism is fighting for women to have equal rights with men. That's it–that's exactly it–no more, no less. I never thought of burning my bra, but then it was a different period."

"What are some ideas to make real changes in the world?" she reads.

"There are so many. The first is education. We should be taught all religions and languages in school. Knowledge fosters understanding. The next thing is that if you have an equal number of women ruling a country, and by that I mean the Parliament and supreme courts, everything that matters. We get a lot of women ministers, they're named. Ministers are named; that, to me, is not enough. Where you don't get enough women is in elected positions. The problem is political parties, they're the ones that lock the women in their parties."

"It's still the boys' club."

"Oh yes, so that would be the first thing to really insist on parity. Parity is not about quotas, parity says half and half, fifty percent. Now the

Scandinavians, the Swedes started out with quotas of a third. We have to have at least 1/3 of either sex in Parliament."

"Ah, of either sex!" I say.

"Well, that was a good way to do it. And they were told, as always, suppose you don't get a third competent people, and they said then we will start our own women's party. That scared them off and they knew they would do it. There was no problem for them. So they said ok, ok and that was made a law. So, of course, Sweden was the first country to have political parity, to have 48%. It was 1995, and we were in Beijing, for the women's conference, we got the news, and we had a ball, it was wonderful."

"What other countries have parity?"

"A country today that has more women in Parliament than any other country is a country is in Africa, it's Rwanda. After the genocide, they have 56% women in Parliament, the highest in the world. It was the Rwandan delegate, I found about it in the UN, oh that was great!

"Most of the Scandinavian countries come close. The French are way below everyone, incredibly. It's the same reason, it's political parties. So I would say, political parity is very important. But in this country, around the world, you can only fight for it in democratic countries. There is no way you're going to get it otherwise, and I'm not talking about Islam, I'm just talking about totalitarianism.

"None of them are for women. I remember in the old days of the Soviet Union. They would always come up and say, not just the Soviet Union, that the situation for women was wonderful in their country. But where decisions are made, where the power is, how many women? We have lots of women deputies, but they don't make the decisions. In short, where the power is, women are not. In any totalitarian country, in Cuba, with or without Fidel, in China, Russia, the women aren't in power."

"One step forward, two steps back. For every triumph, there is another failure. If you think we have it all, that's mistake number one. We never do. When I was a child, I had read a fairytale about the Glass

Mountain and I never found it again, but it existed, and the hero was told he had to go to the top of this Glass Mountain to get this treasure. How do you climb a glass mountain?

"It's one step up, two steps down. He couldn't do it, until he was helped by a witch, or whatever. Anyway, there was trick. Otherwise, you couldn't manage it and I always thought that about women's rights; whatever you achieve, is always being threatened. Nothing you achieve is ever achieved for life."

THE FIRST THING, CEDAW

"But what do you do when you're an NGO at the UN and you hear all these things but you can't decide anything?"

"I don't know, tell me," I say smiling as Bernice is a wonderful storyteller and everything she has said up to this point has been so enlightening and so powerful.

"There are NGOs, which are rich and powerful and sold out," Bernice says clipping the words sold out, "like Amnesty International, who has never taken a position on prostitution. They put out a book a few years ago, with great fanfare, and a lot of money. They had a huge gala evening, to which we were invited because we had given them a lot of information. It was an evening dress. Everybody got a free bottle of perfume, *Guerlain*, which is not cheap, a large bottle, and they announced that evening that they had discovered violence against women, and therefore they had decided to publish a book. And I looked around me and they were women whom I knew from all kinds of important organizations and they were like stunned.

"Well, what do we do? They said it's not possible. Well, they got away with it. The newspapers loved it, ate it up. In the book there was not one word about prostitution. And we contacted them, we had been in touch with them because they had asked us for information. So you have NGOs like that. When you see their statements, they're not going to say something their majority of their governments don't like. All right so you have NGOs like that, they're not going to say anything that isn't popular."

"So what was the UN's stance on prostitution initially?"

"Initially the UN was very good about prostitution, they did a convention in 1949, and that convention says, it says one very important statement, it's against trafficking, it's against prostitution, whether or not the victim consents. That's important because it was recognized at the time, any trafficker can say, 'Oh, but she told me she agreed,' go prove it! Go prove she didn't. The burden of proof is then on the victim. And so the UN convention of 49 says, whether or not, because that's just not something you should do, put the burden of proof on the victim."

"Also you had people who drugged the girls, and crossed borders, or not makes no difference. And if ever there was a complaint, but look at the way she's dressed, and made up, I didn't know, she told me she's eighteen and she wanted to," Bernice says raising her voice in a seemingly innocent manner.

"So, it's too easy, that's one thing. Another thing is, you do have families who sell the girls into prostitution, because they're desperate for money. You have a number of countries in which that happens, and therefore the UN said whether or not the victim consents. This is buying and selling human bodies and it's not honorable. It's a modern form of slavery. And they set up a working group in the UN, which is what you do when you want something to really be implemented. They set up a working group on contemporary forms of slavery and it met in Geneva and it auditioned countries and asked the to report on what they were doing. So it was very important."

"Later on in 1979, the CEDAW convention came out, and that's the most important convention for women's rights it's article 6," Bernice gets up and comes back with a little blue booklet in less than a minute.

"CEDAW's article 6 is really very short, it's one sentence. *"Les Etats parties prennent toutes les measures appropriées, y compris des dispositions législatives, pour supprimer, sous toutes leurs formes, le traffic des femmes et l'exploitation de la prostitution des femmes."* It's short, concise, and to the point. You get rid of it! That's it! You get rid of trafficking; you get rid of prostitution. That's it! So that was fine. That was 1979, and it confirmed what the convention of 49 had said.

"They set up a CEDAW committee, and it worked in New York until a year ago then they transferred it to Geneva, which I feel is a pity, I really do, because most of the women's structure is in New York, and I think it was important that they be there, but they transferred it on the pretext of human rights, and seeing what's happening with human rights. I think it's a bad idea, but however it's there. Anyway it exists. The countries are asked to report to CEDAW every four years, and the NGO's can put out shadow reports on every country that ratified the convention.

"However, after the convention on Children's rights, which is the most signed convention, this is the second most ratified."

I'll take a break here, to explain what does it mean to be ratified and what is CEDAW?

CEDAW is the Convention on the Elimination of All Forms of Discrimination Against Women. Basically, it is an international bill of rights for women. As I write this, 187 UN member states have signed and ratified this bill.

The only developed nation who have signed but not yet ratified it is the United States and Palau. Not surprisingly, Palau's monetary system is the US dollar and their government is in free association with the United States, an indication of why Palau and the United States are together in their non-ratification.

Those who have not signed CEDAW: Iran, Nauru, Somalia, Sudan, South Sudan, and Tonga.

The one non-UN member who has not signed is Vatican City, while the Republic of China has ratified it within their own legislation. It is unfortunately not recognized in the UN.

Why has the US not ratified this important bill? How could CEDAW, a bill of rights which literally almost every country in the world has signed and ratified be seen as controversial by the US?

A SENSE OF URGENCY

I f there is no sense of urgency, it is challenging to get people to
act. Sure, women make 17% less than men, but it doesn't seem
life or death. Sure, a national law enforcing maternity leave
doesn't exist in America, but it's not really a big deal. Sure, they're
always trying to cut funding to Planned Parenthood and the National
Endowment for the Arts, (which isn't a direct attack on women per se,
but an attack on spaces which allow for freedom of expression where
people who may not fit into traditional gender and sexual orientation
roles usually flourish isn't a far stretch), but that doesn't really concern
us. My attempt at satire here is an effort to add some lightness to
discussions that are very heavy. It's a dangerous luxury, the lack of
urgency for women's rights.

But for those that are marginalized, it is very urgent. When Claudine
tells me to be vigilant, I don't quite grasp the magnitude of what she is
saying. When Bernice says take nothing for granted, rights can be
taken away, that is true, like what has been happening in the United
States and elsewhere. I just don't believe it. But we can easily go backwards, more easily than we think; however, if there is any silver lining
to the 45th president, it's that people became active. People realized the
urgency and took action.

FIVE-PARAGRAPH ESSAY

Initially, I wanted this book to have a thesis, something to prove, which would mean that I would structure the book like the classic five-paragraph essay, which would mean an introduction, three main points which prove my point, and a conclusion, which is ironic because that is a very linear, masculine thing to do.

The book would have gone like this:

- Part One: This is What A Feminist Looks Like
- Part Two: Lean In and Break the Glass Ceiling
- Part Three: We Can Do It (Yeah, We Know)
- Part Four: Having It All
- Part Five: It's NOT A Man's World (Anymore)

This structure in five parts is reminiscent of James Joyce's A *Portrait of the Artist as a Young Man* and is led by my personal story of transitioning from being a single unemployed expat to an immigrant wife to a career-driven mother, all while staying "independent."

These changes of identity correspond with five key phrases that reign when writing about women and in this way, I hoped to impose my own narrative on my manuscript while exploring the implications of why we believe independent women are so in fashion today and revealing that, in fact, autonomous women are always *à la mode* and we always love the subject of women with a side of ice cream.

But my book is not a five-paragraph essay; it is a quilt. It is all inclusive, all-encompassing, and it wraps around you to comfort you. It is spherical, it is peripheral. To create in words the effect of seeing an image all at once. Like the iconic image of Rosie the Riveter, the idea of independent women inhibits our psyche. These are the women we are told to be, but we are no longer the audience for the image of Rosie the Riveter. Perhaps we never were; we know *we can do it.* What we need is others to believe it. *They can do it.* The poster should say, women are not the audience, women are more and more convinced of their own empowerment.

It's Maine-based artist Abigail Gray Swartz who updates the famous Rosie the Riveter image after the Women's March in 2017 for the cover of *The New Yorker*. She makes Rosie The Riveter Black and adds a pink pussy hat. The original, done by Pittsburgh artist J. Howard Miller, was commissioned by the War Production Coordinating Committee of the Westinghouse Company to boast morale at for their current workers. Essentially making it emotional propaganda at the time. It's wasn't until the 1980s that the image became associated with feminism.

This may seem obvious, or may seem unquestionable: we want monetarily self-reliant women, and, therefore, empowered and educated women.

These five key phrases still dominate the feminist conversation about financially independent women. Whether or not someone famous claims to be a feminist, and what does a feminist look like? Can she be naked? What is feminism, anyway? And do we still need it?

It makes headlines to tell women to *lean in*, and to search for proof that there is indeed a *glass ceiling*. The phrases *Lean In* and *Break the Glass*

Ceiling degrade until they are just a debate on whether it's women's fault that we're not where we should be.

And it doesn't matter whether women show up at the table, but that they have to say something while they're there. This is where equality gets confused with representation. This comes up for race and other marginalized identities as well. This is not to say we don't think we want equality. If we did, men would wear dresses and still be "masculine." We want equal pay, sure. We want parity. Equality is not synonymous with power. And we want power, too.

Everyone wants to *have it all*. Who doesn't? Or who doesn't care? Men. No one is asking them. *Have It All,* but only if you're trying to balance a career and motherhood; you clearly don't have it all if you don't have both, or you do *Have It All* because you didn't do both.

And finally that *it's a man's world.*

But we have it wrong: women are survivors.

We need to educate the men.

Everyone operates under the umbrella idea of *It's a man's world.* And that is our greatest misstep—continuing to believe that it's a man's world. Which is why we've gotta stop saying it's a man's world. I love James Brown, too, but listen to Aretha Franklin, and I think if there is ever any doubt, one should always listen to Aretha, "They may say that it's a man's world, but you can't prove that by me."

BAC À GLACES

On a sunny day, I meet Claudine at an intimate restaurant called *Bac á Glaces,* which literally means tub of ice cream. Though it is really Claudine's place, to me it becomes our place. Claudine knows the owner there, as they are renowned for making delicious gelato. It's across from one of the major shopping malls of Paris, *Le Bon Marche*, which means cheap and is anything but. I get lost walking down the boulevard Raspail, thinking I've gone too far when I haven't gone far enough.

When I find the place, I do not have time to look at the menu, a condition that will become familiar for every meal Claudine and I have together, and I will more often than not order what she is having. Today, it is a crepe with smoked salmon and mache, the petite salad that they serve and sell everywhere. Claudine is not well; she wears, as she always will, a huge down beige coat, and underneath several layers of pink. Pink blazer, pink sweater, and a Hermes scarf that was her mother's.

Our talk is rapid, another element that will become standard for every meal we have together. Claudine is talking about her office and one of the men she works with.

"Augustine, he discovered that I signed the Manifesto, so now, you see, he doesn't like me or trust me anymore."

The Manifesto Claudine is talking about is the *Manifesto of the 343*, sometimes crassly referred to as the *343 Salopes*, meaning the 343 whores or sluts or bitches. It was written by Simone and was published in the French magazine *Le Nouvel Observateur* on April 5, 1971. It was a manifesto in which every woman who signed it had had an illegal abortion. Claudine, even though she hadn't had an abortion, signed it in solidarity.

At twenty years old, she was the youngest member of the women's movement. Signers of the document included Simone de Beauvoir, who wrote the document, actress Catherine Deneuve, writers Françoise Sagan and Marguerite Duras, and Marie Pilet (Julie Delpy's mother). Julie Delpy, the woman who made the hopelessly romantic films of *Before Sunrise* and *After Sunset* with Ethan Hawke, and later *2 days in Paris* and more recently *2 days in New York*. There is a fantastic scene in the film *2 Days in Paris* where the mother tells the boyfriend she was a whore, and is one of the *salope*s who signed the document. This document legalized abortion in France.

After lunch, Claudine calls Catherine Zviloff for me, as making a rendezvous in French over the phone is incredibly challenging, and not in a good way. What it means is I can't really do it.

Claudine gets Catherine on the phone and sets up the time. When she hangs up, you would think it was her who was going to do the interview, she is so happy for me.

WHICH IDENTITY IS YOUR PRIORITY?

Emma and I go to Catherine's office and she, like many women, is quick to preface the interview with the idea she is not involved in the philosophy of feminism.

She is not an intellectual, but she is involved in the activism part of it. Catherine Zviloff is the lawyer who tried the case that made female circumcision illegal in France.

Emma and I are both nervous. I try to ask my question in French, but my pronunciation is so bad that I ask Emma, "How did she get involved with women's rights?"

"I used to be naïve, but to be naïve is also good. To be a lawyer with the idea to be against injustice. I was very sensitive about injustice, even as a child.

"We, as the French, are very demanding on some of the small details for equality, because we already have equality. Women who are the boss, they are on the top of society, for the outside world it is seen as privileged, high-level women, all about careers, positions in the company. Details, they want the perfect equality, no one is working in the ghetto."

"Quels sont les plus dangers pour les femmes?" Emma asks as I try to imitate the way she pronounces the sentence in French and remember that it means. "What are the greatest dangers for women?"

"We should not take it for granted, so we don't go backwards."

To exist in a country that is not their own, immigrants have to claim their own nationality, their own culture but their culture is based on the inferiority of women so that is the problem. The rules of inferiority are their way to exist."

"What is the biggest challenge for women?"

"The same problems still haven't changed. Nothing is granted. We have the right to vote, it will be a revolution if we go backwards on this right. There is still inequality, abortion, the main danger not to go backwards, you have a very secondary role in the society. There are many countries where women are voting but they are not masters of their lives, so we have to be careful not to be satisfied of the visible rights that we have. You have to be the master of your life. A daily equality she would prefer that more than the right to vote. There are so many countries where they have the right to vote, but they are nothing. Even in faraway countries they are thinking about their rights, they measure the distance of their daily life.

"To have the conscience to exist and not being able to exist. When you can't choose your activity, your husband. When they are aware it's very hard, they are aware of what they can't have, in Algeria, Magreb, Saudi, Egypt, Africa."

Emma says, "She goes there for dramatic cases. So she can touch the reality over there. Her job is to provoke debate."

"Is that how you start to make changes? What advice do you give young women to make change?" I say.

"You can't accelerate history. As globalization becomes a reality, there will still be resistance, but in most of the world, equality will be worldwide more and more. In Saudi Arabia, they are aware of equality, all women know about these rights. They want to be first Saudi and then women, but they pay the price. Once they have the taste of freedom, they never go back. So they claim their inferiority to claim their nationality."

Simone brings up a similar idea that women choose their class system before they choose other women. This is why she says it takes so long to get anywhere, as the women of higher classes wouldn't unite with lower-class women for a similar cause.

Catherine continues, "So you are in the system or you are out of the system, but in order to be in their cultural system, they have to be inferior. If they don't, they will be excluded. In France, the way to exist is to claim their nationality. Globally, the majority of women want to have rights. When they step into the system, they don't want to go backwards."

"Who are some of your role models?"

"I don't know who is going to be a model, if you go back fifty years, there was no equality for women, which is why you have no women heroes. Bu nothing is totally new. Power is not something that you share, it's not men and women, if we had the power we would do the same, money is power, power is money. Marie Curie, she was courageous, intelligent, very free, but she paid for it full price."

After we leave, Emma and I go for coffee, and she tells me she is dating a new man. "When you are working, it is more attractive for men. Men want to commit with women when they are working."

"Yes, that's the advice a lot of my friends have given me, is to appear busy."

Emma says, "Johanna's mother thinks that they have less respect when the girl is not working." She continues, "I met Fred when I started doing this part-time job, and he is into that because he says, 'You are doing your thing.'"

So I keep myself busy. I go on several interviews with and without Emma. I meet Marie-Helene Vincent, a divorced Catholic feminist artist with two young children in her home in the 7th arrondissement. She is also an art teacher, and she takes me to the Pompidou to see the new exhibition on women artists, elles@thepompidou. It is the first time a major art museum has focused a show entirely on women. As we're walking around together, there is a group of school children standing in front of the Méret Oppenheim's fur cup, and I think *Yes, I could have children here and have them come on a field trip to this museum.*

My next interview is with Nathalie Pilhes. Luckily, she speaks perfect English. Nathalie is active in making changes to her country. She is working for President Nicolas Sarkozy, which means I get to go to the second house of the president, as he has chosen not to live there. A guard greets me at the gate. The metro stop is Miromesnil, and this is the fancy part of Paris. I am dressed for the part, I wear a white pinstripe skirt suit ensemble. I am received differently, with more respect, even in the tabac, when I am dressed a certain way.

I bring a box of seven *Pierre Hermes* macaroons, and we eat them with espresso on the gold-plated table in her high-ceilinged office. Nathalie says that the most crucial thing for women to do is to network. She is more than willing to help in any way she can.

Nathalie's father is a well-known French writer, laureate of some of the most prestigious literary prizes, one of them for the novel called *L'Imprecateur*, on the dangers of big financial investments, which was an enormous best seller and became a movie.

"How do you feel being a woman in politics?"

"Last year, I was elected as deputy mayor of the 13th arrondissement. It was very difficult, because this world is very violent and is organized for men. Everything is organized during the evening, during the weekend. It's an archaic organization, because these men have a lot of time to do politics, so we have work, we have family, and we have politics. And that's why it's very different for people who work. I chose to work, because I chose to be free, to be free to choose my position on different subjects. I don't want to be the instrument of a political party. So I want to say what I want to say every time I want to say it. So that's why I work. And to be independent, to be financially independent, from the party, from politics. That's something I advise the young people who begin in politics.

"And my son," she says with a smile, "he is seventeen and he wants to be a politician. But I tell him he has to work. He has to work because he has to be financially independent because he has to be free, as sometimes, he has to be able to say that he disagrees."

Afterward, I walk to the Tuileries on a gorgeous spring into summer day. I sit on one of the lounge chairs by a fountain and talk with my dad. I tell him about the interview and then ask him if I should call Eric. Even as I remember this moment, the anxiety of falling in love rushes through every part of me.

Eric answers the phone and says to come over, and I will be so excited to figure out how to take the bus directly to his house. He thinks I'm sexy in my white pinstriped outfit.

LET THE MAN CARRY THE MONEY

Hélène Monties, the assistant to the French Ambassador in India, says that it is impossible to be independent once you decide to share your life with someone.

Hélène was awarded the French Legion of Honor in 2009 for her work in the Ministry of Foreign Affairs as well as her work with children. Claudine, having won the most prestigious medal in France herself, gave Hélène the reception in her home. Shortly after, I go to stay with Hélène and her husband, Jean-Noel, in Besançon, near Switzerland.

Fall is just beginning, and the leaves are just starting to change. The train ride there is lovely, and there is that brisk prick in the air. Their house is a cozy farmhouse along a little river. It is cold, brisk, that definition of brisk autumn crisp air. That I've been invited to stay by this woman I've just met seems natural. Claudine has told me, "You'll see, Augustine, she's like a grandmother. She'll take good care of you."

Helene is a short heavyset woman with kind eyes. She met John-Nöel when she was thirty-one. In three weeks, he had proposed, and three months after that, they were married. Stories like that can make you believe in the power of love.

When I arrive, we sit at her kitchen table and she tells me the story. Together, we speak a combination of very broken English and French. She seems to think that, as a woman, it is equally important to know what you want and don't.

"As women, we can always propose other options. That may be our job," Helene says. "You should write something that helps women and men understand each other more." So far, that's what everyone says.

At night, I stay in one of their children's rooms and read *Animal Farm* by George Orwell. It's the only book in English. I see a tiny mouse before going to bed hiding behind the bookshelf. I let it be. It's just a small country mouse. I've had mice in my New York apartment before.

When I leave, we sit at the train station together, waiting for my train. Hélène gives her money to her husband to pay, just like my mother. She remarks on this, "Even if we're independent, we still let the man pay." Why? Because it still looks better when the man pays. I do the same. I let the man hold the money so that he can pay for the ice cream later. Will it ever look good for the woman to pay? Does it have to? Do we even want it to? Sometimes we want to feel like we're being treated to dinner even if it is just the guise of being treated cause it's our money. A lot of women still want flowers and chocolate and diamonds. My husband loves when I bring him flowers. The value is not the thing but that the person thought of you. What is important now is to take responsibility for those things. Men follow women's lead.

AU RELAIS-RELAY

When I come back from Hélène's house, I have a birthday card from Eric in the mail.

I'm happy to know he's thinking about me. I can't fault him too much as I've done (ahem) the same thing—tied up loose ends in New York and Los Angeles. Let me explain.

When I first move into my new apartment in Montmartre, I ask Eric if he'll take my spare key. Imagine my surprise when he says, "No."

"Why?" I ask.

"Well, I've been meaning to tell you something. A friend of mine is coming, an ex-girlfriend, and we had made this promise months ago that no matter what happened, she would come. And I've been meaning to tell you. And I can't break my promise, but obviously I didn't know if you were really coming back to Paris."

I don't quite know how to respond. I'm shocked. Here I was about to give him my extra key, and he's about to go off on a love fest with some ex. In my head it's all just wrong, wrong, wrong.

I don't quite know what is said after that. I plead my case. Definitely don't have your ex come to Paris. His case is if I break this promise, how will you know I won't break promises to you in the future? How will you ever be able to trust me? A good point.

In the end, he goes. With her. Whoever she is. And I cry in the bathtub thinking, *How could I be so wrong?* I envisioned my entire life with this person. I'm so madly in love with him it hurts. I planned for us to take baths together, in this tub. I saw it in my mind. This just isn't how it's supposed to be.

To be fair, when Eric goes, I don't rest on my laurels. I go to a party at Mariel's boyfriend's house where I meet Jean-Jacques (not his real name). A very sexy, skinny, white French guy with smoker's teeth and sandy blond hair, who loves to travel and loves the States, and is thoroughly interesting. Just my type, sort of, or my type for the moment. We flirt for three hours, and as we're about to leave to walk home, he casually mentions his girlfriend. Could've mentioned her before, buddy!

Regardless, we leave together as we've already got our coats on and are heading out the door, though now I have no intention of going anywhere with this person but to the taxi station. There is a crazy line for the taxis, as is typical this time of night when the metro closes and the bars open their doors to let everyone out. He leaves me there waiting for a cab with the rest of the suckers.

I decide not to wait and walk home to my new apartment. I don't believe it's too far. Or perhaps this is the night I end up sharing a cab with some other guy I meet in line who says he's going to Montmartre but where we actually go is rue du Montmartre in the 2nd arrondissement, which is not the same thing.

I walk home through Pigalle in the witching hour, past the prostitutes who still stand on the corners. If I spoke more French, I would be so tempted to talk with them. I think about one day when I can speak French doing this. I never do. I'm not brave enough to infiltrate a world of which I know nothing. Just like I want to do a photo project of the different hair braiding shops that line rue Poulet in my new neighborhood because if you look closely each one represents a different country. But I never do.

Back to Au Relais. it means Relay, but I don't know this. Eric comes to my place, and we walk up the street. Eric's eyes are wide. The square is unbelievably charming. At the intersection of rue Feutrier and rue Paul Albert, there are three cafes, *L'Eté en Pente Douce, Au Soleil de la Butte,* and *Botak Café.* There are lights in the trees so the mood is set. What other words are there for romance?

"Wow, you better write the next American Masterpiece—you don't have any excuse not to—living here," Eric says.

No pressure! I think in my head.

He's looked up a good restaurant to go to for dinner. It's closed. We walk back up the hill, past a group of men who may or may not whistle at me or say something inappropriate in French. We keep walking and end up at a French bistro in the shadow of the Sacré-Coeur, Au Relais. There is a live band in the back of the six-table restaurant. We sit by the window at a table for two. The restaurant is cozy. And it's here, over roasted Camembert cheese with honey, one of the most amazing things I've ever tasted, that Eric and I make a choice. Our choice. He wants to be with me, and I want to be with him. *Ça tombe bien,* which I learn in French comes from the hemming of a pair of pants or skirt, directly translated means, *it falls well,* but is used often to say, perfect timing, it worked out, what luck!

AU MARCHÉ

Now that Eric and I are official dating, not sure what we were doing before, we settle into a habit of going to the open-air market by his metro station every Sunday morning. I let him *bavard* for me, meaning to be talkative or to gossip but I think it really means to schmooze, as I try to memorize the over four hundred different types of cheese. He takes to calling me *Chérie*, so I mimic that as well. As the vegetable vendors get to know us, they call us *les amoureux*. It sounds so incredibly romantic to my untrained French ears, I don't quite catch it all the time that it's said, but Eric will point it out to me. Paris is the city for lovers. Random people on the street don't feel awkward saying, *Ahhh les amoureux*, the lovers.

We buy rotisserie chicken and potatoes, where the man with the chickens will always ask if we want *le jus,* the juice, and we always say yes. Along with a homemade pear cider, our Sunday lunch is mellow. Or Eric will make one of his specialty grilled cheese sandwiches, which are unlike any normal grilled cheese. Eric is a precise chopper, he can get the onions, pickles, tomatoes super thin, with *bleu d'auvergne*—a special un-pastuerized and better than your average blue cheese, *comté, morbier*—recognizable by the fine line of ash running through it, with mustard, and mayonnaise on a crusty baguette we sit in their apartment and listen to jazz. Heaven.

That first year, Rasul and Eric live in a very nice subletting HLM, the name for social housing. Rasul is kind and a vegetarian with one long dreadlock going down his back, and together their house is homey, comfortable. His girlfriend, Katy, a petit piano player also from America who is sparkling with energy and that her and Rasul play together at various gigs around Paris is so cool that I like them instantly.

This is my world, or the world I want to inhabit, that of the cool smokey jazz clubs visualized by Digable Planets in their music video, "Cool Like That" but also lived in my imagination from stories of my father as a young man seeing Louis Armstrong play in the village in New York in the 60s. These are my people. So it becomes part of our history, Rasul and Katy witnessing firsthand Eric's and my love affair beginning. It is in this way that they claim our story or are part of our story for themselves, too. "We were there," they say with pride, "when you were first falling in love."

TWO MONTHS LATER

H ands down if you have something important to say, but don't say it while sober, you'll definitely say it while drunk.

Two months later, a friend comes to visit, and this trip marks the end of our friendship. She's exhausting! After years and years of listening to the same problems, I run out of patience. She feels I'm full of myself and selfish as I don't ask about her life, her problems. It's the first time someone will ever accuse me of this, and it feels out of place. I am having a wonderful time in my own problems of somewhat deciding between two men. Though I've already definitely made my decision. But I'm not sure about Eric so I'm still keeping a plan B.

We go to a cocktail party at Laetita's apartment. We drink way too much, and somewhere on our impromptu dance floor, I tell him I love him. I say it in French, *je t'aime.* I double down and say it in English. He doesn't say it back. Now it's out there.

It doesn't go well after that. It starts to rain. It's November. We leave. Eric is smart enough to put us in a cab and says he'll call me tomorrow. My friend and I fight. A viscous, ugly fight. We go to bed. We make up the next morning. Whatever happens after that I don't remember. We're sad. Her visit has definitely not gone as planned. We've grown apart. We haven't been close in a long time. We always had some difficulties that we didn't want to admit to. She flies back to LA. Perhaps we see each other a handful of times and try to put things on the mend. She changes her life. She moves to New York. We see each other while I'm pregnant five years later, and all that's left is love. And if love is all that's left, you're lucky.

Love. There is no plan B. You have to be willing to be vulnerable. To put both feet in strongly, firmly. This is what my therapist, Diane, says. This is good advice. There is no plan B with love. When Eric and I see each other again after this debacle, he is sweet and sensitive and says, "About the other night, I'm happy to hear it. Maybe it wasn't the best situation, but I don't want to take away from the sentiment. It's a wonderful thing to hear. And I think you're pretty amazing, too."

It's not exactly what I want to hear. I know I'm amazing. I want to hear "I love you, too." I'm willing to wait. I'm willing to put my heart out there, because there is no other choice. I'm two feet in, firmly planted, not going anywhere. If it doesn't work out, I'll deal with it then. But for now, I don't want anyone but him. This is a big choice. This is a new thing for me.

WRITING A BOOK IS LIKE FALLING IN LOVE

Is a book like a new lover? And the process of writing or reading a book like falling in love?

You have to know someone's past to know their future. In the beginning, you start out with the idea, the preconceived notions of what love is, what the book is, what it might teach you. You use all the tricks in your repertoire. If you're writing it, you may play games with the reader as if he were your lover. You act mysterious to keep one reading, to keep having second or thirds in hopes of coming home. Perhaps you're coy, coquettish even, withholding till the last possible moment or maybe by the first act you've already jumped in the sack—revealing, in essence, the hidden ending in a series of metaphors.

If a book is like a new lover, the conclusion is not the achievement of love; rather, this comes along early, and love is all the rest of it. The good and the bad, the mistakes and imperfections—the entirety of love. The start of my love story could begin with learning how to ride a bike; Eric would teach me. But that's not exactly the beginning, and it's not exactly the full story. Our love does begin in Paris, and though French is said to be the language of love, the French do not use *amour* lightly; instead, they use the verb "to like," *aimer*. *Amour* is not even a verb but a masculine noun, and it is not a word they use commonly. In

English, we say, "I'd love to." The French do not use this expression, nor do they use the expression "I feel." They' say, "I have the impression of" —*j'ai l'impression*—not "I feel." Feelings are reserved for how one physically feels, because feelings were considered a feminine weakness in French, not "I feel like a book is a lot like love."

SHEROES

We train our daughters to be princesses, not queens. (Until *Frozen* comes along in 2013 and Elsa is queen.) This is one of the more intelligent things I've written over the years, and I hold on to it like a buoy when I'm lost out to sea. Which is a cliché metaphor and not nearly as enlightened.

What is enlightening is the research done by linguists Carmen Fought and Karen Eisenhauer in an article in *The Washington Post* in 2016, "Despite being a story about two sister princesses, men claim 59 percent of the lines in that film." The article begins with *The Little Mermaid*, who literally has her voice taken away.

> *"In the classic three Disney princess films, women speak as much as, or more than the men. "Snow White" is about 50-50. "Cinderella" is 60-40. And in "Sleeping Beauty," women deliver a whopping 71 percent of the dialogue. Though these were films created over 50 years ago, they give ample opportunity for women to have their voices heard."*

Though the greatest take away from their research is to praise children on their skills and accomplishments and not their looks, this is where the newer films are positive—there are more compliments based on ability rather than appearance.

Later, after I have two children, I amend it to say we should train our sons to be queens, or rather when my son can go to school dressed as Wonder Woman, then I'll know we're in a more equal world. It's all fine and dandy for my daughter to come dressed as Superman, or Batman, or any masculine hero, as we're used to emulating men. All we've been taught is men, so we have to emulate men. It's become socially acceptable for a girl to dress up as a guy, but we still have a way to go before boys can dress up as girls, as women, and have it be seen as cool.

"It's for girls," is still said as dismissive and not as cool. But the minute my son can admire women as a heroes, I'll know we've arrived. So when he wants to paint his nails, or pick the pink one, I tell him, "Anything boys can do, girls can do, too. And anything girls can do, boys can do, too."

PRETTY WOMAN

A NOTE ON THE MODERN FAIRYTALE

Naomi Wolf, author of *The Beauty Myth* and super feminist, calls us passé to believe that fairytales are un-feminist. In an article in *The New York Times*, "Mommy, I want to Be A Princess" on December 2, 2011, she writes:

"The second wave of feminism deconstructed the Sleeping Beauty narrative and other princess myths as a form of hypnotism, designed to seduce women into marriage and passivity, and structured to teach them that their real lives only began with the kiss of a prince. Even today, I meet right-on feminist moms horrified at the enduring appeal of this story to their egalitarian-raised kindergartners: Why, they ask me, is my daughter obsessed with being a princess?

I would tell them not to worry: Second-wave feminists have it wrong. If you look closely, the princess archetype is not about passivity and decorativeness: It is about power and the recognition of the true self. Little girls are obsessed with princesses for the same reason little boys are obsessed with action heroes What other female role model can issue a sentence and have the world at her feet?

Claudine adds another important element to the table: "It depends on who is reading you the fairytales." We come to the understanding that with fairytales, it's how we now interrupt them. So Wolf goes on to say;

Interesting that when fables are filled with actual narratives of female power, assertion, and heroism, they are still read as being about beauty and passivity. Don't worry if your five-year-old girl insists on a pink frilly princess dress. It doesn't mean she wants to subside into froth; it just means, sensibly enough for her, that she wants to take over the world."

It may be all right for them but "Modern Intelligent Independent Women" are not supposed to believe in fairytales, not even the popular film *Pretty Woman*, though everyone loves that film.

We should dismiss them. We should worry about the hidden message it's sending. Cinderella didn't doubt she was the nicest and most beautiful, even though she seriously victimized herself (but let's not victim-blame Cinderella) and most likely had a strong case of Stockholm syndrome. She wasn't that self-aware. She doesn't need to work on herself like we do.

One of the things that inevitably comes up when discussing women is fairytales, and these fairytales span all cultures even though they don't all portray women the same way or follow the same structure. We can all draw upon them to refer to. The message of the film *The Princess and the Frog* is a perfect example of the temperature of the society we live in, that women cannot just work hard alone, that love is still important, and this message is perhaps not a bad thing. However, is there something pervasive in this training? It was her dream and her father's dream, and she wanted to carry out the dream she'd inherited. In the end, though, marriage is still the redeemer.

Which is why it appears we'd be hard-pressed to find a single woman who would admit that if a modern-day Prince Charming came riding up on his white horse, like Sting reportedly did for his marriage to save the woman from the evil sorcerer, stepmother, prostitution, whatever, she wouldn't want to be swept off her feet. Both men and women love to play pretend; as adults, we just become better at it.

Is it something about chivalry, perhaps? It's as if we're the ones now chasing Don Quixote. No matter how independent we may be, we love shiny armor or when men open doors for us. But is this seen now as more a sign of respect? Of good old-fashioned chivalry? Chimamanda Ngozi Adichie, the author of *We Should All Be Feminists* has the answer. On *The Daily Show with Trevor Noah*, she says we should open doors for everyone because opening doors is a nice thing to do.

AN OBJECT OF VISION

I don't do many touristy things when I first arrive in Paris (unless you count starting a fling with a half French/half American man), but one of the major things I know I must do is go back to the Musee d'Orsay to see Manet's 1863 painting, *Le Déjeuner sur l'herbe*, that so moved me when I was seventeen.

Back then, the painting was on the fourth floor in the last room with a bench right in front of it. I was so taken with it, I remember sitting there unable to move, looking at the scale of this work. How the woman's eyes follow you no matter what angle you gaze at it from. To go and sit on the same bench and look at it again is something I've been looking forward to since the moment I left. So it was unfortunate to discover the painting had been moved, and was now on the first floor, and there was no longer a bench to linger there. To me, this was the painting that surely solidified women's place as an object. All right, admittedly, women were objects before, but clearly this one painting affected the global way of thinking. Why is she naked and the men are not?

When I was seventeen and had just read *Ways of Seeing* by John Berger, I understood what he meant when he said:

> *"Men act and women appear. Men look at women. Women watch themselves being looked at. This determines not only most relations between men and women, but also the relation of women to themselves. The surveyor of woman in herself is male: the surveyed female. Thus she turns herself into an object — and most particularly an object of vision: a sight."*

Women can take a certain pleasure in being looked at, and more so define themselves by that pleasure. Men look and women watch themselves being looked at, and it's from there women get their power. This is something I inherently understood, as if it was in my DNA. Berger's little theory about men and women was something I instantly related to. What Manet's painting really did was solidify the female gaze. Carol Armstrong, a Professor a Yale writes in her article, *"To Paint, To Point, To Pose"*:

> *"It is indeterminable whether she is challenging or accepting the viewer, looking past the viewer, engaging the viewer, or even looking at the viewer at all. This encounter identifies the gaze as a figure of the painting itself, as well as the figure object of the woman's gaze."*

I grew up knowing the smell of turpentine and linseed oil, how to stretch and gesso a canvas, how to mix the paint so you didn't end up just with brown, how to soak and staple watercolor paper to a wooden board so it wouldn't curl.

I grew up knowing the name of several artists, what they painted, their particular themes, what artistic movement they were in, and where they lived. (Of course, more often than not, it was France.) Picasso, Monet, Manet, Degas, van Gogh, Toulouse-Lautrec, all the greats (all men). That, combined with an admiration of this European lifestyle meant it only makes sense that my developed dream would be to live in Paris to be an "artist" in this way.

To me, male artists had more fun, but then I only knew of male artists.

The only female ones I knew were the muses of these famous artists: Dora Maar, Picasso's lover, Lee Miller, Man Ray's lover, and Camille Claudel, Rodin's lover, all of whom suffered from depression with tragic consequences. Maar never receives recognition she deserves and dies in solitude in 1997.

Lee Miller does her own rendition of *Le Dejeuneur sur l'herbe,* in 1937, a fantastic photograph that in 2013 I can buy for five thousand euros in a gallery in St. Paul de Vence if only I had an extra five thousand dollars. Miller who was a well known World War II photographer ultimately suffers from PTSD exacerbated by her husband's longtime affair with a trapeze artist.

It should be called the Claudel Rodin museum in Paris. Claudel is locked away in a mental institution for the last thirty years of her life, though now records show that her doctors appealed to her family to have her released as she was not mentally ill.

It didn't occur to me there might actually be female impressionists: Rosa Bonheur, Berthe Morisot, Mary Cassatt, Eva Gonzalès, and Marie Bracquemond. I just assumed there weren't any women painters.

This also translates to the value we give to women's art. Georgia O'Keeffe's 1932 painting *Jimson Weed/White Flower No. 1* is purchased by the Crystal Bridges Museum of American Art in 2014 for forty four point four million making it the highest amount paid for a female artist. Versus the four hundred and fifty million for Leonardo de Vinci's *Salvator Mundi* in 2017. Or Paul Cezanne's *The Card Players* sold for two hundred and fifty million or Paul Gaughin's *Nafea Faa Ipoipo* (When Will You Marry?) sold for two hundred and ten million both owned by the State of Qatar. On the list of the eighty-nine most expensive paintings there are only three non-Western artists. These are by Chinese artists Qi Baishi and Wang Meng. Qi Baishi's *Twelve Landscape Screens* is sold for one hundred and forty million in 2017. With prices like these, O'Keefe doesn't even make the list.

Everyone loves the iconic Guerrilla Girls image from 1989, which should be outdated but seems to be more relevant today, which asks "Do women have to be naked to get into the Met Museum? Less than

5%of the artists in the Modern Art Sections are women, but 85% of the nudes are female."

Women were the muses, the wives, the lovers, the mistresses, the sex workers. France does a good job of making the women artists known: The Museum of Montmartre, where Renoir lived, was also where Suzanne Valadon lived, and the focus is on her. I didn't for once think this meant I couldn't be an artist, just that I'd have to behave like a man to do it. And their behavior towards women was less than exemplary, to say the least. I'd just treat men the way they did women. When I was a teenager, it didn't occur to me this might lead to a crisis of identity. When I was a kid, it didn't occur to me not everyone could name who painted the water lilies and haystacks versus *Mademoiselles d'Avignon*.

Yet standing there in front of Manet's masterpiece, *Le Déjeuner sur l'herbe,* I'm still blown away. All the gender identity theories go out the very stylized windows, and I'm glad to be a woman. If I had the money, I would recreate all the famous art pieces with naked men. Women have been battling nudes in museums for centuries. Being the observed, Cindy Sherman turns this on herself with her early self-portraits of *Untitled Film Stills* and then recreating *Playboy* foldouts by always having the camera looking down on herself. One that is a particularly good example is *Untitled Film Still #6,* but they are all masterpieces in my mind.

What does it mean to always be judged on your looks, or to know that you're always judged on your looks, or to know that everyone else knows that you're judged on your looks? It's a cultural problem we're trying to fix. Sometimes it's a lot to wrap your head around, but who doesn't want to be an object of desire? Like Kate Winslet in the film *Titanic.* Who doesn't want to be seen as a muse? I did. So much so that for the first years of my dating career, I only dated artists. (Somewhere, there might be a nude drawing of me in my high school sweetheart's sketchbook.)

∾

When I first meet Eric, he doesn't know a lot about art. He's a musi-cian/sound engineer/music producer; clearly I'm branching out. He took only one art history class in college. So even before we're married, we get a Louvre membership. This allows us to go to the Louvre any time we want. We talk a lot about art, and wonder if we did a survey by the *Mona Lisa*, how many people would know who painted it. Next question, would you rather be distantly related to the *Mona Lisa* or distantly related to Leonardo de Vinci? Part of us believes it would be split down the middle; women would rather be or be related to *Mona Lisa* and men would rather be or be related to de Vinci. Though surely this is an antiquated idea.

"He treats objects like women, man," says the dude from *The Big Lebowski*, talking about Jackie Treehorn, the pornographic film producer who lives in Malibu (as evidenced by the slow-motion shots of women on trampolines). This quote is so succinct it needs no further explanation. Julianne Moore as Maude Lebowski does an exquisite job playing a female artist in the film. When we meet her, she comes at us full-frontal nude making the definition of suggestive sounds in creating her art. Her portrayal is clearly a bit tongue-in-check; however, later, in my life, as well as in the film, when we see her again on the phone talking about the Venice Biennale, her portrayal, I learned (being a lowly event planner for major high-end art events and having the chance to go to Art Basel, the US equivalent of the Venice art fair), is spot on. So much of women's art by women is about their bodies, becoming both subject and object.

Yet Sherman herself doesn't call the work feminist. Marina Abramovic as well denies the term. They don't want their work or themselves to be seen (and therefore dismissed) as just Women's Art. But here is where there is the sea change. That's what we want now. The Guerrilla Girls are busy. True, we don't know who they might be. They've removed their identity purposely to focus on the issues, but we know they are women, and that is enough.

These first days in Paris, I spend a lot of time alone, wandering aimlessly, listening to my iPod, riding the metro after drinking too much wine and thereby feeling nostalgic about New York, coming home to write and then smoking too many cigarettes. So Bridget Jones of me.

At cafes, when I meet people and tell them I'm a writer, no one immediately asked if I make any money doing this with that air of condescension in their voice, as they would in the States. Instead, the next question is the more obvious one: "What is your book about?" The responses vary slightly when I say what I'm writing a book about women.

"I'm writing a book about women," I say.
"Aren't all books about women?"

"I'm writing a book about women," I say.
"You can't go wrong there."

"I'm writing a book about women," I say.
"What about women?"

This is always and only said by other women in a highly defensive tone. They're suspicious; what right do I have to write about women? Once I tell them that it's about women's rights and feminism, working with a woman who knew Simone de Beauvoir and Jean Paul Sartre, and what we can do as the next generation of women to help other women, they seem more inclined to be interested, as it might be a book that can help them.

"I'm writing a book about women," I say.

"Wow, big subject." This is only and always said by men who more often than not are trying to flirt, followed up by, "Do you have the secrets to women? Because I sure don't."

Which is then immediately followed up with, "Women are crazy." And this from guys trying to flirt, but of course it is a tactic, the tactic that says, "You might be the only woman on the planet who isn't crazy, and therefore right for me." Instantly men assume I know some secret they don't know, and they want to be let in.

So yes, clearly I hold the secret to women, and why they're so crazy. So all you men reading out there, keep reading. It gets better and way hotter. Do I have your attention now, or should I take off my clothes to prove it? It worked for Lady Gaga, so why couldn't it work for me?

I may just take off my clothes, anyway, but before all of that, let's have some foreplay. For those who are sexually inclined toward the male member, perhaps you're offended I'm not offering you something. Perhaps I need to be giving you what I want to do, which is to replace all the nude women in art with naked men. A Manet-style *Le Déjeuner sur l'herbe* painting, but in a very hot way with the women clothed and then men not. That, I think, would do me just right. Don't get me wrong, it's not just that I want to seek out making objects of men for the fun of it, but I would be down for more male nudity. We've had feminine beauty for a long while, and while I adore the female figure just as much as the next person, I'd be seriously into erect men making a comeback in art, although clearly to make a comeback they would have had to be there in the beginning.

It might be said that some heterosexual women do not want to gaze upon the male member or *bite* which is the vulgar slang for penis. Penis is the same word in French and English so you're good there, incidentally so is vulgar, pronounced *vulgaire* like air, but if someone says *bite*, pronounced beet, like the vegetable you'll know what they're talking about. They'd actually rather look at other women because they see the reflection of themselves.

Riding on the same train of thought, I'll wish that someone would replace the all male figures in Michaelangelo's "The Creation of God" with women, which is what artist Harmonia Rosales does in 2017. Her work features all Black women as an exact replica of the famous piece of the Sistine Chapel. The singer Ariana Grande will follow suit a year later with an important change by placing herself in the position of God for her music video, "God is A Woman." A homage to several other female artists such as O'Keefe, Chicago, Tamara de Lempicka, Frida Khalo, and Kiki Kogelnick, who is not as well known as the others but was part of the Pop Art movement of the 70s. Rosales also recreates Leonardo de Vinci's "Vitruvian Man," with a Black woman as well as Sandro Botticelli's famous painting, "The Birth of Venus" changing the name to "The Birth of Oshun." Oshun is the goddess, spirit of divinity, femininity, fertility, beauty, and love in Yoruba-based religions of West Africa.

Riding on the metro, it's hot now. There's no need for stockings, as if the stockings had the utilitarian purpose of keeping me warm—more like warm in other ways. It's starting to be summer. The proof is also in the ad campaign of Galleries Lafayette. Each year, they use the same very suggestive ad of a very tanned woman with the look of ecstasy on her face. She's gigantic, covering the flagship store on Boulevard Haussmann and plastered in every metro station. In 2009, there is no question that this image is not a good image, for women or for men. And yet in that Paris summer, I feel like this woman. They say the French hairstyle is the after-sex look. That this woman is satisfied, but not from you. And in that way, she is larger than life and she takes up space. She claims the space. She is equal in size to the nude woman of our imagination.

Could this ad be the modern equivalent of Manet's *Le Déjeuner sur l'herbe*, though the female gaze is now removed? There is no debate about whether she is accepting or challenging the viewer's gaze.

Her eyes are closed. She is lying down. She is smiling. She is ours.

In 2009, Galleries Lafayette could get away with it, but let's hope this summer they won't.

MY ITALIAN DOPPELGÄNGER

T onight, I met the mirror image of myself, and I didn't like her. But don't get me wrong it's not her, it's me. She's lovely. But what does that say about me? About her?

Her name is Elena Rossini, and she is an Italian filmmaker and feminist. OK, she's not exactly like me; maybe she's cooler? She's an attractive brunette from Como, Italy, but went to college in Boston, like I did. She suggests we meet on the roof of Printemps. At seven stories high, it's a cheap place to get a drink with the view of the entire city. The golden statues of Harmony and Poetry on top of the Palais Garnier Opera House reflect the setting sun.

It's not that I don't like her, but that I am threatened by her, which is, in a way, being threatened by myself. If she is me, I don't want to share any epiphanies of mine with her, for fear of what? That she will claim them as her own?

Clearly this is social conditioning. This Italian girl—woman, rather—has lived my parallel life. How is it possible I do not trust her or believe her voice sincere? Is this the example of the fate of women, right here? That this Italian woman who is doing the same project as me, but the film version, could be a person I distrust or don't like? Why is it worse that I dislike her? Is that social conditioning, too? We even talk about the dislike of other women and how older women are threatened by us. She tells me about the difficulty in finding women mentors. I realize how lucky I am to be working with Claudine. But I don't offer for her to meet Claudine. She tells me, "The older women I interview don't help younger women."

We talk about the men we're dating, and how living with her has made his sexist radar go up. We talk about the Galleries Lafayette poster, and she's the one who tells me they put it up every year. Maybe that's why she's chosen Printemps as the place to meet, as Galleries Lafayette also has a rooftop terrace.

Is this what women are encountering in other fields? Women who are inclined not to help each other because of competition, territory, jealously? And even ten years later, I feel that familiar sting of jealousy when looking at her website and Twitter. She's followed by Barack Obama. Her film, *The Illusionists,* is a success.

I feel similarly jealous when someone else (and there have been many women over the years) come out with books about feminism, or women, or what to do, or how to behave as a woman to get ahead), as if I have the exclusive on a book about women. Anne Lamott talks about jealously in her book *Bird by Bird,* and it is the first time I hear it acknowledged that it's okay to be envious.

So as I sit there across from this woman I keep my guard up. Perhaps she does, too. Even though our goals are the same—to empower women, to do something to help women—we don't become friends. Despite saying we'll keep in touch, I know I will never see her again.

To see her again would be like looking in a mirror continuously, and not in a good way. I'm not ready yet to look at myself that closely in the mirror. I'm still under the illusion that I adore mirrors, and have no problem with my own image, but it is this image of this woman emerging, a WOMAN all caps, that turns me off.

Have I been trained to eye roll when the word *feminism* comes into play? Why can I not pinpoint what is annoying about her, or even about myself in her? Is it because women have always been dismissed and, thus, I've internalized this so completely that it is unconscious?

What is it about feminism that gets under my skin? Why after all my research am I still hesitant to admit to being a feminist, as if it's something to confess?

The Queen Bee herself, Beyoncé, appreciates the word in 2013 with her song *Flawless*. She boosts author Chimamanda Ngozi Adichie's career when she samples her TEDx speech, *"We Should All Be Feminists,"* which has been viewed more than five million times on YouTube and then became a book of the same name published two years later in 2014. It aims to give a definition of feminism for the 21st century.

Now that feminism has become attractive, cool, sexy even—pro-women without being anti-man—I don't have the same response from women friends I did ten years ago, when asked if they were feminist. But we have to pay attention and listen to make sure the feminism we're practicing is inclusive and is amplifying the voices of women of color who has been systematically excluded and erased. It's asking yourself the hard questions and searching for how can you do better?

When my friend Michelle reads over this chapter, she says to read a fantastic article "Why Do Women Bully Each Other at Work?" in *The Atlantic* written by Olga Khazan in September of 2017.

Ellemers and Derks believed they had pinpointed the conditions in which queen bees emerge: when women are a marginalized group in the workplace, have made big sacrifices for their career, or are already predisposed to show little "gender identification"—camaraderie with other women. (Think of former Yahoo chief Marissa Mayer's quote about another of her old jobs: "I'm not really a woman at Google; I'm a geek at Google.") Women like this, Ellemers says, "learned the hard way that the way to succeed in the workplace is to make sure that people realize they are not like other women. It's not something about these women. It is the way they have learned to survive in the organization."

It's worth noting that some of Ellemers and Derks's findings are not very robust. But other researchers have since published work that echoes theirs. Michelle Duguid, a Cornell University management professor, has explored something called "favoritism threat," or women's concern that they'll seem biased if they help one another. In a working paper, Duguid showed that "token" women who had helped other women in the past avoided doing so again when given the chance. In a separate study, she found that token women in "high prestige" settings were more reluctant to recruit female candidates to join their team than were women who worked in less prestigious settings or had more female colleagues.

As Joan C. Williams, a distinguished professor at the UC Hastings College of the Law, put it to me, "Women are people. If the only way to get ahead is to run like hell away from other women, some women are going to do that." And research suggests that this kind of distancing occurs in minority groups as well, which means these dynamics may be doubly hard on women of color, since they face both gender and racial bias.

In the Spring of 2009, I can't shout from the Printemps rooftops with pride, "I'm a feminist! (It's more of a whisper), and I know it's a problem my friends can't, either. But this woman can. And perhaps to me that is the biggest threat of all, she is ready to wear the feminist label, or as will come later, the Dior "We Should All Be Feminists" tee shirts.

∾

If we were to re-meet now, I wouldn't have the same problem. I'd be excited to see myself reflected. I wouldn't hesitate to share whatever genius epiphanies I'm having.

But even in 2018, that social conditioning about a lot of women being friends and being down for each other without drama like the cast of *Oceans 8*. I watch Sandra Bullock, Cate Blanchett, Anne Hathaway, Mindy Kaling, Sarah Paulson, Awkwafina, Rihanna, and Helena Bonham Carter and something in me is suspicious, I can't imagine all those women being friends. Like Ruth Ginsberg wanted an all-woman Supreme Court. I'm doubtful, and I question my doubt. However seeing all those women on stage together creates a shift so it's not too far a leap to envision an all-female supreme court. The symbol for justice is a woman, after all.

Still, it's not lost on me that an article on female competition is sent to me by a friend.

Different types of bitches. I remember asking my friend Becca in New York if women bosses could only be bitches? She said her aunt isn't a bitch, and this is true. But a lot of our interactions with other women in the workplace matches that in the article.

We've internalized the male gaze for so long. Still the question remains: do I even know what a feminine gaze would be?

18 MILLION CRACKS

I shook Hillary Clinton's hand. She's the only famous person I've shaken hands with, besides having my picture taken next to Angelina Jolie at the *Laura Croft* premiere and with Don King the night before. There is something to be said for shaking hands with someone. It's true what they say—you can feel her energy. It was a good handshake, a firm one, a real one.

In January of 2009, right before I left for Paris. I'm invited by my friend Becca and her Aunt Suzanne to Washington D.C. for the inauguration of President Obama. It's a great day. I'll never forget watching George Bush's helicopter fly away over the crowd and the cheers and boos. Cheney was there in his wheelchair, still looking like a curmudgeon of evil. And like that—he and Bush were gone.

Standing there on the lawn, in the freezing cold, even though the day is incredibly sunny. As the Greeks say, it was like *sun with teeth*. You feel warm because the atmosphere is hot with possibility. You believe you're part of something grand. Real change. Someone we believed would make a difference. "Yes, We Can!" We believe in Obama and his lovely family at the helm.

The outrageous joy! People dancing. It's magical, a real movement. Everywhere there is something for sale with Barack or Michelle's picture on it. People from all walks of life coming together for a single cause, hope. The streets and freeways in the center of D.C. are closed off to cars, and everyone walks under tunnels usually reserved for traffic. You're alone with your ticket. You're supposed to be back in New York for a meeting about the Gay Center event, but you call it in because you can't miss this. When I get back to the apartment where we're staying, no one is back yet. So I quickly write down some thoughts:

It was in the dark days of America, a time when we had no hope, no faith in our government, we knew they had lied to us but that wasn't very new from our experience. More importantly, it felt that there was nothing we could do about it. And then from out of nowhere came our savior, Mr. now-President Obama. The amount of joy and hope this man has instilled in the nation, in the world, is inspiring and was exactly what we needed.

To finally feel the country is moving in the right direction overwhelms us all. And all of this feels like it was meant to be, that the dream of Martin Luther King has come true.

I was there, that I shook Hillary Clinton's hand—all these once-in-a-lifetime moments leave me with such a feeling of gratitude and humility. And yet right now as I put my thoughts down, I know what makes me most happy is to be sitting here writing. It is again the confirmation I need, the proof this is what I am meant to do with my life and I will continue and persevere until I am a successful author.

After all, if President Obama can do it, then I can do anything. I know that having them in the White House inspires family values in a different more real way. I think people see this happy family that actually loves, cares for, and respects everyone. It is something to see and want to emulate yourself. I believe it is auspicious they have daughters, as the next step is to rid the world of violence against women. Goddess protect this first family, protect us all,

*and give us peace, or rather you have given us the tools for peace and I feel it
may finally be attainable.*

Reading it over again, I realize how wrong I was. How we may have
had eight years of bliss with Obama, but we were in no way prepared
for what was to come. The dark days of America—ha, I want to laugh.
From 2017 on, we are truly in the dark days of America. But in 2020
there is hope, with Kamala Harris as the first Black and first Asian
American woman elected vice-president. And as her historic speech on
November 7th reassures us, "While I may be the first woman in this
office," Harris vowed, "I will not be the last, because every little girl
watching tonight sees that this is a country of possibilities."

It's emotional, and it's how I felt being part of the celebrations of
Obama's inauguration. A sense of freedom and hope and gratitude
that I'm alive to see it.

The day before I shook Hillary Clinton's hand, I'd never given much
thought to shaking a person of power's hand before. It was that
moment when I understood why it is a big deal, why people are overwhelmed when they have the opportunity to meet someone they truly
admire. I admired Hillary Clinton, sure, but I hadn't really given her
much thought beyond wondering if her response to Bill's transgres-
sions and lying had been the right thing to do.

She is one of the guest speaker's for Emily's List Inaugural Luncheon.
Hillary—or, rather, Clinton—is the last one to speak, as she had been
stuck in traffic in the causeway. She is very apologetic, but very enthusiastic she's made it there. She speaks about women, of course, about
the importance of Emily's List who from their slogan on the website,
"Ignite change by getting pro-choice Democratic women elected to
office" and political involvement.

The day she loses the 2016 election, I look back through my pictures. I
find one of the moment right before she comes to me. In the background, it says, "When women vote, women win." And I want to cry.
White women voted, but they didn't vote for her. So it's not entirely
true that when women vote, women win. I specify white women,
because all the ethnicities besides white voted for her. How could we? I

know the answer already. White women don't choose their identity as a woman first. It's deeper and more complex than that. It's almost a mystery because I don't want to accept the answer. In 2020, how could fifty-four percent of white women still vote for that racist, white supremacist, misogynistic evil excuse for a man? The answer is hard to swallow: it's because our country is racist, misogynistic, and violent, and we've been raised in a capitalistic patriarchal system based on scarcity and competition. We've got a lot of work to do.

In 2008, when Hillary Clinton concedes the nomination for the presidency, she uses the metaphor of that infamous glass ceiling: "Although we weren't able to shatter that highest, hardest glass ceiling this time, thanks to you, it has about 18 million cracks in it, and the light is shining through like never before." It's a powerful statement, one still filled with hope but also with the acknowledgement we're still not quite there yet.

Actually, the quote doesn't really make sense because a glass ceiling would already have light shining thru it whether there were cracks in it or not, but I suppose that's neither here nor there.

AMERICANS IN PARIS

We were both Americans in Paris, and this was like being in Paris with someone you already knew.

We found the same things funny, like the way they would translate "great Scott" as "nom de Zeus" in *Back to the Future*. The way the French would talk and talk and talk and talk. We had the same pool of knowledge and culture growing up in California. Though Eric never listened to The Grateful Dead at length, keyword being length, the way I had. We could reference *Seinfeld* quotes at the drop of hat if need be, whereas *Seinfeld* was never popular in France, and most French people had never even heard of it. This became important—not necessarily for us, but for our mutual friend Mariel, who was frustrated she couldn't share this cultural reference with her French man, Thibaut.

Perhaps there is a key to this in relationships, as you draw from a pool of culture to relate to each other, and this is where growing up in America came in handy. We choose our obstacles in our relationship.

It took me a long while to realize that the man I'm dating might be sexist, and upon further reflection, that I might be sexist in some way. It did not, however, take me a long time to know he did not like women too much, or rather he did not trust them. It was hard to realize he might be sexist, to be fair to myself, because he was always making jokes said in jest and aptly taken in jest. But when we discussed the actual possibility of women in power and what that might entail, he was definitely not for this proposition, citing that women are crazy bitches, a line I myself have used several times.

Yes, crazy bitches—crazy, ruthless, jealous bitches who will stop at nothing to compete with one another for the best jewels, furs, houses, and cars. As he put it, the only reason that we (meaning women) wanted such items was to impress other women, not men. If they were to hear another queen or ruler had something better than she or had gossiped behind her back, getting even would take precedence over anything else. (This was maybe funnier when he said it.)

We discovered together that which I already knew: it is hard to say what a world controlled by women would be like, because there are so few examples. We were having this conversation naked in bed after having just had sex, sex that had begun in the kitchen by him coming up behind me as I was about to cut carrots. He said to me, "I know you already know how to hold a carrot." I said, "You're dirty," and by the time we finished chopping, my pants were down, his shirt was off, and we were headed to the bedroom.

Luckily the bedroom is not far from the kitchen in my small apartment. There isn't far to go. And so, there we were, discussing the subject we discussed often. Women—women and power, women and other women, women and men, women, always women, women, women.

FROM RUSSIA WITH LOVE

T he first time I meet Olga, she has met Melis at Alliance
Française. She has come with us to a show for my friends
Barbara and Emma in the Marais. It is cold in Paris. Olga
speaks with a thick Russian accent and smokes very thin cigarettes.

I know this cafe, *Le Progrès,* as it's one of the ones where my very fashionable friend Sophie has told me to go. This is supposedly where all
the fashion people hang out for fashion week, but it's a cafe like any
other. The waiters don't give you much attention. It is a cold day, and
Olga is wearing a puffy short jacket. Her answers are very brief, and
she is bored at the exhibit the moment we walk in. She is also perhaps
in a bad way as her boyfriend, Christophe, is not ready to be married
and so she will have to go back to Russia, which she doesn't want to
do. She can't stay in Paris if they don't get married, so there isn't much
choice.

The exhibit is small, held in an apartment building on the third floor.
There are several people there, and when we walk in, I see Emma, my
translator friend, who has changed her entire look. She has dyed her
hair blonde, is wearing a black dress and red lipstick, and looks like
someone out of a David Lynch film. Emma takes portraits—very

revealing, gorgeous, glossy portraits of people she knows. Later she will publish her own book called *In Utero*.

Barbara is showing her photographs from Berlin. Tiny photographs of automats, in different places. These automats are machines filled with candy or toys found in the most random places. We don't stay long, as Olga is ready to leave. I would love to say that we try to mingle with the French hipsters who are hanging out in the courtyard of the apartment smoking, but we don't. Our French is not that great, and the weather is cold, and it's too intimidating to stay. I still feel sad that we don't stay longer.

That first meeting with Olga, I imagine that she might be someone I never see again. From my first impression, it seems unlikely she'll work it out with the boyfriend, and I certainly don't anticipate that she will become a good friend. But she is so sweet and she makes the effort and calls me even after Melis has gone back to Turkey for a few weeks to hang out.

Olga has red hair and fair skin, and the image I get of her boyfriend, Christophe, is that he is some Frenchman who is not interested enough to make a commitment. When I meet him, however, he is not at all what I envisioned. Instantly one can tell that he is completely smitten over Olga, and a few months later he'll propose, and they'll get married in a French church the following summer. Their wedding will be a main event in our lives, an example of how great a French wedding can be with a block of foie gras for cocktail hour and good French wine.

Melis and I are bridesmaids, and we dance until late in the morning to very Euro music at the wedding in the country along the Seine.

All Olga wanted, growing up in communist Russia, was a Barbie, but instead she had Barbie's Russian counterpart, Steph, who was not as good for whatever reason. She didn't get a real Barbie until she was twelve, and by then it was too late to play with dolls. So she saves it for her little girl. It reminds me of an episode of The Simpsons, where Lisa creates the perfect doll of the new heroine for girls: "The wisdom of Gertrude Stein, the wit of Kathy Giswight, the tenacity of Nina Tottenberg, the common sense of Elizabeth Cady Stanton, and to top it off, the down-to-earth good looks of Eleanor Roosevelt"—only to be outdone by Malibu Stacy, who has a new hat.

It was an American businesswoman, Ruth Handler who invented Barbie, named after her daughter Barbara and based on a German doll Bild Lilli, which in turn was based on a comic strip about a blonde bombshell. Handler was married to Elliot Handler, co-founder of Mattel. They wanted to insist that she be modeled after girls, but she insisted Barbie had to have an adult body.

Girls wanted to play with the women they would become. That was the appeal. That was why it worked. That was what was revolutionary.

My aunt hated to be called Barbie. Perhaps it hit close to home, as she never wanted to go swimming in Lake Arrowhead and ruin her hair. My mother still saved one of the original Barbies, with the smokey coy sideways-looking eyes (important side note, it is not until 1971 that the eyes are changed to look forward) and jet black hair and pale pale skin, white white. She wore a form-fitting black sparkly cocktail dress. Years later, my father would work for Mattel, and his claim to fame from his time there would be that he worked on bendable Barbie, as well as Hot Wheels.

The main thing I think of when thinking about Barbies is that if her proportions were replicated as a life-sized woman, her head would fall over as her neck was too long for her body. I had several Barbies as a kid, bendable Barbies, all with blond hair and fancy dresses. Now, sixty years later, Mattel has introduced the gender-neutral Barbie with a body type, face, and wigs that allow children, both boys and girls, to imagine their own doll, their own representation. A fluidity that certainly didn't exist when I was a child.

But back then, I didn't want to be Barbie. I didn't see myself in her. I was more inclined to the American Girl dolls and the story behind Samantha, the rich Victorian-age girl who did fancy things like tea parties. She was a brunette. She was a girl my age. And she allowed me to imagine what it would be like to live in a different time.

WHEN FEMINISM BECOMES FASHIONABLE

C laudine says the only time of real change is when "society is on your side."

Her example is a story that she tells at many of the lectures she gives throughout France and in other countries. At a courthouse where Simone was called to speak, guards said to Claudine, "We may be in front of you, but we have mothers and daughters, too. We are behind you." It was in that moment Claudine realized the attitude of society had changed.

Machiavelli's theory of social change was that it was only when people believed in the possibility for change that they were motivated to actually act on their ideas. I witness this myself as a year later I am in French class at L'atelier 9, in an old apartment converted to a language school in the 9th arrondissement run entirely by women. A place where they've put French words on everything. In a class of seven women from different nationalities, all of them say that they could never imagine a day when there would be equal parity in government in their country. Because they do not see the possibility, they are not ready to fight for it.

TRANSITIONS

I'll make some big brush strokes: a year goes by, I take classes at L'Atelier 9 in the winter. I listen to Edith Piaf, Françoise Hardy, Camille, Coeur de Pirate, and Serge Gainsbourg with Brigitte Bardot's song *Bonnie and Clyde* over and over in an attempt to learn French. Eric takes me, Mariel, and Thibaut to a Berkley alumni party at the UNESCO headquarters. He invites Sabrina, a woman he works with who he thinks I will like, and he is right. Sabrina and I hit it off instantly.

At my new French school, I meet Natasha Nixon, a fabulous theater director and with Melis, Olga, Sabrina, Susan, and Gosia, we form a group of women who go out every Thursday as a ladies night.

By spring, Eric and I decide to live together.

We pack up all his things and mine and store them under the bed in the apartment with the plan to live in San Francisco for the summer. We find someone to sublet our apartment from a website called A Small World, and it turns out to be the famous singer Danny Brilliant. He pays in cash, four five-hundred euro bills crumpled out of his pocket. We fly to New York and on to California. I work at a small boutique French boutique baby store owned by Eric's friends, we house sit in Dolores Park, we house sit in Portero Hill. We consider moving back. I write, but mostly I spend time in limbo of whether or not to move back to Los Angeles and I field questions from my family and friends: "But Aug, are you really going to stay there for the rest of your life?"

PART III

EGYPTIAN RED RING

What was the music you were listening to when you knew you were falling in love–when you knew you'd already fallen–when you were done for?

For G. it was *Satellite* by Dave Matthews. For J. it was *Paint It Black* by the Stones. For D. it was *Queen of the Savages* by the Magnetic Fields. For C. it was Elliot Smith, *Behind Bars*, standing outside on the subway platform at 125th Street on the 1 or the 9 on a fall day in New York. For E. it was *Sunday Smile* by Beirut, again on public transportation, the metro line 2 on the way to his house.

And for falling in love with yourself it was Sly and the Family Stone, *If You Want Me To Stay* off of the Dead Presidents soundtrack and *Give Me Shelter*, again by the Stones. And Bob Dylan. Always Dylan, *Baby Let Me Follow You Down* and *She Belongs to Me*, that made you think of a version of yourself, perhaps not the best version, but more a way that you wanted to be seen, perhaps by others but more by yourself. That you might one day own an Egyptian Red Ring that would sparkle, that you might be that cool mysterious artist that you made the men who fell in love with you believe they were with. Baby, let me follow you down.

It's good to have been left by a man for another woman, especially when you're younger—that way, you can relate to all the heartbreak songs. Now I can listen to *Untouchable Face* by Ani diFranco and smile. My first boyfriend used to juggle and do handstands to impress me. Now I know I wouldn't mind seeing him again because all that is left is love, not heartache. He got kicked out of school like my father for a prank while drunk. He would've done anything to please me.

I never wanted to be a "good girl." That had no appeal to me. Being a "bad girl" always interested me more. Being considered scandalous, whatever that meant, rebellious—it meant smoking early and cheating on boyfriends. That was the problem with having philandering infidel heroes: you wanted to believe it made you a great artist to have affairs. It's not like I had a problem picking "bad" boyfriends, not till I picked the one who was most like me, my best friend, the one whose demons were the most like mine.

Except I've never been accused of narcissism. Only bending over backwards to please people.

MY INTERVIEW AT THE BACKSTAGE CAFE

"Don't smile at that man," says Claudine.

"Yes, I know, it's the American in me."

"No, really, he'll think you're flirting." It's been two years now and I still haven't learned not to smile the way like a Parisian. No one ever smiles in Paris except the tourists; it's an acknowledged rule. Admittedly I was never trying to learn how not to smile.

We are at the Backstage Café, and Claudine is on her best behavior. She has already apologized to our waitress because on Tuesday she had made a scene. This is Claudine's restaurant: a place on *rue de la Gaite*, on the left bank, in Montparnasse, around the corner from her house with comfy plush purple velvet chairs. This past Tuesday, after a long day at the office, Bernard decided to wait outside for her, and although they had made a reservation, because he was outside, they thought he had left and as such gave away her table to someone else. She was distraught at not having her table and made a scene. Bernard left her there, saying he was too embarrassed to ever go back. French people are not supposed to make a scene. (My family always makes a scene. We are never happy with the first table given.)

Now we are here on a Saturday, and Claudine has apologized profusely. It is January 2011, it is freezing cold and we are here for Claudine to interview me now. On my way to this meeting ,I have been listening to *Rage Against the Machine*. The Egyptian Revolution is in full swing. And even though I am nowhere near Egypt, it does feel like change is in the air. So the music to me is fitting, and yet it still does seem contradictory to be listening to *Rage* while walking through the streets of Paris, as if you should always be listening to wispy French women singers with accordion in the background, I am thinking of how we, as a generation, perhaps did have music that spoke to us. I don't have it in my mind that this is what I will discuss with Claudine, but that is what ends up happening.

"All my life," I tell Claudine, "I've admired the music of the 60s. The protest music that reflected the time of great change. The Beatles, The Rolling Stones, Janis Joplin, The Doors, Bob Dylan, Joan Baez, Jefferson Airplane, and all the music of San Francisco. We wanted to change the world, but we were too overwhelmed to do it."

"Well, Augustine the 60s was a tiny break in the history of the world."

"Yes, but I don't think people will actually protest now unless they feel their very lives are at stake. Like what is happening in Egypt. Unless it is a life-or-death situation." This does become the case with the Black Lives Matter Movement and later with the MeToo Movement, but at this moment we haven't had our revolution yet.

At this point, feminism is still unattractive. Feminists in Claudine's time took the risk to be seen as unattractive, which is not the risk that many Western women would take now. Regardless of that, and I say Western women only because Arabic, Indian, and Chinese women are doing just that they are pressing the boundaries and being seen as unattractive to their culture, but again regardless of that, it seems to me that to not use your beauty is a hinderance. It is one thing to not want to be seen as only an object of beauty or beautiful with no brains, but it is another thing entirely not to use one's beauty as an advantage. As women throughout history have made perfectly clear. It's what women and men have been doing for centuries.

Our conversation circles back, as it often does, to Simone de Beauvoir. We start discussing her work.

Claudine always had a problem with Simone's characters. She would always say to Simone, "Your female characters are not very interesting."

"Why do you think that was? That she didn't write more heroine-type women?" I ask.

"I think it was that she couldn't stand competing with other women. She started with *Memoirs of a Dutiful Daughter,* and then she switched direction. Once Richard Wright became a friend and explained to her the condition of the Afro-American, she saw the similarities between them and women. She wrote to Nelson Algren, 'I'm writing a little book on women, I don't know if anyone will read it.' Can you imagine? At the time her book was published when I spoke to my father about it was the time during the Cold War. You know my father, he is a scientist and is not inclined to exaggerate. He said that when her book came out, we were persuaded that the Third World War was on its way with the crisis in Korea."

Claudine does not believe in destiny or fate or God. When I tell her that one of my friends, Sabrina, is converting to Judaism and she has definitely changed, she responds with, "Freedom is an adult. If it is not God, then you are responsible for your choices. It is very difficult to behave as a free spirit, it really is to be an adult. To accept responsibility for one's self." While religion can teach responsibility, it does not teach freedom. If it were taught that way, it would have no followers.

"What is paramount is to bring men on the side of women. We have now been trained not to trust white males, yet they are still in power just using women as their puppets. We see this happening all over."

"But then how do we make change, Claudine?" This is the question I am always asking. "How do we do it, Claudine? What do we do?"

"We win through public opinion, keeping in mind that public opinion doesn't change overnight. My parents did not talk about abortion. My father is Protestant and my mother was Catholic. They were married simply at City Hall. I was never baptized, which was a big issue when I was in school, because I didn't wear a cross around my neck. I was very proud of not being baptized. My best friend in America was a Black girl at her school in Princeton, which at the time in the 50s was very rare. Now we hear speeches that I would've never hoped to hear. Thirty years ago, women weren't raped. What I mean is they were raped in silence. It's a big victory to say that it exists. So things are changing, Augustine, little by little."

"However, we are going to be facing big problems, the ones who have the minerals are the one with religion. The only negotiating issue for all countries is women's rights. This is where the US and France will negotiate on. It is the subtle conscious revenge of the 70s, I still think that men cannot believe the advancements women have made in only thirty to forty years."

"Is that why there still aren't enough women in politics?"

"The wolves don't eat each other," Claudine says, "Actually, it's still a man's world." Claudine is in the world that I am not. She knows about what goes on behind the closed doors of the United Nations, of her own government, how negotiations are made. In her world, it is truly still a man's world.

In my world, perhaps, and the world that it's becoming, I find that the most revolutionary thing I can say is that it's not a man's world anymore, if it ever was, and give proof. Like religion, to say it's a man's world is to not accept responsibility for one's actions, and while women are often given the blame, it's not the same as taking responsibility for the way the world is going, and I think we see the beginnings of this happening in 2011 and we really start to see results in 2018. Women have said all over the world that we are not going to take this any longer, and it's working.

My interview appears in Claudine's book *Simone de Beauvoir et les femmes aujourd'hui.* A wonderful book of letters written to Simone about what is happening today. In the simplicity of our friendship and Claudine's friendship with Simone, this is the liberation that Simone speaks of, that Claudine transmits to me: women working together with men, making the world the place we want it to be. Young women have said to her, "Every time I have a question about women's issues, I find it in your book."

A MORE SERIOUS TONE

I'm not Angelina Jolie. I haven't gone to war-ravaged countries. I belong to a few women's organizations, but I've never been arrested for my beliefs. I've never been arrested at all. I've never been to Ghana or Haiti, though I've interviewed women who have.

To begin with, as a woman, I've never been raped or physically abused, though almost every woman I know has in some way been beaten by men. Either by an unknown stranger, or a loved one who became a stranger. This makes me write from an incredibly rare place. Nor have I ever been too mentally abused by a man, or suffice to say that the emotional abuse I received was nothing I couldn't handle. I could equally say perhaps I've unwittingly caused mental abuse. No, the most I could say that has happened directly to me by force is perhaps the pressure of a man's hands pushing my head onto his head. So I write from a fortunate place, as most of my girlfriends have undergone at least one of these things, if not all.

I say this because it is important to realize where I am coming from. I cannot write as a survivor of wars and battles ravaged on my body. I can write only from a place of sympathy and empathy and anger that such things exist.

DELLA

While I'm reading *Half the Sky* by Nicolas Kristoff and Sheryl WuDunn I come to the line, "Time spent in the Congo or Cambodia might not be as pleasant as in Paris, but it will be life changing." I'm in Paris while reading this, I feel such a pang of guilt. I should've gone somewhere to actually make a difference. So when I meet Tina Tanglakis at our friend Jackie's bachelorette party, I'm instantly enamored. Tina did just that: she volunteered at a humanitarian organization in Ghana, Africa, and it did indeed change her life.

Tina is the first one to hire me to help her tell her story. We work together, meeting once a week by video to capture the details of the start of her business, how it has grown in order to tell her own story. To write her memoir. We're very aware of the trap of reinforcing the trope of the white savior, or of the magical negro. We don't want to do this. Because Tina is usually the only white woman in the room, she always makes it clear that it's Ghanaian women making the clothes. She starts with the slogan, "Carry Change" as initially she starts just by making handbags and coin purses but very quickly her business grows, and she partners with Urban Outfitters, Toms shoes, and Vans as well.

Here is Tina actually doing the work. Actually making a difference in the world. Tina starts her clothing line Della in 2010. She is a forerunner of creating an ethically responsible business. And the trend of African batiks will appear in France at the Monoprix in 2018. Though in Ghanian batik style, the actual fabrics will be made and sewn in India but the tag will use the words that by buying this product you help a marginalized group of women. Which is most likely true, though essentially helping one marginalized group by appropriating from another.

Tina is not doing this. Tina is the real deal, and she is very adamant about her business—it is a business, not a charity. "We are a woman-owned and woman-run business working directly with a community in West Africa, providing jobs, education, and skills training to our employees. We are driven by awareness of the need for a global market that provides socially responsible, quality products. We are not a charity; we are a business done —and doing—right."

BRUNCH AT CAFE RENDEZVOUS

Claudine and I are out to lunch, and I am starting to cry. I'm not usually a crier, a belief I pride myself on, but Claudine has finished her book, and this is the last time I will see her for at least four months while we are back in the States.

The very minor crying is from envy that her book is finished, and I feel nowhere near completion. I feel frustrated as it's driven me crazy, and Eric has said that the first pages are too aggressive and not gripping enough, so I can't help breaking down a tiny bit as she is giving me advice on my book.

"I was thirty-five when I published my first book," she says. Julia Child was fifty when she became Julia Child. And Simone was forty-one when *The Second Sex* was published. All these ages reassure me.

"Augustine, you must be careful not to give too much power to Eric and his opinion. You should write your feelings about these matters."

"Eric has said the same thing."

"Yes, well, he's right. You can't just tell what is happening. You have to write about your feelings on what is happening. That's what people want to know. That's what makes it interesting, is the human aspect. Is your story. You have to write what you think about these matters."

"Thank you, Claudine, I'm working on it. You're always so inspiring." We take a break and look out the window at the round point of Denfert-Rochereau. We can see tourists starting to line up for the catacombs.

"So, I have a question that I'm unclear about: were Sartre and Simone communists?

Claudine is instantly offended. "No, Augustine, you can't say that! That's just Americans trying to disparage their name."

Claudine continues, "Because you see, communist thought and existentialism diverge. What I mean to say is they could not be further apart. The communists don't believe in freedom of the individual, whereas for existentialists it is all about the individual and the freedom of creativity to write what you want to write. In a communist country, you can only write what they tell you to write. You can only continue the myths of their heroes. You and Eric cannot call them communists as you would be considered not an intellectual, as the moment you said that, people would think that you had no idea what you were talking about."

"OK, I won't call them communists, but they were supportive of the communist party. I guess I always figured, well, when we first met, you had a completely double life and the French government was not inclined to think of Simone and Sartre in a positive way. I assumed it was because of their involvement with Castro and going to China, et cetera. Otherwise, why was Simone considered against the French government?"

"She was considered against the French government because she and Sartre wrote a manifesto, called The Manifesto of the 121, which stated that the French soldiers should drop their weapons and stop fighting because the Algerians had every right to liberty and independence of their country as the French did. This was considered at the time a very un-French thing to say. It was seen as if they were renouncing their country.

"Sartre's apartment on *St. Germain des Pres* was bombed twice because of this manifesto, and when Simone and I would walk around, she would be very afraid if people came up to her quickly. You understand, Augustine, that I am not very big, but when people would come up to Simone she would jump back, and I would be her bodyguard!

"All of my father's friends signed the manifesto. My father did not sign it because he was scared for me. I was eight years old at the time, and I remember my mother every morning opening the front door of our apartment to check to see if there was a bomb on the front door. I couldn't have friends over for two years because they were afraid of bomb threats. It was scary, you understand, as I was only eight years old, but I remember that vividly.

"All of my father's friends who signed it had their apartments bombed or destroyed. Even the Minister of French Culture at the time, Andre Malraux, who was a very fantastic Minister. He was in charge of cleaning all the buildings and making Paris beautiful again. His apartment was bombed. He wasn't in it at the time, but there was a little girl downstairs who was five years old and blinded from the bomb. So, you see, it was a very scary time in the late fifties and early sixties. Even though my father did not sign the manifesto, he was in support of what it had to say and in support of the Algerian Independence.

"Really, Augustine, you can't say that Simone was a communist. This is not correct."

When I interview Judy Chicago she says that she doesn't see other nations burning a feminist flag, but an American flag, and just because they do, people don't say, "I don't want to be an American. I'm going to get rid of the title."

Claudine says that now "Simone and Sartre were extremely critical of every religion, as religion to them was one of the greatest oppressors of women."

After brunch, Claudine shows me where Simone used to live. The shutters are closed, and there is a plaque bearing Simone's name.

Afterward, she heads home. I decide finally to go to the Montparnasse Cemetery where Simone and Sartre are buried together. It is the perfect day for a cemetery, gray and rainy, but not yet too cold in December. At the entrance, I meet the guard who asks me if I am British. When I say I'm American, he asks if I'm from New York or California, and is excited because he has gold and silver bracelets from California. He has a cousin there. He tells me I have a beautiful face, and I am on my way with a map of the cemetery. Serge Gainsbourg is buried here along with Samuel Beckett, who has a very apropos grave: a simple marble slab that seems very suited to the life he lived. I would not perhaps have even noticed it, even with the help of a map, except for an old man with a cane who says, "Beckett, Beckett, il est là."

Simone and Sartre's graves are by the entrance on the other side. They are simple as well. I know at this moment you are supposed to have some revelatory thought, but the only thought I have is how much I do not want to be buried. A giant black crow cackles and flies overhead. It seems so appropriate that there are crows in the cemetery. Two, to be exact, watching from the trees where the leaves still hang on to life in the wind. It is beautiful here, in as much as cemeteries can be beautiful.

Claudine calls me on Monday, not only to thank me for the present I've gotten her (a lavender pillow), but also to read over a few lines for her essay on when Simone and Sartre were opposed to the Algerian War. She says, "This essay attempts to answer this question." I tell her that it is better to say, "This essay answers this question."

"That is OK to say? Because in French it is more polite to say attempts to answer."

"No, it is fine to say that in English. It is better, more forceful." This may be one of the main differences in French and American thought: French can be very flowery and not to the point. Most of the French people I know make a point of saying they are very un-French because they are direct and to the point, blunt. They all say this, and it's clear that they all *want* to be seen as un-French in this way.

Obviously, in "American," we avoid the word "try" as it does not make the impression we want to make. The word try seems to conjure up Yoda advising young Skywalker, "Do, or do not. There is no try." We are people of action: "Just do it," Nike tells us. These are our slogans, and it is not that the French are people of inaction, but they have to do a lot of talking before they get there. Or sometimes it is just seen, as in this instance, as impolite to say what you are doing.

"So if Simone and Sartre weren't communists, what were they?" Eric asks as we walk home from dinner along the rue de Sèvres leading to the Bon Marché and the metro.

"Existentialists."

"Yes, but what political party?"

"Socialists."

"Well, see, there is the problem. In the States, we call communism socialism. They weren't criticizing Obama for being a communist; they are criticizing him for being a socialist, but the meaning is close to the same."

Socialism and communism are both French words, created in the 19th century. Each construct is derived from Marx. Just in case you were wondering, France is a unitary, semi-presidential republic. The United States is also a republic. Like the US, France has two major political parties, the Socialist Party and the Union for Popular Movement. Sarkozy is the leader of this latter conservative party. In the States, we have the impression that the French truly like Sarkozy, but once you start to talk to French people, they equate him to President Bush. They like to joke because Sarko is in love with Obama. Now they equate Macron with the American president as being only for the rich.

A precursor to the #MeToo movement was when Dominique Strauss-Kahn was arrested in New York over the summer of 2012. The French initially were inclined to believe it was a conspiracy set by Sarkozy to eliminate DSK from the race. When I asked Claudine her thoughts on this, she said she had indeed met DSK twenty or more years ago. When she was about to go into his office, his assistant said, "No Madame," that she couldn't go in there alone. He had to go with her. "So he had the reputation for being a sexual predator. This is not news," says Claudine.

When asked about his reputation, Strauss-Kahn's wife, Anne Sinclair, said she was proud of it as that was what made him a good politician. She was one of the most famous TV journalists at the time, and in 2011, a poll in France voted her as the most powerful public figure, winning over Christine Lagarde. Eva Joly, a former judge who had been in charge of investigations against corruptions of financial people, who was then a presidential candidate of the Green party, says Anne Sinclair is not a role model for young women.

Joly writes an essay in the free newspaper *20 Minutes* about the idea of the *Hillary Syndrome,* when women stay with a man because of political power. Who knows the exact reasons Hillary stayed with Bill, or why Anne Sinclair stood by DSK, though she did eventually leave him. Relationships are complicated. The main difference between Bill and DSK is that Bill was not accused of raping someone, and that DSK never apologized.

The DSK debacle was, however, a positive thing for French society: it instilled the courage in women to say they aren't going to take sexual harassment anymore.

I watch as women publish book after book, article after article, about women. Look, they're writing about women, too! Every time, it is like a stab—ugh, she got there before me. This sense of possession from what we now call a scarcity mindset is how capitalism functions. Now, I don't see it that way. There's room for all of us. In fact, there needs to be all of us. That's how you build a movement. And just as Jack Donneghy says to Liz Lemon in the television show *30 Rock,* "A women's organization is where everyone is vice-president." There seems to be no leaders. There are frontrunners, but the movement becomes bigger than them.

In France, #MeToo is called *#BalanceTonPorc,* which means #Denounce-YourPig. It was kicked off by Sandra Muller, who is now being sued by the very person she accused of sexual harassment. Unfortunately a problem in many of the #MeToo cases. Another problem in France there is a law of limitations of when you can accuse someone, so some women missed the window to have a case.

FROMAGES ET RAMAGES

Not only do I learn the word for pig I also learn the words for eyes, *les yeux*, and the plural of eggs, *les oeux*, which are not the same but sound relatively the same. When I go to my favorite cheese shop, yes I have a favorite cheese shop, *Fromages et Ramages* in my neighborhood on *rue Ramey*, I think I'm asking for eggs please but I'm actually asking for eyes. It's so embarrassing. The owner, who also happens to be a writer, thinks this is hilarious. I never make the mistake again. After about a year and a half—two years, I can speak fairly well. Enough to get by. But I still can't pronounce the street I live on correctly *Feutrier,* pronounced like *feu* as fire, Eric will constantly correct me by saying, "Look at my lips, you have to put your lips together." It's a puckering like you're trying to kiss which, after looking at each other lips we do. And any pronunciation at that point is out the window.

BEYOND THE DINNER PARTY

JUDY CHICAGO

New Mexico—Land of Enchantment. To me, it was also the Land of the Big Sky. Because it is the desert, everything is flat, which gives the impression as if it is all sky. Perhaps this is why they do the Hot Air Balloon Festival here every year. The Albuquerque airport is familiar because I lived in Santa Fe my first year of college.

The airport is decked out in Native American motifs the colors of sand, red, and turquoise. The stores feature strands of lights in the shape of red chili peppers and several different kinds of hot sauce. It is July, and it is hot. Ninety-eight degrees hot and dry. There is nothing much going on here, a quiet town with a few streets. Abandoned buildings call up images of the Old West. I rent a car, a little blue number. I say I'm going to Belen. The woman who rents me the car has lived here her whole life. She's never heard of it.

Why would Judy Chicago choose to live here? It is peaceful, that is for sure. And it does have a creative energy—so I suppose that's my answer. For me, I never liked not being near a body of water. The sky is big, so it's true you feel the magnitude of space but you're still landlocked.

On the freeway, I drive behind a truck which has a biblical quote: "Come out of her, my people, that you be not partakers of her sins and plagues."

I drive past Judy Chicago's house. It is an old Western hotel. There is not a person on the street, barely a car in the road. It really feels like we are in the middle of nowhere. Am I nervous about tomorrow? I feel at peace about it. I just hope she likes me. This, apparently, is uniquely a woman thing, that we want people to like us. Judy Chicago is my heroine; of course I want her to like me.

I am aware she is not going to be inclined to discuss her most famous work, *The Dinner Party,* as every interview and even her own book on *The Dinner Party* discusses the fact that she does not want to be known solely for this work. As an artist, she is frustrated this is her sole recognition. *The Dinner Party* is housed at the Brooklyn Museum and if you've never seen it, go, go now. It is an epic work of art featuring 1038 women, and thirty-nine of them have their own "place settings"—that is, vaginal representation on a plate at a large triangular table. The work itself is rife with symbolism. And while I would love to just discuss this work, I have come armed with another project that she has done in 2002, her project on Luga Lake.

"Luga Lake is a remote village in the Yunnan-Sichuan province of China close to the border of Tibet that has been left completely untouched by modern accommodations and conveniences of the past 200 years," Judy tells me. Along the shores of the lake, live many minority ethnic groups. It is the Mosuo, a small ethnic group of roughly 40,000, who are a matriarchal and matrilineal society."

It is one of several matriarchies in the world, though at the time I can't name any. In 2020, the magazine by the association *Femmes d'ici et allieurs* provides a beautiful and informative spread on ten matriarchies around the world.

The Minangkabau People (Minang) West Sumatra, Indonesia. At 4.2 million people, the Minangkabau are the largest matrilineal society in the world, with property, family name, and land passing down from

mother to daughter, while religious and political affairs are the responsibility of men, although some women also play important roles in
these areas.

The Khasi People (1.3 to 3 million people) are an indigenous ethnic
group of Meghalaya in north-eastern India with a significant population in the bordering state of Assam, and in certain parts of
Bangladesh.

The Zapotecs (800,000 to 1,000,000 people) are an indigenous people of
Mexico. The population is concentrated in the southern state of
Oaxaca, but Zapotec communities also exist in neighboring states.
many of whom are monolingual in one of the native Zapotec
languages and dialects. You may know them as Frida Khalo wore their
brightly colored hand woven floral shirts that the women weave which
provides their financial independence.

The Berbers, or Amazighs, (roughly 100,000 to a million people) are an
ethnicity of several nations mostly indigenous to North Africa and
some northern parts of West Africa.

The Navajo, (roughly 300,000 people) is the largest federally recognized tribe in the United States. Also the largest reservation in the
county located around the four corners Arizona, New Mexico and
Utah.

The Himba People (15,000—20,000 people) who live in Northern
Namibia and Southern Angola. They are well known for their ochre
colored plaited hair and beaded jewelry.

With the Trobriand People, (20,000 people) in Papa New Guinea everything passes through the feminine line. Women are also the guardians
of their agricultural resources.

The Guna, (50,000 people) are a politically autonomous society in
Panama as well as a few villages in Columbia. The most sacred festival
is called Diwe Inna, which is when a girl becomes a woman, they also
acknowledge the existence of a third gender for men who feel like
women, called omeggid.

Umoja, which means unity in Swahili, is an all-female village founded on the principles of women's rights in Kenya. Created by Rebecca Lolosoli in 1990, the village is a refuge for women fleeing sexual abuse, and men are banned from the village.

And of course the Mosuo who Judy Chicago worked with and met. What is shocking to me is to learn the population size of these matriarchal societies that are very rarely mentioned. We grow up thinking we have no examples of matriarchal society when in fact there are still some that exist in the world today.

The question Chicago proposes at Luga Lake—"What if women ruled the world?"—is a central theme to Chicago's work. From that question come ten other questions in which over a dozen female artists in Luga Lake create art in dialogue with Judy Chicago.

1. Would God be Female?
2. Would Men and Women be Equal?
3. Would Sexual Freedom Prevail?
4. Would There Be Jealousy?
5. Would There Be Equal Parenting?
6. Would Children Go Hungry?
7. Would Old Women Be Revered?
8. Would Buildings Resemble Wombs?
9. Would There Be Private Property?
10. Would There Be War?

These ten questions are a precursor to her work collaboration with Dior's creative director, Maria Grazia Chiuri (the same woman who made the We Should All Be Feminists tee-shirts!) for the spring/summer 2020 haute couture collection. The questions are reproduced as towering tapestries to form the centerpiece of Dior's runway presentation at the gardens of The Musée Rodin in Paris in January 2020.

∼

Judy wears blue-tinted glasses, a yellow tee-shirt, and dark red lipstick. Her hair is bright red and curly, looking wet and pulled back on top of her head. I've brought presents from Paris: herbs de Provence, a lavender satchel for her lingerie drawer, and a small jar of French pâté.

I set up the video camera while Judy opens her mail. We sit down, and I'm shaking, but Judy isn't really paying attention to me. "So, who is she?" Judy demands of Claudine.

I give her my *schpiel*.

"So you weren't in Paris when you started this?" This is the first time I have evidence she's genuinely interested.

"No, I was living in New York at the time, working as an event planner, but I wanted to do this project."

Judy picks up her cat. "This is Pete, the other one is Repeat."

"That's hilarious."

"When I moved here, I didn't speak any French."

"Oh, really? Where are you from, Augustine?"

"Los Angeles."

"Do you know what's about to happen in Los Angeles?" She doesn't wait for my reply. "I'm in eight of the shows. Pacific Standard Time."

Within the first five minutes Judy has brought up the issue of money. She has no qualms about demanding, "How do you support yourself in Paris?"

Judy is intensely, intensely critical of my project. "So your thesis is that women chose to keep their power at bay?"

For the first twenty minutes, Judy Chicago is interviewing me. She is wondering how on earth I managed to secure an interview with her when I do not have a publisher yet. She says, "You are very lucky, as I normally never meet with anyone until they have already have a publisher."

I swear to her that I will eventually have a publisher. She seems inclined to believe me, and by the end of the interview, is telling me that she believes me to be a real "go-getter."

After fifteen excruciatingly intimidating and embarrassing minutes, I finally hit my stride. I turn a corner with Judy that I do know what I'm talking about when I mention CEDAW.

"The Dinner Party looks at a particular type of woman. Women who were able, because of their class, to stand up to patriarchal society. But were there other strategies, absolutely."

"Well, it all goes back to the Code of Hammurabi, in Mesopotamia and Babylonian times."

"Yes, yes, yes, obviously." I nod my head eagerly in agreement. *Of course, I know the Code of Hammurabi.* I have no clue what that is; Judy is light years ahead of me on this stuff.

"Those were the first laws regulating women's behavior."

"What were women's options? They had no education, no economic independence, they would lose their children if they disobeyed their husbands. So to have agency, access to a little bit of power, they would have to find other strategies, so then they became enforcers of their oppression."

"Like Christine de Pizan."

"This project started because I had so few women friends who said they were feminists. But all my male friends had no problem saying they're feminists, I think because it helps them get laid."

"That's hysterical," Judy laughs. I've made Judy Chicago laugh. It lightens up the room, and we're finally having a conversation. I think that I've converted her to my side.

She is so incredibly articulate, and I still sound like a bumbling idiot, but at least we're getting somewhere.

"I get asked about this all the time, about young women not wanting to be identified as feminist," says Judy with a slight eye roll. "And actually, it's the result of an institutional failure. If you never studied the history of the United States, would you be proud to be an American? Why would you be proud to be a feminist? As Gilda Lerner says, 'Women live in a state of trained ignorance.' They haven't got a clue. Actually I had to deal with this a little bit, I did a graduate seminar, and the male students were much more into my lectures and the women are resistant to me."

"Women don't know what has been taught or thought, so all these young women, to have children and call it choice feminism, they thought they were exercising a choice that was actually socially determined. Men still are not doing fifty percent of the housework. Before they had children, they were the perfect couple and then they had kids, and he couldn't understand why, I still do half the housework, but she still carried the emotional responsibility of the family. Even if a partner does share the tasks, the important thing is that men and women equally assume emotional responsibility."

Four years later when I'm re-watching the video, married for three years, pregnant the second time around, I remember this part of the interview and think, *How would you ever know if your decisions are socially constructed or of your own free will?*

Judy continues, "And that has been complicated by this myth that women can do and have it all. They also were taking on this idea of women artists who were totally victimized and find agency and succeed, and which achievements by which women's achievements were erased out of history."

On the second day, I think Judy and I are both coming down with the flu. After I leave Santa Fe, I get incredibly sick. I've spent the night before up late reading her memoir, *Through the Flower.* I feel embarrassed that I haven't read it before and that it's all there.

I tell her, "I read your memoir last night."

"All of it?" she says.

"Well, except for the last two chapters."

"That's pretty good." I think at least I've impressed her a bit with my dedication.

"I couldn't stop, it was so good. I really related to feeling special being one of the boys."

Unfortunately, this doesn't elicit the conversation that I would like. I'd love to talk more of that feeling, but she doesn't bite, so I move on. We get on the story of the Holocaust as remembered around the world.

"Oh my god, we've seen almost every Holocaust museum all over the world. The story is told differently in different countries."

"In some countries, the story isn't acknowledged at all."

"That's absolutely right, like in Austria. In some countries the word Jew isn't mentioned. In France, it's about the Resistance movement. In Russia it's about the suffering of the Russian people. It's different everywhere."

"How did you keep your hope in humanity?"

"I'm very glad we did it. Because nothing surprises us anymore. We learned so much about the world. It's often said about the Holocaust 'never forget,' and I always want to say, never forget what? How to do it? They're doing it with more impunity. They don't bother to cover it up like the Nazis did or attempted to do."

Considerate Nazis—I've never thought of that.

"You have to think about why people get to such desperation where they don't care if they live or die. That's what we're not addressing as humans. We have to ask, what kind of despair creates that?

"Again, it has to do with assumptions."

"Like Luga Lake, women couldn't imagine the world run by women."

"Where does that come from? It's a lack of imagination. Lack of education."

"It's the same you know, I was in a French class, one of our exercises was to come up with something that you wish for, and I said parity.

Equal men and women in government. And all the women in the class said that will never happen. They were from varied countries, all over the world."

"Really?" replies Judy. "That's discouraging."

"What did you say?"

"I was like, come on, you really don't think it's possible to have equal men and women in governments? They all looked at me like I was crazy and said, 'You're dreaming.'"

"That's really interesting in terms of the questions you are raising," remarks Judy. "OK, if you don't believe that it's possible that the world will be ever be anything but male-dominated, then obviously that leads to the kinds of strategies you're talking about."

Judy continues: "I think one of the problems for me is that I don't operate out of that premise. And part of it is because of my understanding of history. That history teaches us that there has been a long, slow, steady move toward greater emancipation for women. At this point in history, many people acknowledge that economic development is best achieved through the empowerment of women."

As she's talking, I start to hear the Beyoncé song ringing in my head: "Who runs the world? Girls."

Judy leans closer to me. "I think that's really important, Augustine. For you to frame this discussion based on, I mean it sounds stupid to start it from something so personal, but if you describe sitting in that classroom. To be so completely at odds with your generation. If that's the case, then that must mean that they have found ways to operate to go around this, instead of challenging it.

"Yes, but to try and prove that idea…." I trail off.

She insists, "Well, I didn't say to try and prove that women always had power. But I think that one of the interesting insights you've shared is that many women believe that patriarchy cannot be dismantled, and that's a big change from my generation."

"What does it mean to dismantle the patriarchy?" I ask as I instantly fall in love with the phrase, so succinct and to the point—unlike using succinct and to the point in the same sentence.

"Whether that assumption of if it's possible to dismantle it or not. I myself believe it's true. And if the patriarchy isn't dismantled, it'll be the end of the human race."

"Do you still think it's a man's world?"

"Oh, absolutely."

I don't argue because I haven't yet come to my own conclusions. It's a lot to take in, and we are quiet for a while.

"Do you want to go look at some art?" she says.

"Absolutely!"

~

Judy and her husband, Donald, have converted an old hotel into their home and studio. Donald is a photographer and serves as her archivist, as he is quick to follow us when we go into their heat-sensitive storage facility to look at the slides from Luga Lake. As much as Judy does not want to talk about *The Dinner Party*, she does want to talk about how the women of my generation seem to have the idea that feminism has failed them. While many things have changed, it appears the promises our mothers made to us that we could do anything have not yet quite panned out.

This is a revelation to her. This opens her eyes, as this is a sentiment she hasn't heard before. What she has heard before, and she is quick to quote from the opening quote of her book again, is that women who do not know their history are doomed to repeat it, because women are always thinking this has never been done before, so we keep "reinventing the wheel."

After the interview, I go straight back to my hotel room and take a nap.
I can tell I'm coming down with something. I leave the next day.

BACK TO "WORK"

I've let Judy Chicago, and the opinions of my Nana, make me feel guilty for not having a real job to "support myself." So when my friend Sarah, who works at an awesome-sounding job remotely booking travel villas in Greece, Italy, and France, says they are hiring, I send off my resume, and less than a week after my meeting with Judy Chicago, I have a job as a travel agent.

Great Aunt Anita, my grandmother's younger sister, dies that summer. I'm working so much and driving close to three hours a day, so I'm not able to visit her in the hospital before she dies. In retrospect, I should've gone to see her, but even my own mother had to convince my Nana to go visit her. They didn't get along.

My first real job was working as a hostess at Gladstones, the restaurant right on the beach in Los Angeles where Sunset Blvd ends at PCH. It would've been a great summer job, except that year they were doing major construction, and everything was a mess. It was my best friend's mom's boyfriend who got us the job. He knew the owner or something. The dress code was all white, and you had to wear shorts. That was the beachy look.

The summer after my first year in college, my parents sold their house with the intention of breaking up. Dad was housesitting a friend's place in Topanga Canyon, and Mom was staying at my grandparents' house in her old room that had been converted to the TV room with a pull-out couch. I was in her sister's room with the knotty pine painted over in brown that my Nana still regretted doing, sleeping on a very ancient, uncomfortable spring cot, like the ones they use in hotels that fold in half and stands upright.

In this dislocation, my solution was to work. So I also got a job at the new Getty Center on top of the hill, working at the coffee cart in the center patio of the museum. I thought it would be a nice job surrounded by beauty, and on my breaks, I could look at the art. But working is not visiting a museum, and after being on my feet for eight hours, the last thing I wanted to do was stand around. I realized very quickly the reason I got hired was because I was the only young white girl who spoke English without an accent. Everyone else was Mexican. It was clear I was supposed to talk to the customers, take the orders, I was terrible at making coffee under pressure, at being a barista. From the Getty, I could drive directly down Sunset straight to the ocean, then work another standing-on-your-feet shift till 11pm, scarfing an Arby's sandwich in the car on the way. It wasn't sustainable, and I left the Getty Center after a few weeks. But everyone should work in food service, a restaurant, once in their life. Those who've worked in restaurants are so much nicer to wait staff than those who haven't.

Before going back to my grandparents' house, I'd smoke pot in one of the cul-de-sacs around the corner in what, to my mind, was the quintessential suburban American neighborhood of Cheviot Hills. I would drive past where Ray Bradberry lived and think about a time unreachable to me, when there was a deep sense of malaise lurking behind the seemingly perfectly organized safety of cul-de-sacs. Like the Stones song Mother's Little Helper. Or that this vision of America no longer existed. When kids walked to school and all played with each other. To live at my grandparents' was like going back in time.

Almost all of my jobs have been through a friend. Except for my last "real" job at The Gay Center, which I got on my own merit because I had worked with my friend Wilson before at other events.

My first real job, though I don't really count it, was the year before, selling knives for the pyramid scheme of Cutco. They were really good knives.

Even my Great Aunt Anita, whose husband was a butcher or butcher's son, bought them. She was always very sweet to me.

ASKING THE INEVITABLE

And then all of a sudden, I find myself standing in front of the mirror asking a man, "Am I fat? Do I look fat in this? Does this outfit make me look fat?" Clearly, it's the outfit, not you.

I'm getting ready to go out and have changed said outfit twice, and the coat back and forth three times. Now I might be ready to go, but not until after realizing that I've just asked the most forbidden question of them all: "Am I fat?"

I believe I am an advanced woman. I do not succumb to the pressure of glossy magazines. I know they are airbrushed. Yet somehow, something has crept in. I may have enough self-awareness to acknowledge that Eric is pissed I've asked this question in the first place. "It's as if all of women's rights just went back to square one," he says in response to the inadvertent asking of such a question.

But that's what "women's issues" are. They provide us with a grand scope, from the more banal fact of not being paid equally to the hideous atrocities of the virginity test and everything in between.

It's such a broad subject, with so many facets. Where does one even begin? Yet with one simple question, it's as if I've backtracked all of women's progress. Despite being entrenched in feminist theory, I've succumbed to the dreaded demise of so many insecure women.

Eric is pissed. I just want to know if he's going to answer my question.

CHRISTMAS DAY AT THE SACRÉ-COEUR

The sun has already gone down by the time we leave the house to go for a walk.

It's Christmas Day, and we are tired, or I am tired. I haven't been up to Sacré-Coeur in a while. There is a Christmas market there that sells the same stuff as they sell at Abbesses, the same stuff they sell at Champs-Elysées and St. Germain des Pres. Hot wine, hat, gloves, scarves, lots of sausages, raclette, leather handbags that look like the old postman bag, silver and gold coil necklaces that wrap around your neck like snakes. There is such a nice feeling to it all. The festive stands are built out of wood and decorated with fake snow. We walk by the liquor stand manned by a kid who can't be more than eight years old.

Eric says, "You should take a picture of that. Only in France would you find a child sitting in front of all that liquor." He is surrounded by bottles of Jim Bean, cognac, and vodka, the bottles illuminated and looking pretty and tempting. No one seems to mind or find it strange that the parents are not around. When we come back later after the Christmas Mass, the kid is still sitting there, bored. It's not even as if his parents had left him to handle the booth for a moment. No, he is just working there.

Montmartre feels like the village it is tonight. With lights in the trees, the quaint feeling is so much the feeling of Paris— the old and new coming together. We have come to recognize the men who draw portraits for people sitting in cafes. We find a place I have wanted to try, an Irish pub on one of the side streets behind Sacré-Coeur. They have hot wine and grog made with rum. We have a drink and watch the strange outfits on passersby. It's easy to love the life here. We go into Sacré-Coeur right when they're just finishing the Christmas Mass and we watched as they gave communion. The church ia warm and filled with people, there are candles everywhere, and it feels like something spiritual is taking place. The priest tells everyone to turn around and wish peace upon your neighbor.

Being in such a place at this moment, you can understand the church's appeal for the tired and weak. A warm place that is supposedly accepting of your sins. Jesus is there, giant on the ceiling looking down at the congregation. He is a benevolent figure, arms outstretched and open, better than the images of Jesus we saw a day or two ago in the Louvre.

I've never understood the prevalence of the image of Jesus on the cross. To have such an atrocious image as a reminder of the evils of men. I don't think we need a reminder, and this idea of gazing at a man in ultimate suffering is awful. There is a statue of a very shiny Mary with a baby Jesus, and in this one, Jesus looks like a child. It is a strange myth, the Virgin Mary, similar in thought of Athena being born from Zeus' forehead. This idea of creation out of nothing not is not how creation is supposed to be. When Laila and I spoke the other day, she agreed she is spiritual, like me. She believes in something, but not in religion. She is impressed by Sabrina's devotion because it is something neither she nor I would ever do. We admire it, but we don't understand it.

I feel very comfortable with my practicing of religion, I have bought a menorah, the first one I have ever owned. We light the candles every night, because it is nice. When we light the candles on Christmas Eve, because Hanukkah and Christmas are around the same time this year, Sabrina and I say the prayer. It's the prayer I know by heart.

Christophe asks me who taught it to me. I imagine my mom and dad and Nana. He asks me what it means, and really, I have no idea, no idea of the actual translation—just a blessing of the candles to God, I've assumed. Sabrina fills in more of the meaning. Laila says she wants to have a menorah, too, as she wants to celebrate both and teach her child both ways of celebrating. I imagine I will do the same when I have children.

The night before, on Christmas Eve, Sabrina told me about the twenty-one or twenty-two-year-old women who cry all the time because they are single. We are discussing the idea that you have to be happy with yourself first before you can be with someone else.

Sabrina says, "When I have a little girl, God willing, I will tell her to go, go do things, go have sex with different people, go explore and find out who you are first." We are listening to Elvis sing *Merry Christmas Baby*, and Sabrina's father, like my father, is a huge fan of Elvis. We dance a little and take 'family' photos with a tripod in front of the tree. Olga and Christophe pose with Eric's guitars.

The Doors comes on, and we start talking about Jim Morrison. We've had a few glasses of Kosher wine at this point, and Sabrina says, "Jim Morrison. Sex was written on his forehead!"

It's a French expression to say that something was written on his forehead.

"When I was young, fifteen years old, I loved Jim Morrison. To me, he was sex, really. Ah, he was so sexy."

This is something that we have in common. When I was fifteen, Jim Morrison was beyond sexy—the voice, his poetry and him. Even watching videos of him now in his tight leather pants and crazy ways, he exudes sex appeal. There was something and still is very mysterious about Jim Morrison. You never knew what he was going to do. I made the pilgrimage to his grave in Pierre Lachaise with the two musicians I knew when I was twenty in college, visiting Paris.

The conversation drifts in and out between religion and music, the difference between the States and here. I drift off, too. Things written on foreheads or being born out of foreheads. They've been playing James Brown constantly on the radio as it is also the anniversary of his death. James Brown never ceases to remind me of my ex, and for a moment in the lull of the wine and warmth, I again acknowledge how much I miss my friend. It's not that I want to be there or with him, but I feel the loss of a companion, as I have felt the loss of all the people who are no longer in my life. But I've already moved on.

A NEW TRANSCENDENTALISM

While Starbucks, McDonalds, and Coca-Cola are signs of American corporate domination in a global world, they are also beacons to world travelers looking for something that will always taste the same. Here, Eric and I sit looking at all the tchotchkes of Paris.

Eric says, "I would hate it if I had to sit and sell this crap all day. All this crap made in China for nothing, and here the Chinese come to buy it just because it says Paris, but it can't say it's made in Paris because nothing ever is."

But back to real art. The idea of a Renaissance is appealing, but is my generation already too old for such an endeavor? We had such big dreams when we were young, but we got bulldozed by just how hard it is to live. There might still be time. People are doing creative things. Everyone has the forum now to express anything they want. It seems, though, like with everything, it's been created and then parodied so many times over, it's hard to know what is genuine.

What will future generations do with all that we have been document-ing? All the blog posts, Facebook tags, digital photos. Will we move away from the screens or move more towards them? At the moment, it appears that there is no artistic trait which holds us together, no move-ment except this one, which is to continuously and constantly docu-ment life at almost every moment that we are living it. The videos I have of my youth are priceless because they reveal how I used to talk (pretty much the same), what I used to look like (much tinier), and what was important to me. They are also priceless because they are so rare. I wish that I had videoed more, and even now as I try in my daily life to do so, I still don't realize how great they will be until the moment is gone and that is all you have left. While we're living in a moment, it seems as if it will go on that way forever, even as things are changing. But it doesn't happen that way, and all of sudden that period of life, that person you were, is no more. Will the children grow up with a different proximity to their past than we do? Their past will always be readily available. Every instant since the moment of their conception has been recorded and posted on Facebook. Will they rely solely on these images alone, or will their own memory play a part?

It's not for us to decide what the next great movement will be. Perhaps a return to transcendentalism, or the revival of an urban transcenden-talism, like Thoreau wanting to be one with nature. But we have to acknowledge that living in a city with our modern conveniences leaves less of a carbon footprint than living out in no man's land.

If we start with mutual admiration for each other, it is easy to build on such a foundation. Initially, it seems that was what men and women started with—not just a fear of and confusion about each other, but a reverence, an admiration for that which the other could not do. Women could give birth, possessing a power that men did not have, and men could hunt, possessing a strength unknown to most women. We were in awe of each other, I imagine, but in the complications of labels and rights, of a person's *place* and God-given gifts, we've lost some of that awe we so often hear about safeguarding. It's easy to say, "Oh, yes, just return to that wonder, that amazement, that awe, and everything will be all right." It's a start, at least, but not at all sufficient.

No, you have to do all the work of it, too, but we have to start somewhere, don't we?

AN EVENING IN A MONTMARTRE CAFÉ

"The year was 1968 at the Sorbonne. I was nineteen years old and met Sartre. The movement was all men, not a single woman. Quickly, I decided to quit the masculine left party and joined the Women's Liberation Movement, the MLF, and this was how I met Simone."

Claudine will say this is such an engaging way: *"C'est le rêve de ma vie."* She arrived at Simone's apartment in Montparnasse, and knew that Simone was very precise, so she was told not be late. What she didn't know was that Simone had a clock that was set seven minutes fast, so when she arrived at the door at 17 heures sharp, Simone opened it, her eyes even with Claudine's as they are both the same size—*les grandes dames petites*—and the first thing she said was, "You're late."

When Claudine met her, Simone seemed such an old lady. Now Claudine will say humbly, *"Je suis la vieille dame."* Whenever Claudine tells this story, those listening (at this moment we're with a group of women bloggers) will politely laugh at the joke.

In 1970, Simone published *La Vieillese, The Coming of Age*, in English, which Claudine now deems equally as important as *The Second Sex* because of its "profound modernity."

There are certain things which are very particular and peculiar to Simone. One was that she never wanted to be late to meet Sartre. Claudine believes, as I do, that if she had had the choice, she would have wanted Sartre all to herself, but it did not work out that way. I am remembering the time Claudine recalled that Simone was like a little schoolgirl when the radio called her and Sartre a couple.

When the women bloggers ask Claudine about her advice for women now, she responds with two things: one, she believes there should be a mandatory class on women's history in all schools; and two, the world is running out of minerals, and whoever owns the minerals is going to own the world. I'm surprised when she says this opinion to the women. Perhaps in my own way it is because I had felt this was information that she had shared only with me. For the first part, it is definitely agreed by several women that women's history should become part of the curriculum, that gender studies should be incorporated. As well as Bernice's idea that we should study the history of religion, as it seems you can't have women's history without the mention of religion. That is where Claudine sees the real danger. That women's rights are always being negotiated.

The women in this meeting see becoming a housewife as the modern trap of young, educated women. Judy Chicago has said that we are conditioned to believe we want children, but one day, women will wonder if that was really what they wanted. Judy didn't have them, and neither did Simone, Claudine, Virginia Woolf, or Gloria Steinem. In this way, I know something about being a woman they don't know. I know what it's like to breastfeed, to give birth, to acutely feel the loss of my independence from the birth of a baby.

But enough of women's empowerment; we need to be training the men. We need to change the language that we use. We've taken men out of the picture, and that's where we are going wrong.

Women's empowerment can take many forms, which means that under the guise of girl power, what we believe to be for women's rights can be actually harming the cause. We want to portray that we can, and do, have anything and everything, but still complain about the burden of having to do everything.

Feminists (or anyone for that matter) pick people out of history and use their narrative for their own means. I myself am doing this to build a case that women were more in control of their fate than we give them credit for, because I think this is more empowering. But then, do I need to be more empowered?

Why did I think that French women knew the answer to how to do something for women? Because they were sexy? Because they had stayed sexy? Because they weren't trying to be men, like their American counterparts were supposedly trying to be? Because France had a long history of women in politics, women in positions of power?

Eliane Viennot, a French historian who has written several books on the subject, is filled with information and quotes that she can give at any moment. During our interview, she shares about Voltaire and the woman before Voltaire, Catherine Bernard, who no one knows, whom it is said that Voltaire plagiarized. She teaches me that this female French playwright was extremely successful in her time and wrote a play called *Brutus*. Thirty years later, there was quite an uproar in Paris as Voltaire published a play of the same name, and it is said he in fact stole lines from her. Yet now, no one hears about her. How did she disappear from history books? Was she ever there?

On a side note, I think about my French class at the Sorbonne, how it is ten women and one man, and the teacher, also a man. When we study logical arguments, there is an exercise about women in politics. We are supposed to put two phrases together: the event of *"Une seule femme a été nominee minister dans le nouveau gouvernment,"* and the problem of *"La place des femmes dans la vie politique."*

In a class filled with women, no one wants to put together that problem. Our teacher, surprised and unsure of how to handle the dead silence of the class, tells us that we are not feminists. Still no one answers; it's as if we are tired of the problem, and seemingly uninterested. Is that the case? There is something about having too many women in the room, how our teacher, on the second day of class, expressed his feeling that he was in the minority. All of these foreign women starting back at him. One of the first exercises he brings to the class is about recipes—hey, this is France. Every class I have has talked about recipes. This essay is about the kitchen and life of Versailles versus the peasants. He prefaces the article by saying that he didn't bring in something about cooking because we are all women, and he loves to cook and he is not being sexist. This is important for him to point out.

In the morning, talking about the article, I say to Eric, "I have expensive tastes." "Well, I'm of the finest quality," he jokes.

He tells me, "If you include lines like that it your book, it's sure to be a success," so I've included it here.

LE JARDIN SECRET

I look for a table next to no one so as to be super quiet for Claudine.

She hasn't arrived yet, which is rare, but I have made a point to be early. Claudine likes these established French places; despite being very modest, she appreciates grandeur. The Hotel Lutetia has a long history involving World War II, but when you think about it, what doesn't have a history with WWII in France? Lutetia was the original name for Paris; it didn't become Paris until 360 BC.

The hotel has a beautiful tea room. The couches are in plush burgundy velvet, and there are crystal chandeliers, which today are covered with a thin see-through mesh covering. We decide that this is an attempt at avant-garde art. For all its oldness, the hotel's attempts at modernity are shown not only in the chandeliers, but also in the large photographs mounted on plexiglass that are portraits of unusual-looking people taken in the dark, against black background illuminated by fire. We've come to the Hotel Lutetia several times before, but today we are lucky as it is quiet and the waiters are nice—also unusual. One small child has been roaming about, a blond boy in overalls. This makes me nervous; it's not that Claudine doesn't like children, but she has very sensitive hearing and doesn't like the noise children make.

I've found us a good table, so when Claudine arrives, she is happy. "You've gotten the best table, Augustine, and you've left me the couch." We haven't seen each other since I left Paris four months ago to return to the States. From the moment she sits down, we have to order. Claudine at first grabs the menu of cocktails, but no, none of that for her. She doesn't drink and always orders Earl Gray tea with extra hot water, *extra chaud.* "It is so difficult to get hot water in France," she says because it always takes anyone a long time to succumb to her request.

At that moment, while we are still waiting, the second parlor room opens up. Claudine, per usual, would like to move tables, but today I don't feel like moving. Ordinarily I would let us move, but I do something perhaps very un-French when the waiter comes with the tea when she asks me if I'd mind to move. I just say, "C'est toi, c'est toi," which is perhaps not very appropriate, yet is more polite than saying, "No I don't want to move."

So we don't move. We stay right where we are, and it is fine. Claudine has been working for the past fourteen days straight at UNESCO. They have just finished their major global conference of the year. She stretches out her arms to the end of the small couch and says, "I'm sorry, I didn't have a chance to do yoga this morning. So, tell me, my dear, how are you? You're back in Paris, and you're happy to be here."

I've come back to France after four months working as a travel advisor in Los Angeles. I haven't looked at my book since leaving France.

Claudine used to come to the Hotel Lutetia with a lover of hers when she was younger, but she whispers this is in her secret garden. *Le Jardin Secret.* This is a very important expression to know. One lives their life with secrets. These secrets are blooming, and to discover them is like entering a place unknown to others filled with growth and potential.

"You are growing, Augustine. You may not think so, but you are. This time is good."

"I hope so." I mention something off the cuff about perhaps getting married so that I could work in France.

"We've been talking for exactly seventy-two minutes, and you now just mention that you're going to get married?"

"Well, not exactly, he hasn't asked me, I don't have a ring, we're not officially engaged, we've just talked about it." I haven't asked him because I know he wants to ask me. I haven't asked him because I know I want him to ask me.

"Men respond to action," she says and this sounds very definite and persistent, something I imagine I will remember her saying for a long while.

Claudine comes up with a strategy. She says, "This is Parisian, this is the Parisian woman." In other words, manipulative. But I keep it in my secret garden. I don't do her strategy; I do my own.

MARRIAGE, ISTANBUL, TURKEY

Melis and her new man, with a name I'll never remember, walk towards us at the taxi stand of the airport in the frigid cold.

Melis, as usual, looks glamorous, out of film noir movie in color. She wears a turquoise scarf, a deep brown short fur coat, and her signature Isabel Marant sneaker heels. He is a good-looking man, tan, hair cut short, not too tall. Together, they look like a good couple, already at ease with one another. After introductions and hugs, there is a game of Tetris to fit the suitcases in the back, and then we are off, driving the highway into Istanbul.

"You can sleep when you get back to Paris," Melis says. These words will prove to be true for all of us as we all embark on our journey to get me and Eric married by the week's end.

Eric, Sabrina, and I are tired from the long day of travel. We woke at three in the morning to catch our flight from Paris, and now it is six in the evening, Istanbul time, but dark as if it were five in the morning. When we arrive at Melis's house, there is luckily a space, and we go down two flights of steps to enter Melis's modest home. It is not an exact replica of her apartment in Paris, but the feeling is the same—a space crammed with things, though there appears to be some order to the way that papers and trinkets and spices arrange themselves throughout the apartment. As is tradition, we take off our shoes after being greeted with big hugs and smiles from Melis's sister, Funda. Funda has dark hair pulled up in a wave on her head and a casual burgundy sweater. We all receive a pair of slippers from hotels that Melis, her mom, or Funda have stayed at.

We've been speaking a combination of French and English. Wine is opened, Kosher wine for Sabrina, and we toast to our welcome and our wedding. It will not be the last toast to our wedding.

Sabrina decides to go outside to smoke and starts to put back on her coat, but the ladies of the house say stay and open the window, which looks out to a street with a sharp hill. We will discover that Turkey is made up of these hills. Seven hills make the city of Istanbul, a sprawling city that straddles each side of the Bosphorus, but we haven't seen the Bosphorus yet. Instead, after a glass of wine, we walk up the hill to a fancy street with restaurants and shops for a light dinner at an American chain restaurant. The street is the same as all streets I imagine in a globalized Western-centric world. There is Prada, Louis Vuitton, HSBC bank, a bar/restaurant chain that is throughout Turkey called The House Cafe. It's like a little Champs Elysées or Fifth Avenue. The dinner is dinner, nothing special to report, but after we go to a typical Turkish dessert place, where they serve us a gelatinous cream-type blintzes made with chicken. It is tasty but the baklava is clearly something sinful. I imagine the calories it must contain. Melis says, "You may be on vacation, but I am not." I take another half slice as it would be equally a sin to let it go uneaten, or so is my rationale.

We have an early appointment at the American consulate, so after dessert we are back to Melis's cozy house and to bed early. The American consulate is a fortress of a building, on the top of a hill looking down onto the city. It is the only time that we will be in this area. We arrive an hour early, and after the burly man at the security gruffly says, "Only one, only one!" Eric and I are in, leaving our friends behind at one of the small cafes across the street, beginning the adventure. We are nervous, our hands sweating as we hand over our cell phones, cameras, and watches. Through a passageway that is outside and then into an elevator to the third floor. When we enter, it is filled with Turkish citizens requesting visas, and the room is packed. It primarily looks to be filled with men, with only a few women in the mix. The room to the left with no one in it is the notary. We have gotten a number, and the number is above the window already. A woman, clearly the woman that we have both spoken to on the phone for her cold demeanor, gives us the paperwork to fill out. It is a simple page declaring that we are celibate, single, and free to get married. We question whether or not we should put the last name first or the first name last for our parents' names. We say we will ask them, but each fill it out our own way. Eric writes his mother's last name first and a line for his father, I write their names in the order they are spoken. This one choice will ultimately change our fate. We don't know this right now, as we are too excited to know anything except the very clear fact that we want to get married.

There is a couple in front of us, and the bald man behind the window is joking with them as they swear in front of him. "Now are you sure you really want to get married?" he asks. "Usually I like to joke with couples just to make sure they are really sure." The laughter lightens the mood. She is blonde from North or South Carolina, teaching English in Turkey, and her future husband is Turkish. "I say that I came to Turkey and not only got a job but got a future husband as well," she jokes.

There is another young man, out of breath, sitting in the back relaxing as we go up to pay. He tells us he ran all the way down to the sea to find a bank that had US dollars. This will be his story of marriage, that he ran all the way down to the sea for his love. We return with the papers and she tells us to pay one hundred US dollars. Unfortunately, their credit card machine is broken, and obviously, being the American Consulate, they only take American money, so we take back our passports and are back outside hoping to find American dollars.

Luckily, in one of the stores that take overpriced passport photos, there is a large man with a one-hundred dollar bill, and he just happens to know the exchange rate: 195 Turkish Lira for 100 American. You haven't seen a one-hundred dollar bill in a long time, and for a moment, even after glancing at the light to make sure it isn't counterfeit, you wonder if you could really tell after all. But this man is in front of us in line, headed to the consulate himself, so we seem to feel sure that it's real.

It's at the US Embassy that we make our mistake, a mistake that we won't know about till the end of the week. On French forms you always put the last name first. On American forms it's the first name first. One of us puts our parents' last names first. We even ask the guy if that'll be okay. He says sure. He's wrong. But on this official paper that we carry with us everywhere, which says we have the right to get married, will be wrong.

The rest of the week is a whirlwind of tourist locations, official and not so official governmental buildings. In my journal for the week, I don't even have the time to give eloquent details. Tuesday: A blood clinic (because we need proof we don't have HIV for some reason before we're married). The Medusa cistern, and the Hagia Sofia. I don't know that Princess Theodora built the Hagia Sofia. It would've certainly resonated more had I know that information at the time.

What impresses me is the cistern across the street from the Hagia Sofia, which has two huge Medusa sculptures in it. From the plaque in the cistern no one knows why.

On Wednesday, Eric has surprised me and reserved us a very chic hotel. On Thursday, I've written in shorthand, *Starbucks 7am, chest x-ray, Sultanahmet, lunch at kebab place, dessert at tea shop next to the pudding shop, buy our wedding rings.* We buy our wedding rings from a jeweler that Melis knows, we keep them simple. I want them in platinum, but there is not enough time, so we get them in white gold, though after the years has worn away so that now they are gold in color.

It's Thursday, the day when Sarkozy has passed the bill stating that Turkish people must acknowledge that they committed genocide on the Armenians. In every taxi cab we get in, if we are speaking French, the taxi cab driver says to us, "I love the French, I hate Sarkozy."

We are at a dessert place after having eaten delicious cheap kebab, and now we are having coffee, real coffee, and baklava. We haven't read anything of the situation or why now, all of a sudden, this bill has come to pass when it has been so many years since the genocide. We learn that it is so Sarkozy can get more votes with the Armenian population in France.

Melis explains, "Our first president, Mustafa Kemal Atatürk was very smart, you know. He was the one who made Turkey a secular state, although it isn't now. He questioned whether he wanted Turkey to be part of Europe because at the time, they wanted Turkey to be included, because we have the path for Russia and Iran to get oil. He wanted to build up the east side of Turkey. Now, of course, we are begging to be let into the European Union. But they don't want to do it because of the east side of Turkey."

We see pictures of Atatürk everywhere, in every coffee shop, restaurant, and store that we go into. During Atatürk's presidency, women had equal civil and political rights and achieved full universal suffrage in 1936, eleven years after the founding of the Republic of Turkey.

On Friday, we wake up thinking we're getting married, and it's snowing. We go to the city hall, nervous and excited. We meet the woman who is supposed to marry us, who looks at the first form we filled out from our American embassy and says it's wrong. She can't marry us. Then all the papers will be wrong. We have to go back to the American Embassy to change them. The embassy is only open half days on Fridays. We'll never make it, even if we could get an appointment. Eric cries. It's the first time I've ever seen him cry. We spend the rest of the day smoking Niagara, the Turkish word for a hookah.

The next day, we fly back home defeated and unmarried, and the minarets pierce the cold sky.

DECISIONS SET YOU FREE

I t was Sartre who told Beauvoir to write a book about herself, and *The Second Sex* was what she wrote.

She started out writing an autobiography and found that the first thing she had to say was that she was a woman and that her youth and education had been different from Sartre's. That was the shock of her life. She found that curious—why should that be necessary to state? This became her book on women, which has little of Simone's "autobiography" in it. Her voice is there, to be sure, very academic, but in terms of the actual events of her life—she leaves them out. It seems from the text she wrote in a fury, in anger at her discoveries. By contrast, I started to write about women and found that what I was really writing about was myself.

"I think there should be a chapter in your book about decisions," Eric says after asking me if I'd like blueberries in my breakfast. It's a mundane decision, and I'm not that hungry, so it takes me too long to make. When he says "decisions," what he means is decisions, or lack there of, by women. I'm still deciding if I want to include my indecisiveness here.

I used to be an indecisive person. I attributed it to the idea of being flexible, and that surely being flexible couldn't possibly be a bad thing, as I could be happy anywhere. All my life, I remember being this way, except for one incident as a child when I was put in a group without any of my friends and made the teachers move me. I remember the teacher told my parents they were surprised because usually I never complained. That was me, go with the flow.

When Eric says "decisions," it resonates with me as a personality trait/flaw I've had to overcome. I'm not alone on this one. I'm reading *Fear of Flying* by Erica Jong, amazed they didn't have us read this at Columbia as the counterpoint to Philip Roth's *Portnoy's Complaint*, and I find this passage about indecision beautiful:

"I thought back to my days of having fantasies of men on trains. It's true that I never did anything about these fantasies and wouldn't have dared to. I wasn't even brave enough to write about them until much later. But suppose I had approached one of these men, and suppose he had rejected me, looked away, shown disgust or revulsion. What then? I would have immediately taken the rejection to heart, believed myself in the wrong, blamed myself for being an evil woman, a whore, a slut, a disturber of the peace. More to the point, I would have immediately blamed my own unattractiveness, not the man's reluctance, and I would have been destroyed for days by his rejection of me. Yet a man assumes that a woman's refusal is just part of a game. Or, at any rate, a lot of men assume that. When a man says no, it's no. When a woman says no, it's yes, or at least maybe. There is even a joke to that effect. And little by little, women begin to believe in this view of themselves. Finally, after centuries of living under the shadow of such assumptions, they no longer know what they want and can never make up their minds about anything.
And men, of course, compound the problem by mocking them for their indecisiveness and blaming it on biology, hormones, or premenstrual tension.

Is there a biological reason women may have a harder time making decisions than men? Is it that women's emotional hormonal core is continuously in flux and therefore the ability to overanalyze enhanced? Does this lead to complications deciding anything from the sometimes incredulous stupidity of what dress to wear or if I want blueberries, to the more challenging "real life" decisions? For years, women's emotional state has been the excuse for their inability to do things, the reason they can be excluded from social activities and endeavors. Now, new research is saying men are just as unstable as women, if not more so. That the testosterone levels in men inhibit their ability to make clear decisions. To go even further, the cause of the economic crisis is men's irrational testosterone chart, or so one study says.

Is it that we just haven't decided what men and women are biologically good at, and even if we did, we wouldn't agree? Most people have had enough blaming biological factors for women's lack of freedoms or equality. True, some women carry a child for nine months, which can put them out of the workforce from three months to three years, but is that any reason they should get paid less? It's an arbitrary question. One could explain away any response, and they have.

We could go the route of saying women are more inclined to be better listeners and more passive, and are thus more specifically attuned to being better leaders. To go this route—that women are biologically enhanced because of their passivity and therefore better leaders in the modern age—is to do the exact same thing which kept them out of the workplace to begin with.

It is much better instead to say women should make up half of the senate and half of the decisions in government because women are half of the population.

We focus now instead on the best and worst countries for women, in the spirit of equality, but we don't investigate the best and worst countries for men. It's assumed wherever men are, they have rights and opportunities no matter what, but that may not be the case. Men were the default for what it meant to be human, and women had to be studied separately.

My parents taught me no matter what decision I made, it was always the right one. Whether this was the right thing to do can be discussed elsewhere, or in fact it's the realization that later you get to choose, but the belief that I was always on the right path, even when it didn't seem like it, is strong and, without sounding too New Age, gave me a posi-tive outlook.

As my father would always say, "All decisions set you free."

By this logic, I could never go wrong, and even if I did, there was something to be learned, a reason for my fuck up. In this way, every-thing could be seen as positive. I realize not everyone was brought up this way. I had the control to believe that said decision was in the end positive because it gave me knowledge I most likely needed. Positive in the best of hippie ways. From this attitude, I adopted the phrase, "Everything will work out; it will all be fine." Because it would; I would make it be fine. This type of thinking is a luxury of rich coun-tries, particularly because I'm a fair-skinned Western woman. For the one billion poor people who are living on less than a dollar a day around the world, it is a different issue.

I understand while saying this that my privilege is showing, and that even the word privilege now is pejorative. In Gay's 2012 essay on the website *The Rumpus* entitled, "Peculiar Benefits," she speaks to that effect:

> *Privilege is a right or immunity granted as a peculiar benefit, advantage, or favor. There is racial privilege, gender (and identity) privilege, heterosexual privilege, economic privilege, able-bodied privilege, educational privilege, religious privilege and the list goes on and on…. The problem is, we talk about privilege with such alarming frequency and in such empty ways, we have diluted the word's meaning. When people wield the word privilege it tends to fall on deaf ears because we hear that word so damn much the word it has become white noise.*

For me, coming from so much privilege sometimes makes me want to curl in a ball and make myself small. I feel guilty that I have had so much whereas others have had so little, but this knee-jerk response to hide is not the right one. I have the responsibility to make myself big, to take up space, to make my voice heard, as Gay articulately continues:

You could, however, use that privilege for the greater good—to try to level the playing field for everyone, to work for social justice, to bring attention to how those without certain privileges are disenfranchised. While you don't have to do anything with your privilege, perhaps it should be an imperative of privilege to share the benefits of that privilege rather than hoard your good fortune.

If I shrink because I have been fortunate, I help no one. I want everyone to have the advantages I've had.

Still, no matter the adversity, this psychology of having a particular mindset of survival, of knowing you will handle what your face, is a good one. It gives you the freedom to confront life's challenges by coming from a place of mental strength.

BETWEEN FLOORS

I usually take the stairs.

It's a mild day in Paris, yet I'm still wearing a peacoat and sweater and scarf, as Eric and I walk down to the City Hall of the 18th Arrondissement with our *dossier,* all the necessary papers, and passport to go and pick a date for our wedding. I am nervous. On our walk, I've said, "I'm worried that maybe we won't do a party in LA after we're married because what would be the point?"

"Oh, right, because you don't like parties," Eric says with a grin.

I love parties. I used to plan them for a living. "OK, but promise me that if we do get married at the *Mairie,* we will still have a party in the States."

"Oui, chérie."

The *Mairie,* the word for City Hall in French, of dix-huiteme, is gorgeous. It's like an old train station with the wrought iron and glass ceiling you see at any of the train stations in Paris or the Musée d'Orsay, which used to be a train station. Once you enter the space, you feel the grandeur of the high ceilings and light, which floods in even on a gray Paris day. The marble staircase wraps around in the center of the space, leading up to the offices on either side.

The hall where we will be married is illuminated by chandeliers and yellow and green stained-glass windows, complete with red carpeting on the stairs and throughout the room. You could never find such a building in the States, and if you did, it would most certainly not be completely free to get married there. I imagine all the City Halls in Paris are certainly beautiful, though this one is ours because we live in this arrondissement.

At first we take the grand staircase, only to get to the top and realize that the door which leads to a reception bar area, complete with original paintings by Utrillo, the famous Montmartre painter, is closed. So back down we go, and as the smaller staircase on the side is closed for painting, we decide to take the elevator. At first it is only the two of us waiting, but then several others appear. I stare at the elevator and now five other people are waiting, and I motion to Eric that we could take the other stairs on the other side. I know I don't want to get in that elevator. I'm claustrophobic, a malady that never seemed to bother me until I was hungover and trapped on the L-train in New York underneath the East River for forty-five minutes. My boyfriend at the time, who was hungover as well, was no help. He said, "You're freaking me out, I'm going to throw up on you if you don't go stand over there."

It sounds pretty cruel when I write it out. The tone was much more a joke, but it was no help at all. That one moment in my life where I literally could not handle being stuck under the water in the subway completely changed my feeling of being trapped, of knowing I would be the worst person to be stuck with in a catastrophe. After that, I took the bus in New York or taxis. But when I moved to Paris, I didn't mind the metro. Your cell still got reception, unlike the New York subways at the time, and you always knew when the trains were coming, usually every two minutes.

I'm not one to not to face my fears, so when Eric says, "Well, now we've waited, and the elevator is here," I agree to get in the elevator. Six of us fit in, and there is one man left standing out, but someone in the elevator calls to him that there is space, he can fit, so he gets in with us. I look at the weight limit of the elevator, eight people. I count. We are seven. *It should be fine,* I reassure myself.

There is a woman in the corner to my right holding her nose. Clearly the new man who has gotten in smells, though I can't smell him. There is another woman in front of me, and she must be blocking the odor. It seems clear that all of us in the elevator cannot wait to get out the moment we get in, or perhaps that is my projection as I try to push the idea out of my head of being stuck in the elevator with these people.

The doors close, the elevator starts rising and then falls a few feet and stops.

"Aww, shit." The guy in the baseball cap to the left of me looks at me with that kind of expression you see on someone's face when they swear in a drawn out way. Kind of smiling, in a joking way.

Immediately, the elevator's female voice starts speaking: *"S'il vous plaît, supprimez l'obstruction des porte."* She repeats in the same non-reassuring tone, "Please remove the obstruction from the doors." There is no obstruction in the doors, just us.

I look at Eric. "Honey," I say. I've already started shaking. Everything is shaking—my legs, my feet, my hands. I've started unconsciously taking off my coat and my scarf. "Honey," I repeat, looking at the ceiling of the elevator the corners. There is a flat ceiling with lights, no opening, no trap door, just seamless at the top.

"It's okay, cherie, just breathe," Breathing helps, but in my mind all I can think is, *I knew it, I knew we were going to get stuck in the elevator! Fuck facing your fears, I knew it all along. You should listen to your instinct instead.*

We've tried to press the button to go up again and have dropped a few feet again. The other man by the buttons has pressed the call button, and soon there is an actual live voice speaking to us. She seems incredibly calm. She's not stuck in the elevator.

She asks what our elevator number is. Now the woman in front of me can feel my legs and whole body quivering, and has turned around to give me a smile. Perhaps I smile. Perhaps I don't. I can't remember. I can't remember what she looks like. I want to say she has a nice round face, braids in her hair, and that she is young, but I remember more her gray coat and that I am trying to press myself more into the wall so she can't feel me shaking, but that's of no use.

Eric is now on the phone calling the number next to our elevator number. Meanwhile, the two men in front are working on prying open the doors. I may have asked they try this, as we're not getting anywhere with the other elevator lady who is sitting comfortably wherever she is answering calls about elevator catastrophes. Just to be clear, the elevator is the size of an airport bathroom stall.

The men succeed in prying the first set of doors open, and we can see we are stuck between floors. Even this makes me feel somewhat relieved that at least we are close to getting out. But the second set of doors is still firmly shut. The men are banging on the other doors, saying, "Hey ho, we're stuck in the elevator. Help us."

At first, the top doors won't open, so they try the bottom doors, and with luck now those are open too and we can see the ground of the floor we started on. Everyone starts climbing out, the men helping the women jump down. Eric hangs up the phone. "Leave your stuff here," he says to me as now I am entangled with my coat and scarf and purse, but all I can think of is to get the fuck out of this elevator. We are the last ones out. I jump down, not so great on my knees and now Eric is beside me. A woman who has been standing in front of the elevator, knowing we were trapped, asked me, "How long were you trapped for?"

I say just five or ten minutes maybe, but long enough. Eric and I walk away from the elevator and into the large space of the Mairie. Where our compatriots of trapped-dom go, I have no idea.

"Maybe we're not supposed to get married," he says, smiling.

Ironically, the first signs of my claustrophobia started in France when I was five with my parents, and we stayed in a beautiful hotel in St. Germain des Pres. The hotel still exists. I remember we were on the top floor of the hotel and the elevator was so incredibly small, so I would race up the stairs to try and beat my parents to the top. I usually won since I was so young.

The feeling of that voyage comes back to me with all the exoticism travel brings. How the doors of the hotel were all painted with pretty pictures, how the hotel had a little white dog, and my first little Paris outfit my parents bought me: a deep green and navy blue striped shirt and pencil skirt, with a little navy sweater. The doll museum and my first *Corolle* doll with curly hair, how she smelled of vanilla.

My parents didn't tell me Venice was a city on water, so when we arrived, and they said we would go take a cab, and instead we got in a motorboat, I was completely astounded. Taxis weren't boats in my mind.

Certain memories I know I remember, like the time we got robbed in the train while we were sleeping and woke up to our clothes and everything in a big mess all over the room. Certain memories I'm not sure if I remember or if I just remember the stories of them, like being robbed by Romanis on the bridge overlooking the Ponte Vecchio in Florence while my father painted. I thought it was exciting we'd been robbed, as that was the first thing I said to Dad: "Dad, we've been robbed!"

They say that being homesick makes you indelibly nostalgic. Not only do you miss your family for the events you miss while you're away, but those who find themselves in a foreign country have a tendency to over-romanticize the past. To look backward more than looking forward.

"Maybe we're just supposed to go through some obstacles first," I say with a smile.

We're both taking deep breaths and kind of circling around each other. Now we kiss, and hug, and I run my fingers through his hair. We look into each other's eyes, and together walk across the room to the other set of stairs.

In the office, there is a new woman we haven't worked with before. We tell her of our elevator debacle. When we leave, she says not to take the elevator, and that she won't either. We give her our file, and she takes our passports and documents to the corner of the room to make photocopies. While she's gone, I say, "Thank God you were there. There is no one I would rather be trapped in the elevator with. You were so good with me, honey. Thank you."

Eric takes my hand and says, "I'll take care of you."

"I'll take care of you, too," I say.

And this is the moment that engrains itself on my brain because I tell myself to engrave it. This is the moment when I say yes, this is the man I want to marry—the man I want to spend the rest of my life with. I am sure, there is no doubt, no indecision, and all is good.

The moment I met him, I knew I wanted to marry Eric. Well, not exactly the moment I met him. The moment I met him, I thought we'd be friends, but somewhere between our first kiss and a month later, I became beyond smitten, to the point of imagining him in a tuxedo at the end of the aisle. He'd look so good in a tuxedo.

Eric is quick to remind me I didn't believe in marriage when I met him, and I believe this is true. I was never a girl to jump to ideas of marriage. I was never in a rush, never imagined every detail of my wedding, and even though I'd considered marriage with every serious boyfriend I'd had before, I was imagining the party, not the marriage. I never actually envisioned who was waiting for me to say, "I do." Or in this case, "*Oui.*"

You could say perhaps it is Paris. You get swept away with the accordion players riding on the smell of buttery croissants. The city doesn't have to try hard to persuade you to fall in love, it's true. The lights on the River Seine, or the Canal Saint-Martin, lights glimmering on water, with a light breeze, lights glimmering anywhere, really. If there is one thing Paris is good at, it's lighting.

Everything seems to be in order, except she says there is no way we can get married in less than a month. She proposes April 20th. Eric and

I are not stoners, but for whatever reason 4-20 is symbolic of a stoner holiday. It's also Hitler's birthday, which is odd because Holocaust Remembrance Day is the day before. I'm leaving for Los Angeles on the 18th.

She tells us we can't decide the date now, anyway, as our file has to be reviewed. We have to come back Thursday to discuss, and we leave completely disheartened it may not be possible to get married before I leave because I don't have a visa, I'm only allowed to stay in Paris for three months, and my three months is up since we've come back from Turkey. In which case we'd have to wait, in which case I'd have to go back to the States to apply for a visa.

It's now 4:30pm, so we decide to go get a drink at the *Place de Tertre.* There may still be some sun there.

BAC À GLACES

On a gorgeous Spring Friday, hot, Claudine and I meet at the *Bac à Glaces* across from the *Bon March*é.

I know where it is now, and the women there know me. Claudine has written about the ice cream artisan who works there and creates interesting flavors such as passion fruit with anis vert (green licorice), almond cookie or ginger and cinnamon combined. A stout woman with straight golden hair, she gives us a taste of this new flavor along with another vanilla and hazelnut cream.

The instant Claudine gets there wearing a purple Chanel-type skirt and pink jacket, we begin reviewing her notes of the first sixty pages of my book. She does not have as many notes as I thought she would. She loves the part about my family and has written "excellent and beautiful" on several pages. This is a good sign.

Previously, she has said she doesn't like the beginning—I need to add more of Paris in it, "more atmosphere." In my effort to avoid clichés, I left out Paris completely. "Add the clichés if you want, but we have to feel we are in Paris, Augustine. You should reread the chapter I wrote in my latest book with Laurent. I really describe Paris; perhaps that will help you."

She has told me I need to start the book with a funny and nervous anecdote. "You're funny," she says. "You will think of something."

I am pleased that today I think I have found my anecdote, which is, of course, being stuck in the elevator on our way to the marriage office.

"We're getting married on April 16," I say, "It's a Monday. Unfortunately, there was no way we could do it on a Saturday."

"Augustine, this is perfect. This is how you should end your book, getting married on a Monday in Paris."

I am very hesitant.

"Well, don't you think it is the perfect end to your book to end with your wedding?" she asks.

"Yes, but the problem is all of these French books, or women's books, end that way."

"Oh, well I, didn't know that."

"Yes, they all end with the happily-ever-after fairytale of the woman falling in love and ending up with the man of her dreams."

"Well, you could end it here with us talking about it and you could say how Claudine was so impossible, and wanted me to end the book with my marriage and we got in our first fight about it, because Claudine was being so impossible," she jokes.

"Yes, that might be good."

In France, everyone gets married at their city hall, and then you can do a religious ceremony or celebration after that. Sometimes you do a simple ceremony at the city hall and then plan a huge celebration later, like my friends Olga and Christophe do. They get married at their city hall in the 15th arrondissement on a cold winter's day with just a very small group of people and then in the summer they have their wedding at the church when it's warm. Our friends Mariel and Thibaut do everything on the same day, their city hall marriage in the Marais and then a reception in the Buttes Charmont, a gorgeous park in the 20th.

That is our plan, too. We'll do the civil ceremony in France, just so I can legally stay in France and begin to work and then do a celebration in Los Angeles. So, two days after we get married I fly to Los Angeles alone with the intention of planning a wedding there. On a later reflection I realize it's more apropos I'm going on a honeymoon alone to Los Angeles to plan our other wedding, and what better way to reaffirm you love someone and you want to be married than to leave by yourself for a month?

Or could that just be the true sign of independence?

HAVING IT ALL

While feminism undoubtably ushered in several positive effects on society, it appears there are two major downfalls to the theory: it left men mildly confused of their role, and women became and are still mad at feminists because now they have to do everything.

It's taken for granted that feminism is to blame because they gave women the myth they could and should "have it all." Anne Marie-Slaughter writes an article entitled "Why Women Still Can't Have It All" about the myth of "having it all," in the July / August 2012 issue of *The Atlantic* magazine, and people get so pissed. So much so that Ms. Slaughter rescinds and decides never to use the term "having it all" again. People were pissed on several levels, one of the main ones being she is still in a much higher economic status than most people, though she makes no claim to be otherwise and is very clear in the article that she is writing for a "certain type of demographic." People were pissed that even asking the question increases female stereotypes.

The question also implies that all women want it all, the "it" being the family, the career, the 2.5 kids, the American dream. Not everyone wants the "it."

It appears to be only a woman's problem to have it all and do it all. Men don't seem to face this problem, as evidenced by the several interviews of successful working mothers who are continuously asked how they balance work and family life. Men are rarely, if ever, asked this question.

For a while, there was a trend on the red carpet of *Ask Her More*, because men were rarely asked to only talk about who they were wearing.

Because of this article in 2012, Slaughter becomes a reference in the US on gender issues. Five years later, in *National Geographic's* 2017 special issue on gender, alongside Gloria Steinem, Slaughter is interviewed to express her views. Her phrase, "cultural norms sustain inequality," will resonate. Later that year, another article makes waves, Gemma Hartley's "Women Aren't Nags, We're Just Fed Up," in *Harper's Bazaar.* Overwhelmingly, women relate to Hartley's sentiment of the mental load of housework. Around this same time, an anonymous article goes viral with the title, "Why I Don't Help My Wife." It will be a nice counterpoint to Hartley that perhaps it is in the language we use that makes the difference. To use the word "help" suggests that it's not equally your responsibility to manage the mundane tasks or running a household.

Now it appears even harder for women, as compared to the days of specific gender roles. Now they have four full-time jobs instead of one. The way we see being a housewife has shifted, each task recognized and separated. The full-time job of being a housewife was discredited as being one job when in actuality it is several: grocery shopping, meal prepping, laundry, dishes, staying thin and young (now called self-care), and being a mother. Now we add a career on top of that, and it's exhausting. But this white narrative itself is deceptive because women of color were already working and doing all these things. It's important to question when we think about what we've been taught about women entering the workforce in the 60s. Still, men's role of fatherhood wasn't necessarily enhanced at the same time, but hey, at least some white women now have their own money.

In 2019, during the Conference on the Status of Women, UN Women's Instagram page posts statistics like 208 million women still need modern contraceptives, women do 2.6 times more care work than men, only 41% of new mothers receive maternity benefits, 2.1 billion people lack access to safely managed water in 2015, and 80% of those depend on collection by women and girls.

However, Slaughter remarks on a new shift in her 2017 article for National Geographic, "Imagine a World Where Gender Is Neither a Plus nor a Minus"

Given the gulfs between us, is it possible to write about "the state of women" collectively? We do not all bear children; we do not all love men; we do not even all have the same genitalia. But women do all at least have one thing in common: we are all prisoners of our cultures.

Women are still trapped and oppressed in so many parts of the world, forced to submit to the dictates of men. But men also are trapped, forced into culturally defined roles.

Watching our sons be twisted to fit society's expectations of men, even when those men wield power, can be as frustrating and counterproductive as watching our daughters be denied the ability to fulfill their potential.

The concept of gender fluidity remains alien, even abhorrent, to many people in Western society. But that concept is accepted in nations around the world, and it opens doors. Once we recognize that gender identity and expression exist along a spectrum, why should we cling to the rigid categorization of men and women? The ultimate goal, surely, is to let all people define themselves as human beings, to break out of assigned categories and challenge received wisdom.

Without the weight of gendered expectations, each of us—women and men— can "develop the full circle of ourselves," to borrow Gloria Steinem's lovely phrase. We can work to extend equality and opportunity to the entire human family.

I've done my best to use gender-inclusive language. But we're all human and I may make mistakes. And in these terms, the blanket term "women" encompasses those who are gender queer because they also face discrimination. Not all people who menstruate are women and not all women menstruate.

I truly believe we are on the path of acceptance of a third gender, that of non-gender, or that the wave of the future (and I use wave purposely here as feminism also comes in waves) is to a gender-fluid identities. That the very concept of gender and race and all the systems that seek to divide us will become outdated. But we are not there yet.

The wight of gendered expectations: that is what we have to challenge. Eric is quick to remind me that when I first meet him, I didn't want to get married. I wasn't sure I wanted kids. It was because I met him that I wanted those its.

I don't ask him to marry me. In hindsight, I wish I had. It's not very feminist of me, versus my friend Laila, who planned out a romantic dinner of Spanish tapas to recreate the meal they shared when they first met.

Eric and I never have a wedding party. If you can believe it, it's not fun to plan a wedding when you don't have a job. Nana wants to help and gives me a budget of ten thousand dollars. But my bat mitzvah was thirty thousand dollars more than fifteen years ago, so it's not a realistic budget for Los Angeles. Nana has her 95th birthday party at Lawry's instead, which works out better. My parents and Eric's mom don't come to our wedding in Paris, much to the continued chagrin of my parents. Eric's mother was taking care of her sister who had dementia so she couldn't leave, and we didn't want one set of parents there if the other one couldn't be. We said we would do a wedding, but we ended up buying our apartment instead. I'm still holding out for a big wedding, but I've got to make money first.

BIENVENUE EN FRANCE!

France and US history are similar in that they both had revolutions, America taking the lead in 1775 and France in 1789. For both countries, this is where "democracy" started. We're told these countries were formed by creating a written document entitled a Declaration, and *voilà*, you have a country. In principle, the idea is a good one. Write a list of what we believe to be true, and then continue from there.

The Declaration of Independence (in America, 1776) and The Declaration of the Rights of Man and Citizen (in France, 1789) have many similarities, chief among them that both excluded women from the unalienable rights. When Israel and India were created after World War II, they included in their constitutions the right for women to vote within a year.

Women did not gain the right to vote in France until 1944 and did not literally vote until 1945. A year later, with women now at the helm of voting in France, they made brothels illegal. That was only sixty-six years ago. So it seems obvious to me at least to wonder what the fuck were women doing from 1791 to 1945? Were they continuing to fight for this natural right? That's 153 years.

When I am welcomed into France, after marrying a Frenchman, our teacher for the day's history lesson explains, "Women would have gotten the right to vote after World War I, (like the United States) but then there was the Depression, and then the start of World War II, so they were busy with other matters. But then we got it right after the war."

She was wrong, of course. We know from many feminist history books that the French suffragettes fought every day between the two wars to obtain the right to vote. There were a few times it went to the National Assembly and was going to be adopted, but the congressmen, including the socialists, found every excuse to postpone. But in 1936, three women became cabinet members, including the Nobel Prize winner Irène Joliot-Curie, daughter of Marie Curie, and it finally passed.

In the room with other immigrants like me, we spend the entire day learning about French history and culture through a PowerPoint presentation. In it, they focus much of their attention on the rights of women, making it clear to us that women are allowed to walk around without a companion, that women share equal responsibility of the decisions of their children, that women are allowed to own property, making it clear that some of these rights are not afforded to other countries.

In 1893, New Zealand became the first self-governing nation to extend the right to vote to women. In Saudi Arabia, women finally get the right to vote in 2015. That was the last remaining country in the world that prohibited women from voting.

It took over 200 years to abolish slavery, and most people would agree slavery was worse than the conditions of women. However, if you compare the conditions of some women, there are remarkable similarities. They had no money, no power, were often beaten by their owners (husbands), and were not allowed to be educated. It's no wonder so many women were inspired by the Civil Rights Movement and that the two coincided. Still, in the mix of these discussions, we can't forget that white women had slaves and then later continued the debasement of domestic work by employing Black women for low wages to take care of their children. We can't forget either that Black men in Africa sold other Black people to the slave traders. That women as brothel owners put other women in impossible situations, that grandmothers are the ones most likely to enforce female circumcision on their grand-daughters. But as Claudine has said, "there is no word for apartheid for women."

In 1920, women finally secured the right to vote, which means we haven't even been voting for more than one hundred years. Wyoming did have voting rights for women, as did Kansas. We think of the States as being one of the first to initiate the right to vote, but when looking at the actual dates of how long it took from the start of a nation to the law providing the right, it's very close to most all of Europe. Particularly because even though the 19th amendment, giving women the right to vote, was granted in 1919, it isn't until the Voting Rights Act of 1965 that Black women were fully granted the right to vote. Also important to note when we discuss American History is that Native Americans weren't granted citizenship until 1924, but state policies still prohibited them from voting. In 1948, World War II veteran Miguel Trujillo filed a lawsuit giving Native Americans the right to vote in New Mexico and Arizona, but it wasn't until 1957 that all states allowed them to vote. So this is all recent. In my parents' lifetime. This is not common knowledge, I learn this when watching Rachel Cargle's, "Unpacking White Feminism" lecture and reading Evette Dionne's 2017 article in *Teen Vogue,* "Women's Suffrage Leaders Left Out Black Women: Despite what you may have learned in school." This is exactly it, what we learn and don't learn in school. Cécile Fara and Julie Marangé of Feminists in the City express a similar idea about their high school education in the early 2000s in France that they never learn about Louise Michel in school. Even though the square in front of the Sacre Coeur may be named after Louise Michel she is still considered an anarchist and not taught in schools, they'll say.

IT'S NOT A MAN'S WORLD. WHY?

Try telling that to the Rohingya refugees who were raped, whose homes were destroyed, and whose husbands and children were murdered in front of them. Try telling that to the girls who are forced into marriage, who are forced into circumcision, who aren't allowed to go to school or are shot in the head if they do. To say it's not a man's world is insulting. It comes from a very privileged place. And yet, could these women one day say that it's not a man's world, it's our world? I imagine they are much stronger than I am, so I do think it possible.

I say it's not a man's world because believing that is more beneficial for my mental wellbeing and the wellbeing of the world. But just because I want it to be true doesn't mean that it is. As my friend Michelle put it, just because you say that the world is flat doesn't make it so.

It's a man's world or it's a woman's. Or, there are two worlds, and we've just been taught that one isn't as important as the other. But now people are starting to take notice of this whole other world, and that may be important, too. The third option is it's OUR world.

When I say it's not a woman's world, either, I breathe a sigh of relief. Thinking that men are not actually in control is quite destabilizing, as if everything as we know it is now up for grabs. That's how I feel, anxious. If straight, white, rich, men aren't running the show, who is? To say it's a man's world, though, seems to automatically assume it's run by the wrong kind of men. And we really wouldn't be too hard-pressed to find them. So we replace man's world with the patriarchy, with white supremacy, with the system.

This is a woman's world because she is in fact Mother Earth. Father Time has had his time, and now it's time for us to train the men to be fathers. The comparison between women's place in the world and the state of the planet is an easy comparison. Women are in a rage, and the planet is raging along with them. We're literally raising our temperatures in anger. The world has been raped and pillaged and pummeled. Her precious resources have been destroyed, and yet she rejuvenates. She perseveres. Concern for the wellbeing of our planet coincides with concern for the wellbeing of women (and men).

So, no, it's not a woman's world, either; it's our world. The message of inclusion we started off with when we were kids was a good base. We are equally responsible for this mess we're in, and we are in a mess; there's no doubt about that. And yet, we've been in a mess before. Much worse than this—at least we're not beheading people in a public square for the most part, and at least we've stopped sacrificing virgins; well, not quite, we don't kill them now, we just marry them off. But we are getting somewhere. It does appear that the savagery of past generations has subsided a bit in many locations of the world. And I don't mean just savages as in a western orientalist way. Western civilization has had plenty of savages—our American founding fathers to name a few. But we don't need to call names. What we need to prove is why it's our world. Who's in charge?

Women consume more media.

Women are the majority of teachers and medical staff.

Women control supply and demand.

Women are the buying power of the household.

Women create the demand for luxury items.

Women are the influencers, and it has never been more clear than the images that have propelled women to power.

WITCH HUNT

From Leonard Shlain's 1465 - 1820 timeline for *The Alphabet Versus The Goddess:*

- *After the Bible, the next bestselling book is the Witch's Hammer; a how-to book for the rooting out, torture, and burning of witches.*
- *Witch craze breaks out only in those countries impacted by the printing press.*
- *Germany, Switzerland, France, and England have severe witch-hunts. All boast steadily rising literacy rates.*
- *Russia, Norway, Iceland, and the Islamic countries bordering Europe do not experience witch-hunts. The printing press has a negligible impact on these societies.*
- *Estimates range that between 100,000 women to the millions were murdered during the witch-hunts.*
- *There is no parallel in any other culture in the world in which the men of the culture suffered a psychosis so extreme that they believed that their wise women were so dangerous that they had to be eliminated.*

This line haunts me. A mass psychosis which resulted in 100,000 executions of women because of the publication of a book.

And yes we all known that the best-selling book in the world is the Bible, but who ever thinks to ask what was the second best-selling book? The *Malleus Maleficarum,* still in print, is the original name of *Witch's Hammer*, written by a "self-proclaimed expert" on witches. This was at a time when women were allowed to own property, live alone and knew the secrets of medicinal herbs. So guess who got the woman's land when she was proclaimed a witch by her neighbor? That same neighbor who reported her as a witch. *Cheers.* Isn't that convenient.

A mass psychosis, let's hope there never is one. But there is one right now. In 2017, roughly 87,000 women were killed by domestic violence, 50,000 by an intimate partner. To put it another way, 87,000 men became murders of the woman they professed to love. We learn that it's the witches that were hysterical, but it's the other way around: it was the society that surrounded them.

LEAST VIOLENT TIME FOR WOMEN

This leads one to wonder when was the least violent time for women, and which country has the least crime against women today? Judy Chicago knows the answer immediately. "Empress Theodora of the Byzantine era." I unfortunately do not know this epoch off the top of my head like she does. Byzantium was an ancient Greek city founded in the seventh century BC. Today, it's known as Istanbul. Theodora was an empress who ruled from 522 to 548. That was a long time ago for the least violent time for women. In Chicago's book *The Dinner Party*, she writes:

Theodora passed laws nullifying theater contracts constraining actresses' freedom and broke down the barriers that kept them in a socially interior role. She issued an imperial decree making it illegal and punishable by death to entice a woman into prostitution, turning one of her palaces into an institution where ex-prostitutes could go to start new lives. She helped raise the low status of women in marriage, improved divorce laws in their favor, instituted legislation protecting women from mistreatment by their husbands, saw to it that women could inherit property, and instituted the death penalty for rape. Moreover, Theodora's insistence that all these changes be enforced created a legacy that benefited the lives of Byzantine women for many centuries.

Pretty amazing stuff, yet we rarely hear of her. Theodora and her husband, Justianian, who had his uncle change the Roman law stating that government officials couldn't marry actresses just so he could marry her, together created Constantinople as the greatest city of the time, building the Hagia Sofia. She was perhaps the most influential and powerful woman in the Roman Empire's history, though we rarely learn about her.

We rarely learn about Justinian as well, unless specifically studying Ancient History. This dynamic duo is a significant team to remember because it is believed that their relationship was one of love and equality.

BIRTH CONTROL

All this time, I've been managing my apartment in New York. Now it is finally time to give it up. The plan is to spend New Year's Eve in New York, but Eric and I both get the flu on Christmas, so we stay past New Year's. When we do finally make it to New York, I am more emotional than usual.

It's a joke, because I'm not usually emotional, but since I'm a woman by default "I'm emotional," which is clearly a bad thing. This is what we have to be aware of. This is our awakening, our reminder that being emotional can be okay, that we don't have to dismiss it.

Still, I'm not acting like myself. Eric knows something is up, and when I'm five days late, I take a pregnancy test. My plans of partying it up in New York one last time are dashed, and now all I want to do is sleep. Eric stays to pack up all my stuff and ship it back to Los Angeles.

When we return to Paris, I start searching for a doctor. It's impossible to find one who doesn't require waiting for at least two months.

Luckily, Mariel recommends me to *Group Naissances*, a collective of twelve midwives, three doctors and two psychologists running out of the maternity clinic *Jeanne d'Arc* in the 13th arrondissement in Paris.

Five years ago, I would've never imagined I'd be able to pick a midwife who didn't speak English.

Francine is lovely and joyous, like a grandmother wearing Birkenstocks and is happy to discuss the history of midwives with us.

A midwife is different from a doula because they are medically trained. A doula is there to give support, but they don't actually deliver the baby. For forty euros per visit, we meet with Francine for an hour a month. She talks to us about taking advantage of being just the two of us. We, like most new parents, can't really wrap our heads around having a baby or how our lives will change. People joke about not sleeping in on Sundays, but the shift of identity is not possible to envision until you're there. And if you didn't really want the baby and didn't really feel that you chose this, then parenting, which is already super hard, would be even harder. How lucky I am that I was able to make the choice.

CONTRACEPTION IS THE ANSWER

While we in the States vehemently argue for our right to an abortion, I wonder if we are fighting the right fight.

What if women today decided they no longer wanted to take birth control? We still do not fully know the effects of long-term use of birth control pills, as we are still in the guinea pig stage. There are only two or three generations who have been on it.

I stop taking birth control pills shortly after we're married. It's the first time in my life I'm willing to take the risk of being pregnant, and it was the first time in my life where I realized if I were to get pregnant, I wouldn't have an abortion. You spend your whole life trying not to get pregnant and then when you want to get pregnant, you're not sure you can.

Fast forward a few months to October 2012, and I've bought the book *Taking Charge of Your Fertility* by Toni Welscher. It's not a pregnancy book per se, but is used as such to understand the times when you are most fertile. In the book she raises a few excellent points, the first being while men are fertile all of the time, women are fertile roughly seventy-two hours every month. But here's the catch, sperm can live for a week. No one ever told me that! So why is it always women's responsibility to take drugs which affect their bodies in unknown ways? The answer is obvious, because women are the ones who are going to have to deal with being pregnant.

She says, while the pill was supposed to give women freedom, what it really did was further entomb the idea it is only the women's responsibility. Why did no one teach us about our cycles? That the window to get pregnant is such a small one?

Education is something no one, not yet anyway, can ever take away from you. So shouldn't we be educating today's women and men instead of just putting them on medication?

There is no question to me that being pregnant, giving birth, and breastfeeding compromise your ability to be active, and we shouldn't feel bad about that. Instead of trying to rush back to work, we should in fact take more time. Our partners should take more time, too. In France, you can take a maternity leave for up to three years, particularly if you have two children, which allows you a third of your salary to take care of your children. Some women don't want to do this, and that's totally fine, but we should be given the choice, and most women feel they don't have a choice. Some women take the three years, and some women go back to work after three months, which they can do because France has a national daycare system unlike the United States. Additionally, they have no problems taking time off before they give birth. It is socially acceptable to take it very easy before giving birth.

Eric, as a teacher of English, is under the status of an *"auto-entrepreneur,"* so he is afforded eleven days off. In the Nordic countries, women and men can take up to an entire year off from work.

ACTUAL COSTS OF GIVING BIRTH, ASIDE FROM THE OBVIOUS

In 2013, *The New York Times* says that the United States is the most expensive developed nation in which to give birth, an average of forty thousand dollars. They've found a way to monetize each aspect of giving birth so that giving birth to the infant is one price, and giving birth to the placenta is another price.

In France, I pay out of pocket: 1600 euros for my son, Noah, and 1000 for my daughter, Evalie. This is exceptional. That money goes directly to Francine and Sidonie, my midwives. The cost of the hospital is completely reimbursed by the French government. For Noah, Eric and I stay in the hospital for a week because he has jaundice, and because we're not pressured to leave. I don't think people like to admit what they pay in hospital bills in the States. It seems embarrassing in some way.

In Santa Barbara, my friend Evan finds an all-natural birthing center that charges 5000 dollars for a one-night stay, basically just for the delivery of the baby. However, if there are any complications, such as I had with Noah, and a doctor needed to be called in, she would have to go to the hospital as the center has no actual doctors.

In London, my girlfriend Michelle goes to an all-natural birthing center that costs about 4400 pounds, so just shy of $7000. However, it is almost fully reimbursed by her private insurance, provided for by an American company. If she had had an emergency and needed to go to the local hospital, the National Health Service would have covered it. Alternatively, they could have just gone through the NHS and it would have been completely free.

That's what my girlfriend Laila, a teacher in Australia does. There, for the birth of her two children, she pays absolutely nothing. Sheila Aminmadani, a high school teacher in Brooklyn, New York, belongs to the United Federation of Teachers (UFT) also pays nothing to give birth, but for her first child in 2016 she has only six weeks unpaid maternity leave, then in 2019 the union succeeds in securing six weeks paid maternity leave but it is the union not the government funded public school that will pay for it. In both cases, she can also take all the personal and sick days she has accrued—they just have to be used *before* the 6 weeks start. There is also a childcare leave, but it's unpaid and you lose your health insurance.

In France, you can refuse to take the total of sixteen weeks for maternity leave for your first child but you are obligated to take at least eight weeks maternity leave minimum—two weeks before the birth and six weeks after. And you do have the option to take more, particularly if you have more children with the maximum of up to three years leave with reduced pay. In 2020, France will increase paternity leave to twenty eight days. By comparison, Germany and Sweden have the most in the world with fourteen months or four hundred and eighty days paid leave which can be shared between the couple.

CLINIQUE JOAN OF ARC

At a quarter to midnight we get in a cab. My contractions are five minutes apart. I'm not listening to the radio, I'm watching the lights of an empty Place de la République, past Marianne. It seems fitting to be on my way to give birth at the Clinique Jeanne d'Arc. On the radio they are reporting the harrowing story of a woman who gave birth on her own under a tree as she crossed the border of North and South Sudan. She cuts the umbilical cord herself with a stick. Women are so formidable or *for·mi·dable* as they say in French meaning the same thing, so powerfully impressive. I can't imagine.

I'm not listening to the story. I'm focusing on squeezing Eric's hand to stifle my screams from the pain as it's been rumored that cab drivers will kick you out of their cab if they realize you're in labor. Eric is listening and he knows or reassures himself that no matter what happens we are not going to the same conditions, we're not going to be in a similar situation. But this reassurance isn't totally assured, birth is always a life or death situation.

PART IV

BECOMING A MAMA

A nd then I think I gave birth to a nine-pound, six-ounce baby without an epidural in four excruciating hours. I can do anything.

Most people with kids will say there is life before kids and life after. Two separate entities, two separate existences. This is true. Before, I was concerned about the feminist existence. After, it seems like a single people's problem at best. Gloria Steinem, Virginia Woolf, Simone de Beauvoir, Claudine Monteil—these women never had kids. Those first six weeks, priorities shift. You're just trying to keep this little person alive. Who has the luxury of time to contemplate women's condition? I'm living the woman's condition.

The due date is September 8, but there are no signs of labor. I feel exactly the same. So I keep having to go to the hospital every forty-eight hours. Francine gives me homeopathic medicine I put under my tongue, old remedies from midwives. The process of pregnancy and birth is very feminist. by which I mean naturally and primarily occupied by women. Francine is a *sage-femme*, literally translated as a wise woman. Later when Noah learns to speak French, we say to him, "*Sois sage*," which means "be wise."

Noah arrives exactly a week late, supposedly, but when he is born, Francine says he arrived just on time.

There is a point when I think I'm going to die. The pain defines excruciating. I'd read that in *A New Active Birth,* which said that this thinking at a particular point in labor was necessary so that it got your adrenaline pumping for the final push of the baby. At a certain point around that time, before or after, Francine says that the baby is still doing fine, and I think to myself, *I don't give a fuck, just get this fucking thing out of me*, but then logic kicks in, and I am relieved.

And then finally, Francine says, "*Prends le!*"—take him—and I do. And he's on me, and Eric is crying. And that's the moment I would savor forever if I could. That's the moment I would relive.

I try as hard as I can to hold it, engrain it in my memory, before it is gone.

FIRST SMILE

How much fun it is playing with Noah when he is awake and calm.

How amazing to watch him sleep beside me and wonder what he will do when he grows up. Will he like boys or girls? Will he experiment? Will he have an orgy like his mother did? Will he get a tattoo? A piercing? Several? Will he like Bob Dylan? Will he play guitar? He is mesmerized by Eric's hanging guitars. Will he look like me? Like Eric? Eric says he has my cheeks and chin. Will he rebel against us? What will that look like? Will he borrow his Dad's old tee-shirts? Will I see him get married? Have kids of his own? Will he be an only child? Will he like to read? I have to start reading to him more and more. What will he study? Will he respect women? How can I make sure? Will he learn Chinese? Will he like to cook? To travel? To adventure?

So many things to wonder about. So much joy.

A REGULATORY SUBSTANCE?

Noah and I meet Eric in the pouring rain at the HSBC. Under the fog of intense hormones, I feel the banker has insulted my mothering. There are several times where well-meaning people have given advice, and it feels like a direct attack, like I'm doing something wrong.

I always said I never wanted to raise a child in a city with snow. I'm Jewish, so therefore slightly neurotic, and I wasn't raised in the cold weather. The first time I saw snow was when I was fifteen, except for the one exceptional time when it snowed two inches in Los Angeles when I was a kid, which doesn't count as it was more like a layer of frozen hail, like making a snowball out of crushed ice and not the soft, shushing whisper-melt on your fingertips-type.

Almost all of my worries about my son stem from his temperature. My husband says the only thing I worry about is him breathing. So when I walk up the street and the man at the cafe who always gives me an extra glass of wine or a free café crème tells me it's too cold for infants, I'm instantly worried I'm doing something wrong, and the implied context is I'm a bad mother. I don't know if he has children. I know nothing about the man at the café. I don't go there that often. I imagine they do this in all other countries. Everyone wants to give you advice on how to raise your child and what you should or shouldn't be doing.

The instant reflex in me when someone tells me something that questions whether I know best, or whether the choice I made is the right one, is to want to smoke. I haven't smoked in eleven months. But when someone, anyone, makes a statement of advice about my kid and temperature, I'm instantly as sensitive as if I weren't wearing gloves or a scarf or a hat, which of course I am.

What right do people have to tell you what to do as a parent in that condescending way that only people who think they are trying to help can manage? It happened the other day when we were leaving the bank, when we got into the stairway. A cold gust of wind blew in, and instantly I thought I should've put a jacket on Noah before we left the office.

Years later, Eric retells this story to new parent friends, and we laugh because we know I'm not that hormonal anymore. The mother can relate, as for years she was too scared to bring her son to a park for fear that he would be stolen.

But it gets easier.

RÉÉDUCATION PÉRINÉALE

Her name is Charlotte, and she has an office near Madeleine. I'm referred to her by a friend about three months after Noah is born.

No one ever told me that after childbirth, you would pee just a little when you sneeze or cough abruptly. Worse yet, vomiting after you've birthed a child pass also meant you would inevitably have to change underwear, unless you do some serious exercises down there.

More than just Kegels, Charlotte guides me through a half-hour session focused on the awareness and tightening of some powerful muscles that could easily go unnoticed. It's called *Reeducation Perineale*, for the *perinée*. I don't know what the *perinée* is in English, or that it even existed, until I'm offered by my midwife to put my pelvic floor muscles back in order.

Since 1985, the French healthcare system has covered roughly ten to twenty sessions with a specialized *kiné*, physical therapist. France is one of the only countries in the world where this is on the health services menu for women. Though this is a profession in other countries, France is the only one whose health insurance covers it.

As Pamela Druckerman so aptly puts it in her article, "Perineal Re-education Rocks" for the *New York Times*:

"In France, making mothers good as new is a matter of national interest. The state health system pays 60 percent to 100 percent of the cost of re-education for all women after they give birth, and private insurance plans typically cover the rest. I finally solved the mystery of how Frenchwomen fit back into their skinny jeans six weeks postpartum: The state pays for abdominal re-education too."

Some people use the wand, which is like playing a video game with your vagina, or so I've heard. I don't do that method. Charlotte follows the method of Dr. Bernadette de Gasquet, who has written several books on the subject and has her own institute in the 14th arrondisse-ment of Paris, which provides training to midwives as well as classes for new mothers. Nicknamed "Madame Périnée" because she preaches that the pelvic floor muscle is the most important. She revolutionized French hospitals so that today eighty percent of French maternity clinics use her method of giving birth. Her bestselling book, *Abdom-inaux, arrêtez le massacre!* has sold over 200,000 copies and discusses at length the best exercises to strengthen a different kind of core.

Could this be something that other countries should adopt? Most defi-nitely. Druckerman goes on to say:

"I don't doubt the rewards of re-education, but what about the costs of a system that would provide such a seeming luxury? Well, France spent $3,464 per person on healthcare in 2004, compared with $6,096 in the United States, according to the World Health Organization. Yet Frenchmen live on average two years longer than American men do, and Frenchwomen live four years longer. The infant mortality rate in France is 43 percent lower than in the United States."

That Druckerman uses the term "luxury" is telling and an indicator she is writing to an American audience. But vaginal reeducation should definitely not be seen as a luxury. It's apropos then that Druckman ends her piece by saying,

"Another poll found that just 54 percent of Americans want a European-style national health care system, and only 53 percent want to require everyone to have insurance. Perhaps that's why Democrats use the word 'choice' as often as they can, but describe their plans for the new state-run option modeled on Medicare in only the vaguest terms.
But I'm thinking the magic wand can change some minds. This American has certainly been converted. Do I want the government in my crotch? Of course I do."

We're supposed to get the joke. American women want the government out of their vagina, not in it. This speaks to America's distrust in its government. And this is one of the major differences between France and the United States. I was raised with an inherent distrust in the government. Who knew what the government was there to do, but it was definitely not to help us. Though the French may have a distrust in politicians, they do not vehemently distrust the actual support of the government, as Americans do.

To the French, the government is there to support them by providing free healthcare, free education, free daycare beginning at three months (versus the virtually non-existent daycare for children ages three months to five years in America), monthly compensation commensurate with how many children you have, and vacation discounts to all-inclusive family-friendly resorts. These are just a few of the benefits that are too numerous to name. This all comes at a cost, of course—and a very high one at that, according to the French. They pay an average of twenty-five percent in taxes. However, there is an understanding that you get what you pay for, and the French government is there to help you. This is socialism: that services such as healthcare and education are a common right, not just a privilege for the wealthy.

Another article, "The French Government Wants To Tone My Vagina: Inside my amazing and embarrassing postnatal'"perineal re-education' class, paid for by la France." written by Claire Lundberg for *Slate*:

"Despite the occasional embarrassment, these sessions actually work. There haven't been extensive studies done, but what studies exist show that la

rééducation significantly reduces incontinence and pelvic pain at nine months after giving birth. Frankly, I'm happy there's a medical professional paying attention to what happened down there. Rééducation périnéale gets scoffed at in American and Canadian publications as one of the most lurid examples of the indulgent French welfare state, but as far as I can tell, we do exactly nothing in the United States to help women get back into shape after giving birth."

And this is true. When I go to my friend Nicole's bachelorette party in Los Angeles and tell them about this, they can barely believe it. Not a single one of them, out of ten mothers, has ever heard of doing any type of specific exercises after childbirth, let alone with guidance. When I tell them what Charlotte has told me, that you should avoid crunches as it destroys the muscles down there, no one has ever told them this before. If you are really attached to crunches, Charlotte clarifies that you must engage your pelvic wall, which most women aren't told to do.

I remember seeing Kate Winslet on some late-night television show and she was afraid that she was going to sneeze right before coming on. She says to the host that, after three children, it's not a good idea to sneeze. Lungberg goes on to say,

"An American woman gets her six-week postpartum checkup and, if nothing is seriously wrong, she's cleared to have sex again and sent on her way. If she's lucky, the doctor or midwife reminds her to do her Kegel exercises, but without much guidance. Meanwhile, at least in the experience of many of my friends, she may still be experiencing a variety of symptoms that, while not medically serious, sure are annoying, embarrassing, and strange, and not at all conducive to reinvigorating her sex life. Elective 'vaginal rejuvenation' through plastic surgery is on the rise in the U.S., though this surgical reconstruction is largely aesthetic and pays little or no attention to returning sensation or control to the woman. Americans' lack of attention to the female body after giving birth is our own version of the modesty gown or the word vajayjay; we're covering our eyes and pretending there's nothing there to see, until it can no longer be ignored."

This is not a luxury. We must play the woman card. We must take care of ourselves. This is one of the many examples of how French women have managed to make workplace advances while at the same time guarding the sense that they are certain non-negotiable needs. This, to me, is one of them.

FEMME POTOMITAN

W hile these issues of postnatal care are important, they're still a luxury. Pregnant women around the world are just trying to stay alive. In the United States, Black women are 3.2 times more likely than white women to die because of complications related to giving birth. According to the CDC from statistics of 2019, 60% of pregnancy-related deaths in the United States are preventable. In 2018, Serena Williams writes an important article for CNN about how she almost dies giving birth because she is not believed, and in August 2020 leaders in maternal health like Latham Thomas and Chanel Porchia-Albert will team up with Rachel Cargle's Patreon's *The Great Unlearn* to provide a syllabus of what we can do.

This is on my mind in September 2020, when I interview Claudine's dear friend Gisèle Bourquin, president and founder of the association, *Femmes au-delà des Mers.* This is quite a poetic name for an association as it means *Women from Over Seas.* Born in Martinique, Gisèle moved with her family in 1956 to Paris where she would eventually study at the Sorbonne. There she meets Aimé Césaire and discovers the high-brow intellectual and philosophical movement of negritude. From there she travels all over the world, living in Africa, where she teaches French in the Democratic Republic of the Congo and then on to Iran where she stays for six years, teaching and learning Persian as well.

Her passion for education also takes her to Afghanistan, Pakistan, India, Thailand, Mexico, Australia and New Zealand.

Gisèle has just been awarded the prestigious honor of The Senate Delegation for Women's Rights for her years of commitment to women's rights.

"Yes, it's my pleasure. Usually when it's from Claudine, ça passe."

We start by speaking French but switch to English. Though we are on Zoom, Gisèle's warmth and generosity come through the screen.

"For me, education is paramount. The way I work, I prefer to give models. To show what worked. You can't change everything just by protesting. You have to know you are going step by step. The way I work is to show there are other ways to advance and to take your right place."

"Why did you create the *Femmes au-delà des Mers* association? What are the goals?

"I decided to start in 2007 because I worked for the *Minister of Outre Mer,* I was organizing cultural events."

Claudine interrupts to say "It's a very important ministry in France because it represents Tahiti, New Caledonia, French Polynesia, Guyana, Guadeloupe, Martinique, La Réunion, St. Barts, Saint Martin, Wallis et Futuna, Mayotte Saint-Pierre and Miquelon. It's really very symbolic. It's really an important ministry."

"I made a few events for them, and I tried to have people from all over the world. For instance, whenever I had the theme World Heritage, I tried to have somebody from each part of overseas."

"We are all French, not different, we are something more." She laughs. "I had a big round table about nature as part of world heritage, as UNESCO says. The moderator was from Tahiti, from the scientific center of France.

"From Guayana, from Amerindians. They have a different culture. And he was a journalist, very well known in France. That's very interesting. They have the same education, the same programs. But they have their own culture, and I find this very interesting. Because this shows you how to work. How to go forward.

"When I finished, and I thought it was time to retire. But the work was not finished. I had started something. And really I must confess I think I was the only one to do it." Gisèle smiles. "Why? I had the opportunity to live in many countries. I lived all over the world. Also, when I came from Iran, I worked for fourteen years dealing with family demographics. For me that was quite interesting.

"When I worked for this organization I was occupied with the problems of women. When I worked with the ministry, I dealt with culture. We have to take care of the women. I worked for a lot the organizations including the French Institute of National Education Demographics, know as INED, I worked there for fourteen years.

I did many events and I realized I created a movement around the women of Outer Mer. The work was not done. Now I'm taking care of the women of the Overseas, Outer Mer, as we say in French."

"I'm very interested in this particularly because in the United States we keep track of the demographics, with Covid, they see the areas for Black Americans are hit worse than the rest of the country.

"In France it's quite difficult to have that information. For INED all of France included overseas, sometimes they can make ethnic statistics, but it's illegal. For instance, in Martinique, it's quite difficult to share this kind of thing. With statistics, it was everything included."

"In the United States, one of the major problems is the Black maternal health as three times as many Black women die in childbirth than white women but as France does not have these statistics, how can we monitor if this problem of racism exists in France and for women beyond the seas?" I ask.

"In fact, I don't think in France we have this problem. Even overseas, except Maillot. We don't have these kinds of problems. We might have them in Mayotte, not because the system is not good. But because they are so numerous."

Claudine interrupts, "But the French government is trying to make sure everyone gets health care in a decent manner."

"For instance, Matrimoine des Outre Mers, was quite a successful symposium at the Senate and for the CLEE. What we wanted to show was that women can advance no matter what the situation. Women from overseas have a talent to advance and move on and to find solutions no matter what the circumstance. They can preserve the tradition, but they are also educated and they grow.

"In Martinique, and Guadeloupe also in La Reunion in the French departments, we have an expression: they are the "*Femme Potomitan*." This is quite important. Is a big pole that you have at the middle of the house. When we say *Femme Potomitan*, it means everything goes around them. You cannot avoid this potomitan."

"I love that!" I say.

"Yes, I love it, too!" Claudine chimes in. "J'adore."

"I was tired of this expression because all the time they *parle femme potomitian* but here we never speak of it. The image we have of women over there is *Femme Potomitan*. They are strong and you can't avoid them!"

Claudine laughs.

"Well, you need them to hold up the house!"

"Exactly!"

SOLO ADVENTURES

When I first came to France, I couldn't speak with authority about the French, about France. Who knew what the French did or do or thought? Certainly not me. Much of my writing stems from those precious three months. I didn't understand it as deeply as I do now. Everyone had told me to live each day like it was my last, but I didn't fully understand what that meant.

What it truly means is this: what are the activities you want to be doing, had you to die at the end of the day? At twenty-eight, this was not yet a concept I'd fully grasped. What I believed it meant at the time was taking advantage of my place and time. It still does mean that, in a way. But if you live each day like it's your last, how do you build a future? Though I was writing every day, I didn't believe yet that I was actually a working writer.

There's a story I like to tell when I meet young women who are traveling by themselves or have come to France in search of adventure and romance and independence. All of these searches can be lonely. I remember walking along the bridges of the Seine, the *Pont des Arts*, or the beautiful bridge behind Notre Dame where I once met a homeless violinist who lived in the *Cafe des Artistes* in Montmartre, and seeing all of the French people with their friends having picnics with wine and cheese and charcuterie—something so natural to them. You walk by so alone, as you can't speak French, and they are just too big of groups, too intimidating to join. Everyone is having such a wonderful time, and I said to myself, *One day I will have friends and picnic on the bridges, too.* And I did, it comes.

Now I can speak with authority, because ten years later, I do know what I'm talking about. I do know what the French do and say and how, to a certain extent, their society and culture function.

IT'S IN THE BOOK

Nana always said, "It's in the book." Meaning that when it's your time to go, it's your time. I fly with thirteen-month-old Noah in October 2014 to Los Angeles. We make it there just in time. She sees me and smiles from the hospital bed that has been moved into her living room under the professional portrait of her and my grandfather and near the fireplace with her three-foot-tall statue of a knight in armor guarding the mantle.

"I'm so happy to be here Nana," I say.

"Me, too," she says. And she gives me that look of relief I know so well.

She is on morphine. I don't know how fast or slow things will go. Someone has said that after the drugs wear off, she'll be more clear. This is not the case. So I don't fully realize that these will actually be the last moments when she is conscious.

We surround her bed—my aunt, my mom, and my son still not walking crawls on the floor. It's serendipitous that he finds the bell she had given him this summer and rings it. It's my Nana who taught him how to ring the bell. He rings the bell.

"I love you all," she says. It's not until the next day we realize these are her last words. She doesn't speak after that, but, ever the fighter, holds on. I make chicken soup thinking the smells will be nice and comforting and to make sure I feed myself and my son. I listen to the creaks in her kitchen floors. Family members and nurses come and go. We play Frank Sinatra and Cole Porter CDs in the player that she never used. In the evening, in the depths of grief, I breastfeed my son to sleep in her bed. I take a shower. My mom falls asleep on one couch, my aunt on the other. I sit next to her and hold her hand. I tell her what I think she'd like to hear:

"It's enough already," I say in her intonation of voice. I want to give her permission to let go. I tell her, "I am so grateful for everything you have done for me for our relationship, I will cherish it always and I promise to dedicate my book to you, Nana. It's going to be called *Women À La Mode*, Nana, and I know you would love it. But it's because of you. It's thanks to you that I was able to do it. It's dedicated to you. Thank you, thank you, thank you."

I'd love to say that she dies like that while I am holding her hand, but she doesn't. I take in these last moments with her the warm of her hand in mine, the feel of her skin, unlike anyone else. I kiss her forehead and say once again, "It's okay, Nana, it's time to go, we'll be okay, we love you." And knowing I have to get some rest, I join my son. A particular sense of calm comes over me and I fall asleep. Twenty minutes later, my mom is waking me up with the words, "Augie, your Nana has died."

She passes away November 3, on what would've been her seventy-fifth wedding anniversary. Ten years to the day before my Aunt Barbara, her eldest daughter dies on November 4, 2004. We put this together, and it gives us a calming effect as if things are meant to be. But there is no consoling my grief.

Evan is instrumental. She arrives and puts up photos all over her house. She helps organize the service. We hire a female rabbi to do the funeral. She is fantastic. We get potato pancakes and mini brisket sliders.

After a few extra days in Los Angeles, I head back to the airport. I eat something while waiting to board. I haven't brought a stroller with me, so Noah rides on my belly in the Ergo. The two weeks in Los Angeles and he's starting to walk as long as you hold his hand. Because I've got a kid, I'm allowed to board the plane first, and the moment we get to the seat Noah proceeds to throw up all over me. Luckily because it's hot in Los Angeles, even in November, I'm only wearing a tank-top, and have a sweater in my bag, otherwise I haven't brought any extra pair of clothes. But I'm still wearing the ergo, covered in vomit.

The woman in the aisle seat next to me across the row is no help.

"I think I'm going to throw up," she says. "I have a very sensitive gag reflex. Maybe you could move to the bathrooms or get the flight attendant to help you."

When you're by yourself, there is no one to pass off a sick child to. So off I go to the minuscule airplane bathroom, and somehow manage to change, and clean off my child one-handed, holding on to him on the changing table, using wipes and soap and starchy paper towels. Obviously, I brought tons of change of clothes for my son. Thus begins our twelve-hour flight back to Paris, which, luckily, is uneventful aside from a disconcerting comment from the flight attendant.

"You really shouldn't let your son crawl on the floor," says the flight attendant. "This plane just came from Africa, where there's an outbreak of Ebola."

"Oh great," I say but in my head I'm thinking, *Cheers, you want me to keep my son who has just discovered walking in his seat for twelve hours? Never going to happen.*

Also never going to happen, traveling by myself, as this is what I tell Eric the moment we arrive safely back to Paris. And I never do. There are many times in childrearing and raising where I have so much newfound appreciation for Eric's mom, Andrea, who did an excellent job and raised him by herself as a waitress and immigrant from France. I have so much respect for single mothers, single parents. It's so hard.

I am fortunate I got to say goodbye, that I have some sense of closure, but with people we love, we are never done having a good time with them. We are never ready no matter how long we have them in our lives.

JE SUIS ET JE NE SUIS PAS CHARLIE

A t 3:45, the church bells start ringing. At 4:30, a helicopter flies overhead. It's a sound rarely heard over Paris. It's January 2015, and the March is going.

Another helicopter or plane overhead, this time louder. There still seems to be a constant ringing now, even an hour later. There is so much discussion on freedom of speech versus racism. So much *parole* (talk) of all of the countless deaths we're not paying attention to, all over the world, of all of the censorship in France and elsewhere. People point to the banning of the hijab as insensitive. People point to anti-Semitic remarks in the fashion industry and ask, "What's the difference?" No one knows where to draw a line. No one knows how to define worthy satire, but no one wants to say you can't do it, either.

On January 7, 2015, two men armed with machine guns kill twelve and injure eleven journalists and cartoonists who create the newspaper Charlie Hebdo because they have published a satirical cartoon of Muhammad. Remember no images of God, as not only in the Hebrew bible's second commandment but also in Islam as well even though that is not written specifically in the Quran. Later that day in related attacks a terrorist will hold nineteen people hostage and kill four at a Kosher supermarket. What will resonate most for me when I discover it, is it is a woman cartoonist with her child the same age as Noah at the time who is held at gunpoint and forced to unlock the doors to the office. She and her daughter survive, but witness the killings of her friends.

So many drawings of the pencil being mightier than the machine gun, but the sad reality is that isn't true. The pens didn't save them or protect them. The terrorists won: France and the world are in terror. This doesn't matter, of course, because it's doubtful the terrorists will ever feel that they've won. To do so would be to lose their purpose. And while they may not care whether they live or die, the one thing they do hold onto is their purpose in life. For them, their meaning, their identity is this narrative of vengeance. Of dissatisfaction. For us, convincing ourselves we are not afraid, that we have won the fight, is not possible, either. And grossly naïve. No one is ever going to "win" because both sides already have.

We live in France because things like this aren't supposed to happen here, but it's clear now, nowhere is safe.

At the same time, I can't help but be struck by how simple it all is. That the power of humor, image, and the written word is still so poignant and considered so dangerous as to be worth bloodshed. Nothing has changed since the beginning of our history. I'm amazed at how fast a slogan, *Je Suis Charlie,* is created and spread around the world. I don't want to be Charlie. Charlie is dead. I want to live. Or are we resigned to accept that Charlie will live on because of the timelessness of the art of the cartoons? Charlie will be immortal, as will the two men who killed them.

It seems so simple as to elicit questions of a conspiracy. One of the brothers left his ID in the car. Who brings a *carte d'identité* to a mass murder? Was it a set up? It seems all too perfect. Newspapers tell us to beware of pushing a secular agenda. But everyone has some sort of agenda.

Women are images. Men are words. The power of images. What is considered most dangerous is what they are attempting to destroy. A cartoon. An image of God. It's from the Ten Commandments. The third one, *thou shalt not make unto thee any graven image.* Anyone who is against the earth is usually against women.

That's why we are in a New Transcendentalism. That's why a renewed interest in the earth is a renewed interest in women. *It's not a woman's world, either. It's our world.*

But while it's wonderful that the world focuses on the gender gap for women, we can't forget men's issues. When we don't talk about men, that's when they become invisible oppressors. We need lists that focus on the best and worst places for a man, just like we have for women.

STOP SAYING VIOLENCE AGAINST WOMEN

START SAYING STOP VIOLENCE BY MEN

W hat would be men's issues?

What comes to mind? The prostate gland, watches, the gym, suits, gym suits? Part of you wants to say men don't have issues. Another part wants to say, women. Author of *The Macho Paradox*, Jackson Katz gave a TED talk to say that men's eyes glaze over and they stop listening when we say "women's issues." But we need the men to listen. He breaks down how the oppressor erases himself from the equation. He takes his research from Julia Penelope, a feminist linguist. For example, he writes on the board:

> *John beat Mary.*
> *Mary was beaten by John.*
> *Mary was beaten.*
> *Mary is a battered woman.*

He goes on to say, now John has left the conversation. We have it wrong when we're talking about women's issues. Violence against women is, more often than not, violence by men. But we don't say that, do we? We need to start saying that. Men's violence. Violence by men against women. We can keep women in the equation, but we have to add the men.

From an article on The World Economic Forum published on November 25, 2020: "As the UK publishes its first census of women killed by men, here's a global look at the problem"

- *Six women are killed every hour by men around the world, most by men in their own family or their partners.*
- *A new report shows that in the UK a woman is killed by a man every three days.*
- *More than half of women and girls killed by men are murdered by their current or previous partners, according to UN data.*
- *The latest UN figures show that 137 women across the world are killed every day by a partner or member of their own family – a total of 50,000 women a year murdered by people they know and should be able to trust.*

Or here's me writing this another way:

- Six men become murders of six women every hour around the world. Most men kill members of their own family or their partners.
- A new report shows that in the UK a man kills a woman every three days.
- The latest UN figures show that 137 men across the world kill a woman who is their partner or member of their own family every day — a total of 50,000 men a year murder women and girls they know.

It makes such a difference how we write this. When we write it in active voice it gives it the urgency this situation deserves. Sex men kill six women every hour around the world. That's 144 men who become murders a day. That's 51,264 men killing women they claimed to love. Clearly there's a problem here.

One of men's issues is violence. It is violent for them to be violent as well. We talk of men's lives being ruined by the violence they caused, as if it's women who ruined their lives. They ruined their own lives by their actions. It's as simple as that.

We have a public health issue of violence by men.

We're living in a time when reading the news makes it hard to tell the difference between a dystopian novel and the history of World War II. This is an indication we still have lessons to learn and we're not doing a good job policing each other, but we're still being very policed and big-brothered. The dictators believe the world is an evil place. Do they know more than us? Are they privy to some classified information that we are not aware of? No, they have chosen to see the world negatively.

After the attack at the Charlie Hebdo office, and the Jewish grocery store, everything changes. Armed guards protect the Israeli daycare at the top of the hill near the Sacré Coeur. Armed guards are everywhere. Walking around Paris, I feel a palpable sadness.

I don't go to the March. Mariel watches it from her window.

Claudine says, "You must include this is your book. There haven't been this many people who have marched since the French Revolution and Victor Hugo funerals."

When the attacks happen again at the Bataclan theater, I'm eight months pregnant and very aware how compromised I am. I couldn't run if anything were to happen. There is a pregnant woman at the Bataclan who is filmed climbing out the window, and someone comes to her aid and pulls her back in. The shooting in November touches everyone. Thibaut, Mariel's husband, knows someone who gets killed just sitting casually at a cafe outside. Claudine's yoga teacher, thirty-two, is killed at a café. His wife and six-year-old daughter were five minutes away.

On the street walking down to our new apartment, we see a couple with two young children who have been killed. There is a candlelit vigil for them outside of the building. Everywhere is tragedy. A video of a husband whose wife was killed, leaving behind her eighteen-month-old son, goes viral. He says to the terrorists, "You will not have my hate."

∼

Two years later, when a policeman is killed on the Champs Elysées, his husband gives his eulogy, echoing the same sentiment: "You will not have my hate." I'm not sure if it is the council of the French government to state this. Hate is such a valuable commodity, as it means they've won, yet I'm not sure how they do it. I don't think I could.

LETTER TO ZOHRA D

When I interview Danielle Michel-Chich, a handicapped French immigrant from Algeria, journalist, writer, activist and mother of four children and grandmother of five grandchildren. We discuss the idea of trying to find a new word for victim, she says, "I hate the word victim, you are only a victim at the moment something is happening to you, but then if you are still alive you are a survivor."

Danielle knows about being a survivor. At the age of five, she lost her leg, and her grandmother died in front of her on September 30, 1956 at the Milk Bar in Algiers terrorist attack during the Algerian war. The attack is done by the Algerian fighter for independence, Zohra Drif, who after some time in prison will go on to become a well-known politician becomes the subject of Danielle's book: *Letter to Zohra D,* published in 2012 and awarded the French Voices prize by the *Bureau du Livre français* in NY in 2013 to promote translation and distribution, the sum of which can still be used by an American publisher.

But we don't start our conversation here. We start by talking about her work for handicap women. As a committed and active feminist, she has been a member of several women's associations such as MLAC in the 1970s, Groupe Femmes, *Maison des Femmes Thérèse Clerc de*

Montreuil, Association of Women Journalists (AFJ), and was president for three years of the association, *Femmes Monde*. Now she is co-president of the organization *Femmes pour le Dire Femmes Pour Agir, women to speak, women for action* for the past two years.

"There is thirty percent more violence against handicapped women. In France, there is a quota to hire six percent of your company must be handicapped, but seventy-five percent of companies prefer to pay the fine than to make the concessions to hire handicap women," she tells me. The work she is interested in now is diffusing the information so that people are aware of the discrimination and what they can do about it.

One of the major changes that she has seen is the way the media reports domestic violence. In the beginning murders of women by their partners would be called a *drame passionel*. Now the newspapers no longer write that. They write "domestic violence."

"So that's an improvement." Danielle says. "But women's battles never end. Feminist activist one day, feminist activist for ever!"

TRUMPED

C linton loses. *Trump triumphs* is the headline of *The New York Times*. I have a feeling it's because of the etymology of the word. Trump. Trump has trumped us.

I feel completely violated, as if he's grabbed my and America's pussy. Trump. He has outshone, upstaged, surpassed, and beaten Clinton, as if he used a trick card in the deck. We're fucked. It's hard to think otherwise. Maybe we didn't realize just how racist, sexist, homophobic, xenophobic, and stupid Americans really are. They'd prefer a macho billionaire conman to a woman. It's hard not to despair. But maybe this is an opportunity.

America's in an abusive relationship. That's what Gloria Steinem says in the best article I read about the election the day after in *The Guardian*. My therapist says something similar: Trump is the ultimate narcissist.

Eight years ago, I shook Hillary Clinton's hand. Now I want to give her a big hug.

Immediately I remember what Bernice said about the Glass Mountain: "One step forward, two steps back." And so, at a time when it seems we've taken a giant step back, how do we now take two giant leaps forward?

For the past eight years, I've been working on this question of what we can do to further equality/human/women's rights. Now, one marriage and two children later, my manuscript is ready to take flight. What are the tactics and strategies that women have used to get ahead?

We've witnessed several changes. When I started working on this project, I felt the need to convince the reader that the twenty-first century is the women's century. Now it seems evident.

If we ever needed proof of America's sexism, now we have a perfect concrete example.

WHAT WOULD HILLARY HAVE DONE?

There is no question to me whether Hillary was the better choice or would've made a great president.

However, I can't name anything she was going to do. Perhaps I am in the angry phase of my grief, and anger's only the second stage. I thought I was a lot farther along by now, seemingly having traversed disbelief, and still admittedly clinging to the hope that the electoral college will change their minds. Or even that Trump himself will admit he didn't want the job after all. Fat chance.

The fact remains, though, that people envisioned what a Trump presidency would be like. *The Daily Show* did a not-so-funny Halloween edition of an apocalyptic vision of the future if Trump won. No one, to my mind, did that for Hillary, or even attempted calling her President Clinton. But people jokingly or quite seriously referred to President Trump as something that should not happen.

Still, I don't know what Hillary was going to do. Trump wanted to build a wall. Trump wants to register and deport Muslims. Trump wants to reverse Roe v. Wade and punish women for having abortions. Whatever Trump wanted to do made news. Whatever Hillary wanted to do, didn't. Except her emails. We can easily blame the media, our social conditioning, the barriers women face and will still face in 2020 when we try this again.

Trump wanted to *Make America Great Again*. Hillary said we're *Stronger Together*. But *Stronger Together* is vague; it's in the ether. Americans don't know what it means. Hillary's campaign was in direct relation to his campaign. Her slogan came as a response to his campaign to divide the country, to build a wall. And somehow, by championing division, he was able to unite white people against marginalized groups. Even if it was for a horrible cause. Even if it meant and now means giving a free pass to hatred.

He was this myth of anti-establishment. Whatever anyone says, to me, Hillary played by the rules. She is experienced and qualified, but she wasn't really willing to shake things up. As a woman, she was in a classic double bind, double standard. But maybe this wasn't the right strategy. She should have chosen a woman vice-president. Looking at it now, I think the media should've banked on the fact that being a woman was the ultimate anti-establishment choice. The media should've played up the woman card. That she was going to do things differently because she is inherently different from all other presidents who had come before. That she was going to put family first. But in America, we don't put family first. We put work and money first. We give that more value than anything else.

Clinton would've made maternity leave a national law. She would've made paid vacation a national law. I believe she would've ratified the Convention of Elimination of Discrimination Against Women. CEDAW. Most Americans, I imagine, don't even know what CEDAW is. She would've put money into the public school system so we could stop creating so many ignorant Americans.

He really is the Frankenstein monster of our own creation.

It'd be easy to say, now that He Who Should Not Be Named has won, that it is, indeed, still a man's world. But we'd be wrong. Women also put him into power. And to continue to say that it's a man's world is to continue to behave like children, to not take responsibility where responsibility is due.

I love Hillary Clinton, but in hindsight, maybe she needed something tangible that people could hold onto, a physical symbol like the wall. Trump led the people to talk about the wall; he created it as an issue. She didn't do anything like that. Trump even got the Pope to respond to the wall. And still, Catholics didn't even care what the Pope thought.

Trump is the exact myth of the self-made American man, the Renaissance Man, like Ben Franklin. That's who we've been taught to love, the jack of all trades. He is a businessman, a reality TV star, and now the president.

What is the myth of the American woman? The Lenny Kravitz song?

It seems pretty clear that the American woman is dangerous. What other songs? *California Girls? LA Woman?*

What kind of country do we need to elect a woman president? The 54% of white women who voted for this clown keep me up at night. How can they vote against their best interests? Is it a matter of just following their husbands? Beauvoir talks of this, that the reason why women didn't band together throughout history was that the women from higher classes, which is what white women are, didn't want to lose what little privilege they had by lowering themselves to raise those with different identities. They didn't prioritize being a woman.

It's such a heartbreak. Though Hillary Clinton wins the popular vote, the system gets outsmarted by a charlatan. Why didn't she pick a woman vice president? She played by the rules, but she didn't play the game, and she got burned. Trump had nothing to lose, whereas she had everything.

Over and over, I watch Kate McKinnon as Hillary Clinton sing "Hallelujah" by Leonard Cohen on *Saturday Night Live*. I just cry and cry. We don't know what's in store for us. We don't know yet that the Russians have tampered with the election. We don't know the coming atrocity of ICE. I can't even fathom children being separated from their parents will happen on American shores, but I wasn't paying attention to the actual history of America, because even though I'd heard the voices of enslaved and Indigenous people, we were told that was in the past and I was still bound to the ideal that America was the greatest country in the world.

A superpower, the one all other countries looked up to, but it was all a lie. It was just the admiration of a capitalist system, and that America has lots and lots of money. We don't know that we will become a country so divided, so hateful, so fractured that we'll become nostalgic for the Bush years because even though he stole the election, too, his reign was mild by comparison.

What is the American identity? Individualism. The Renaissance Man. The Bootstrap Myth. People like loose cannons because they feel they can't be controlled, can't be advised. I'm thinking of Robert Downey Jr. at the end of *Iron Man*. That's Trump, but obviously not as good-looking or rich or ingenious. Hillary was a chameleon. She changed her stance, her appearance, and her identity to cater to what was expected at the time. She should've put more fear in her speeches, as in *"Don't fuck with a woman witch/bitch."*

She should've really played the woman card. The mom card. Nostalgia is dangerous. *Make America Great Again*— that was a great slogan. What was Hillary's slogan after all? Love trumps hate? That was bad because it had his name in it and not hers. She should've run with her first name or even her maiden name.

Feminist is still a dirty word. The depressed voter didn't love the options so wasn't inspired to vote. *Stronger Together*—it wasn't good enough of a slogan because it wasn't active. *Yes We Can*—we were doing something. *Make America Great Again*—it's implied we're doing something. Perhaps people are duped into believing time was simpler then. That roles were easily defined. What they don't seem to realize is that we can't go back to one-income households now. Not without help from the government, which they don't want to give. Maybe this is the last vestiges of the patriarchy, and they're not going down without a fight. Or this really is America, and we were in our coastal bubbles, and even within those bubbles, even within our own families, there will people who will vote the other way because they are racist, because they are sexist, because they rationalize the economy and don't really understand what socialism is. We don't know anything about half of the country. We see the same results in 2020. Half of the popular vote still votes for him.

We are not as inclusive as we think we are because we didn't include them.

LE CHOIX DU ROI

When I get pregnant with Evalie, everyone says, as I push Noah in his stroller, *peut-être ça va être une fille*—perhaps it will be a girl.

Yes, I'll always say, *le choix du roi*. It's an expression that means the choice of the king, a boy and a girl.

Beauvoir says pregnancy is an alienation, and breastfeeding an exhausting servitude. She never had children, but she's not wrong. She says women were seen as weaker because they were physically weaker, and because of their menstrual cycles, their bodies are forever changing, making them unstable. This is fact, she says. But it only means women are weaker if we prize physical strength and violence. It takes a lot of physical strength to grow a baby and give birth.

When Evalie is born on the 13th of December—the 13th being the day that both Nana and Aunt Barbara were born—it seems like a sign that she would have their two names: Eva and my aunt's middle name, Lee.

On the third day in the hospital, it's time to check out, and this time, I can't wait to get home. The doctor comes in to do the final Apgar test. Named after its creator, Virginia Apgar, an American obstetrical anesthesiologist, the test scores a newborn baby's health after birth. The Apgar score is now the world standard.

Each newborn is given a score of 0, 1, or 2 (with 0 meaning distress and 2 meaning optimal condition) in five categories: heart rate, respiration, color, muscle tone, and reflex irritability. Compiled scores for each newborn can range between 0 and 10, with 10 being the best possible condition for a newborn. I am lucky both my children are a 10. I was a 10. My parents used to brag constantly about the day of my birth, saying that the doctor ran through the hospital saying, "She's a 10!" Have I mentioned they're inclined to exaggerate? Though I heard this story throughout my life, that I was a 10, I never understood that this score was from an incredible woman who improved the survival rate of newborns.

She is noted for having said, "Women are liberated from the time they leave the womb." When I turn my daughter over on my chest immediately after her birth to see if she is a boy or a girl, she cries at having been moved. She has nails and hands like my aunt, and the same blue eyes as my son.

I remember her birth a bit more concretely, as it is faster. Eric and I make love the night before, and I know that this has instigated something. At 2:30 in the morning I wake up to contractions. I read about false labor off and on until 5am until I see the telltale sign of what's unappetizingly called "the mucus plug." At 6am, my parents arrive to watch Noah, who is luckily still sleeping. My water has already broken, and we take a car to the Clinique St. Therese in the 17th. At 9:30, I tell my midwife I can't do this anymore, and she suggests going in the bath and that after that, I can have the epidural. I get out of the bath at 10, and Evalie is born ten minutes later.

This final scoring is to make sure that your baby is healthy and ready to leave the hospital. The doctors tell us that there will be a small spot of blood in her diaper, which is normal, it sometimes happens naturally and not to be alarmed. Just like that when the doctor takes her diaper off, there it is, a small dot of blood, a sign that everything is functioning, her first period, twelve years or so in advance.

It's undeniable proof she will one day, like Beauvoir says, "become a woman." This is not exactly what Beauvoir meant. We don't become women with our first period, and we don't have to have a period to be a woman, as we've recently seen. But the idea that the human body is already prepared, and that there is a sign that when the time comes the organs will function correctly, is amazing to me. So much of pregnancy and childbirth is.

A BOOK ABOUT WRITING A BOOK

Eric and I joke all the time that the favorite subject of movies made in LA is about making movies in LA. Movies about making movies is Hollywood's preferred subject.

It took us years to realize my book was actually a book about writing a book, about what it takes to persevere, about the sacrifices one has to make, and never are they more felt than when we have two kids. The sacrifice is felt more strongly by Eric, who gives up any notion of doing music, working out, going out with friends until my book is finished. We can't move on until it is complete. Then, at least, I will be able to say I wrote a book and finished it, when my children ask me what I've done.

There are not too many writers who have children. In fact, *A Moveable Feast* is about writing a book. It may be brazen of me to compare my book to Hemingway, but if I were Hemingway, I wouldn't think anything about it. He says he wants to write one true sentence. I just want it to be finished.

RENDEZ-VOUS WITH DR. W

I t's a brisk morning, and I'm running late trying to put Evalie down to nap.

This doesn't happen, so I rush out of the house. It's too late to take the bus, and ordering a car will take ten minutes. Luckily, there is a taxi at the taxi stand. I give him the address: *"À côté de l'avenue Matignon et les Champs Elysées, s'il vous plaît."* A building on a side street right by the river, and one of the most expensive addresses in town, *avenue Matignon* at the intersection of the Palatine Bank, Channel, and the hotel Georges Cinq.

This fancy address is the address of my doctor. Doctors in France have their offices in old apartments, and Dr. W is no exception. He is on the top floor of a very beautiful building with marble stairs and an undulating red carpet. It's a wonderful time of year in Paris. I am going on the day before Thanksgiving, though obviously the French don't celebrate Thanksgiving. They are already gearing up for Christmas. Every shop has their lights and decorations up. Everything is festive. The feeling is one not quite out of a movie, but out of a collective memory of what Christmas can be, what it should be. It is actually sunny out and not too cold, both rare occasions for this time of year.

My rendezvous is for 9:30. I make it into the cab by 9:05, and arrive just in time. It's eighteen euros, and I only ask for a euro back from the driver as it's the only money I have, and I may need that euro.

There is an elevator, but I take the stairs. A blonde woman is on her headphones on the phone at the top floor with a feather duster, carefully dusting in between each wrought iron design of the banister. We exchange *bonjours*. When I enter, the doctor himself is behind the desk.

"We have a rendezvous." It's not a question. The doctor is thin, cream, most likely going on sixty, seemingly in very good health. He wears glasses.

"Yes."

"Take a seat, I will be with you in one moment."

I think this conversation is in French, though I'm not quite sure now. The secretary returns, and there are two other men in the waiting room. There are several doctors in this huge apartment. I manage to get the secretary's attention.

"Les toilettes?" I ask.

"Tout en fond, à droite." Down the hall to the right. This I know is in French because I am proud to understand where she has told me to go.

"Merci."

The rest of the apartment is empty. The bathroom is a single one, with those very classic French porcelain doorhandles which don't seem to work quite properly. It's a small door handle which fits in the palm of your hand. They've put a padlock on the door as well to lock it, but I don't lock it. I doubt anyone will be coming. I pee quickly. I wash my hands with a good-smelling soap. In the hallway, there is a water fountain, so I pour myself a glass, and the doctor arrives.

We sit down at the desk in his very large and comfortable office. It's all very civilized. There is an L-shaped couch to my left and then beyond that, the chair with stirrups. It's like being in a living room. It most likely was a living room.

"Madame Blaisdell, vous êtes une patiente de Francine?" You are a patient of Francine's?

"Oui, nous avons recontrée une fois, l'année derniere."

He searches his memory, "Ah, yes, I remember, for the sinuses." He says switching to English. "And you gave birth to…?"

"Evalie was born the 13th of December."

"A normal birth?"

"Yes."

"And you came today…" He pauses. "Just for a check?"

"Yes, and also, my husband will have a vasectomy, but he just went to the doctor and we realize there is a reflection period of six months. So I am curious about an IUD in the meantime."

"Yes, of course, you should definitely have it."

"I'm still breastfeeding,"

"So we do a copper one then with no hormones. It's perfect."

"How old are you?"

"36."

"And your husband?"

"36 as well."

"Your children are still young. You both should wait until you're 40 for the vasectomy, and then you decide."

I interpret what he's saying as, "Your children might die so you may want to have another one."

"Where do you come from?" the doctor asks. He is a gentleman, with a kind face.

"Californie."

"Are you ashamed?" The question seemingly comes out of nowhere but I know exactly what he is talking about.

"Yes, devastated. It's a disaster."

"Well, I wouldn't say it's a disaster, but it is certainly terrible."

I'm not sure what look I give him. "He's horrible. It's unbelievable."

"I think we don't quite understand how hard it is for the middle states, and I think there were people who voted against her. They didn't like her," he says.

"Yes, people still don't want a woman president."

"It should have been the other guy," he says. "Bernie Sanders, perhaps he would have won." He gives me a hopeful look. "But he's Jewish."

"Yes, they've never had anyone who has been Jewish before."

"Ah." He gives me a look that is not quite a frown, but a certain under-standing. The doctor is Jewish. In a few weeks, he'll go on vacation to Israel, where he goes often. He gives me a prescription, which I pick up at the pharmacy for twenty-eight euros. I get reimbursed through social security. Because he is a private doctor, he charges me eighty-five euros for a doctor appointment. I come back the following week, so for a little over one hundred euros, I have the IUD, which lasts four years. When I go home, I look up on Planned Parenthood how much an IUD costs. They'll say it ranges from $0 to $1,000, depending where you live. That's quite a range. My girlfriend in Santa Barbara will say it would cost her $500 "even with good insurance."

I'm looking at the election results when Eric walks in the door. Evalie is sleeping. It's the day after Thanksgiving, and we are all very tired. He takes off his coat and hat and bag, and comes up behind me to rub my shoulders. We talk for a moment. It's 11:10.

"What time do you need to leave?"

"Not till 11:30, I have some time."

I close the computer and Eric goes to close the shutters.

"I hope that doesn't wake her up," I say.

As he closes the door, I am taking off my shirt, my bra with the breast pads. Eric has unbuttoned his pants. In a minute or less we're naked on the couch, cuddling. These are rare moments. Naked sex during the day is rare. The difference in energy level is astounding. And feeling like we have the time is rare as well.

I take a shower and manage to put my pants back on before I hear Evalie. She's up in perfect timing. I'm able to breastfeed her and then finish getting ready to go. She is full of big smiles as I kiss her and Eric goodbye as I head out to meet Claudine.

"Tell Claudine it's women's fault Trump won," he says with a smile. It's a classic joke, one that illustrates women get blamed for everything. In this case, it is partially true. It's white women who voted for him.

I walk quickly because it is now 11:45, and it will take at least half an hour on the bus to get there. It is an extremely cold and gray day. One where you can see your breath and the bus is warm.

We are meeting at the *Bac à Glaces*. The usual place. We have been here too many times to count. In a way, it is our place. Perhaps it is more Claudine's place. When I walk in, Claudine is in full conversation with Laurent, the man who works in the framing section in the *Bon Marche* and the waitress.

Claudine, as always, is so happy when she sees me. She stands up and says, "Hello dear!" We do a combination American hug and French kisses from side to side on each cheek.

"Laurent, je te presente mon amie américaine, Augustine."

"Yes, we met before. Ça fait longtemps."

Laurent has become a close friend of Claudine's, as he is a feminist. Raised by a single mother after his father died, he has a deep understanding of the difficultly his mother faced as a woman providing for her family. He, like me, has his own chapter in Claudine's book, *Simone de Beauvoir et les femmes d'ajourd'hui.* In it, he discusses how he became a feminist.

He is very kind and asks about my family. I'm surprised when he mentions his own children, as for whatever reason, I assumed he was single.

I know Claudine will have the salmon crepe, and to avoid looking at the menu, I have the same. It's a fine crepe. Today we order the soup as well.

Claudine, surprisingly, doesn't have any insight to the election. She didn't realize it was white women her own age who voted for Trump.

"Forty-two percent of white women voted for him. Forty-two percent!"

I can tell our conversation is strained because there is a very stylish Black woman sitting next to us. We don't know if she speaks English or not, though I imagine she does. She is young enough to. With the success of American television shows and films, more and more young people speak English and incorporate English words into common-day speech.

I'm so distraught. I've come for enlightenment or a new way to see the results, some new insight I haven't thought of that Claudine always provides.

"How could this happen, Claudine? I'm in shock."

Claudine says in a low voice, "It's immigration, and fear of losing jobs. It was too much to have a Black president, so now it is swinging back the other way."

I expect Claudine to be angry about the American election, but instead she is more introspective. "A week before my mother died, Bernard and I had my parents over for dinner. Her mind was just starting to go, though I didn't realize it at the time, and we were sitting there when all of a sudden she said, 'Maybe you'll see Hillary Clinton become president of the United States,'" Claudine has tears in her eyes. "She said that just all of a sudden, out of the blue. So, you see, I really thought I would live to see this. It meant so much to me because of my mother."

MADAME PRESIDENT

Two years later, I finally have a chance to ask Claudine what it would take to have a French woman as president. She says, "The French are not ready. It is still a sexist country, it is still too macho."

"Too macho? I don't think so, Claudine. French men are some of the most effeminate men, the joke is always are they gay or French. They wear more pink than women. I always thought they embraced their feminine side?"

"Just because they wear pink doesn't make them feminist, Augustine."

"I guess," I say, though I don't really agree. To me, French men are not macho in comparison to American men.

"Who do you think is good as a female leader, then?"

"Michelle Bachelet is fantastic!" It's August 2018, and she was just nominated as the United Nations High Commissioner of Human Rights.

"Yes, I just watched her speech on Facebook." While in office the former president of Chile legalized gay marriage, as well as abortion under certain circumstances.

Gay marriage and abortion rights usually go hand in hand, which "makes sense" as they are both laws telling people what they can legally do with their bodies.

"And the prime minister of New Zealand, Jacinda Ardern, she's incredible. The first women to breastfeed in front of her colleagues." She causes quite a stir in September for her speech at the United Nations. She's a fan favorite. And indeed, it'll appear that there are two prevailing mindsets: one of globalism and inclusion, a positive belief to envision a better future; and the other, well, we know the other one. We're living it.

I acknowledge that, for me, I can believe that it is no longer a man's world, because I am white and educated and privileged and don't live in the States, but one day, I believe people will say other qualifications in earnest.

Claudine thinks I'm too positive, bordering on naive. Several times throughout our discussions, she looks at me with fury and says, "Don't be so naive, Augustine!"

CODEPINK

At her home in Venice Beach in 2011, I interview Jodie Evans, Co-Founder of CODEPINK as well as member of several organizations such as the Rainforest Action Network, 826LA and Women's Media Center.

I start our conversation bringing up what Claudine has told me time and time again about the access to mineral resources and women's right always being negotiated.

"Well, it's a paradox, because as women, what we're seeing right now is the devastation to the lives of women and children because of globalization and capitalism and the violence run amok all over the world over resources. At the same time, what we're witnessing is a revitalization and resurgence of the feminine voice in the form of both women and men. As the changes started to happen. First when you go at something, it's messy. You see that it's not really men, it's about the patriarchy. And then it's about equal rights, so it's not just about women, it's about everyone. So what feminism is continues to both be a bigger tent and a refined definition. So you have something stronger to stand on. One of the things I've been working on with Robin Morgan, (well known feminist, writer, activist and co-founder of Women's Media Center, partner with Simone de B) is how the women's movement is kinda stuck in the 70s, so how do we upgrade it?"

I don't think feminism is stuck in the 70s. Feminism has grown and evolved. Where it's alive and vibrant and creating beautiful change is in the Global South, the underfunded areas, and women of color. And where you find the power and the stuckness is in the North, where it's mostly white, older and higher net worth. We need to democratize, funnily enough, the women's movement."

"You don't have to declare it; you have to be it. It's not about the words, anyway. Look at the people who declare they are feminists and yet are living out of the Patriarchy and trying to be just like the men. It's really not about what you label yourself, it's really about what do you do with your life. And what are you living out of. And what beliefs you have been able to transform. Transform not only in your own life and in the world around you.

"I see this in a reflection of the forty years I have been doing this. This is my work, since I was a maid in Vegas who was freed to use my voice by marching for a living wage. I've never felt more hopeful about where women are."

At that point, she is by far the most positive person I've ever interviewed. I tell her this halfway through our interview and she says, "Well, maybe that's because I work with girls. At Women's Media Center we have this thing called Spark. We teach young girls how to use their voices. And at Global Girls Media, where we teach high school girls how to be the media and we've had super success. Right now, I'm one of the funders of Eve Ensler's play in South Africa and the Global Girls reported on it. Holding the space for a girl to find her voice, which is what happened to me, changes their life. And I'm watching the power they have, it's so inspiring."

Jodie continues, "Out of Women's Media Center, we helped make this film called Miss Representation about how women are misrepresented in the media films, What's sexy and what's sexism? And let me tell you, the young girls know the difference. I get to work with young women, and they inspire me."

Her positivity is contagious. I don't think it's only the effect of the California New Age lifestyle, but after speaking with her I'm inspired and positive, too. Claudine is cautious and believes we have to keep up our guard. Simone impressed upon her this reality even after their celebrated success when abortion was made legal in 1971, Claudine only twenty something at the time said, "Simone, we've won!"

Simone said to her, "Never forget that it will only take a political, economic, or religious crisis for women's rights to be called into question. These rights can never be taken for granted. You must remain vigilant throughout your life."

What a buzzkill, Simone—my words not Claudine's—but the sentiment is the same. Claudine was crushed and has never forgotten that moment.

Is this a difference between the French and Americans? Ruth Ginsberg has said that women in the US are taking our rights for granted, the French seem to rarely take anything for granted, in fact they are more apt to complain that they aren't getting enough. Is it their continuous debate about their rights that keep their laws in place?

TALK ABOUT IT!

I meet Moïra Sauvage, the co-chair of a collective of thirty-eight associations, *Ensemble contre le sexisme, Together against sexism*, for better equality between the sexes, via Zoom in early 2021 the night after white terrorists storm the capitol. "Did you watch the events at the Capitol?" she asks me after we've wished each other happy new year.

"Yes, it's a catastrophe," I say. "I'm so ashamed."

"What really surprised me is that the Americans are surprised. I suppose in France, we're used to these types of things. Beheading people, revolutions and so on…"

"Yes, but I think in France we don't expect them to be so armed."

Born in Dublin to an Irish father and a French mother, Moïra Sauvage is a journalist, Parisian, and mother of four children. She was a member from 1981 to 2005 of the Association of Women Journalists, which defended the place and image of women in the media. For ten years, she was head of the Women Commission of Amnesty International France, where she led an international campaign on violence against women and worked in 2006 on the publication of an quintessential report "Violence against women in France: a matter of the state."

In 2008, she published in French, *Les aventures de ce fabuleux vagin*, The adventures of this fabulous vagina, based on her travels with Eve Ensler, author of *The Vagina Monologues*.

"I love the title of your book!" I tell her.

"Yes, I adored working with Eve Ensler and seeing how the work really changed the lives of women who performed it, who watched it. It really was quite incredible. The more people talked about it and saw it, the more it reduced violence against women. And her creation of "V-Day" as a way to give back to these organizations and raise money was really inspiring."

In May 2012, she published a book on women warriors in the world entitled "Guerrières! Meet the Strong Sex" based on her travels throughout Israel, France, England, Kenya, Rwanda, and USA.

Since its beginning in 2013, she was president of *Excision Parlons-en*, a mobilization of eighteen associations that fight against *excision*, which is female genital mutilation or female circumcision.

"Does female circumcision still happen in France?"

"No, not really. It's illegal, but the young girls, adolescents are at risk, who may go to to their country of origin of their parents in West Africa and it may be done to them by aunts, or grandmothers, even if their parents don't agree. We work to make sure it is still talked about. To tell these girls to pay attention."

"We talked about it a lot in the 80s, but there is a lot of immigration from West Africa in the early 2000s. It is a violence that many women living now in France, have experienced. We shine a light on it so the government doesn't forget. It's a violation of fundamental human rights. Now I've stopped working there, I was president, vice-president because already seven years was good, but the association continues, and February sixth is the international day against female genital mutilation, and we are supported by the press by the ministry for women in government of France. All of the work to understand and to foster the sensibility of what it is."

Moïra continues, "It's not religion, it's not tradition. That's what the women say, that's what the family says, but that's not the truth. The real reason, which is still taboo to say, is to prevent the pleasure of girls and women. So that they will remain faithful to their husband. So that they don't stray. That's the real reason profoundly."

I know this, I've read this, but to hear her say it out loud is a different story. "That's very brave to say that, no?"

"Yes, we know that's the real reason they do it. We know because men say I want a wife who will stay with me." What is implied is that women's sexual appetites and ability to have multiple orgasms means that one man will not be able to keep them satisfied. This is the excuse. This is the thinking.

"And it's usually the women, the mothers, the grandmothers who do this."

"Always," she says, "because they are persuaded that otherwise their daughters won't find a husband. They live in a society where the most important thing is to be married and to become a mother. This is typically how women perpetuate the male domination. But I want to add, we can't put this as this is only something that happens in Africa, far away. We can't forget that in the United States they did this until 1950s to calm women. It was done in Europe to calm hysteria in women, because they discovered this was the erogenous zone. It exists in India, it exists in the Amazon, and it traverses centuries. We found mummies who have been circumcized. So it's been happening forever."

Now I know I've changed from when I first arrived in France. Not only am I carrying out this whole conversation in French, but I am as passionate about female circumcision as I am about sexy stockings.

PASSION

We don't wait until we're forty. At the age of thirty nine, Eric decides to have a vasectomy. This has always been the plan, and since I've done everything else, this is something he can do. This is what he says. This in part because the Copper IUD that I was singing the praises of turns out makes my period last for a week when it used to last for two to three days, and in part because it's always been the plan. He wants to share the responsibility and if I don't have to go on hormones, or run the risk of getting pregnant again—this is the best option.

He does not see it as a lessening of his virility. This it turns out is quite rare, especially in the South of France, as indeed when I meet with a general practitioner who has been a doctor for over forty years, she tells me that she's only ever had one couple whose partner opted to have one and this was because they had literally tried everything else on her—the woman. It was really a last resort. In America and Australia, most of my friend's husbands after their second child have made this same choice not as a last resort but as a welcomed decision of support or as Claudine calls it, "an act of devotion."

The quantity of this sample size aside, France is particular about sperm. Sperm banks as we know them in the United States don't exist, if you want to get pregnant on your own as a single woman, it's not allowed—you have to go to Sweden or Spain to acquire sperm. On the contrary, in vitro is a relatively inexpensive procedure provided you've got a mate, or some sperm handy.

When Eric wakes up from the anesthesia after having the vasectomy on a sunny summer day in Nice, the only thing he can think about is playing guitar. This isn't necessarily a revelation for him, but it does change his priorities. It becomes clear he can't live without music in his life, without playing guitar, that that is the only thing he wants to do, that is his passion. Since the birth of our kids, it's been difficult to create the time for much else besides parenting and work, but after that day it becomes imperative that he must make the time. And he does.

THE FUTURE IS FEMALE: WOMEN'S MARCH IN PARIS

My friend Anne-Louise says we should go. It's January 2017. The unthinkable has happened: an admitted and active sexual offender is the president of the United States.

We take a car to the Trocadero. My mom comes with us but she can't walk very well, and it's wicked cold. We don't march the whole thing. From Trocadero, you look down to the Eiffel Tower, where the march will end. We take pictures. My favorites are the really graphic signs.

There is a woman shouting near the statues, and watching her I'm in awe and believe I've missed my calling. I want to be her. But I'm not her. The energy is thrilling. I'd like to say it keeps us warm. Everyone wearing their pussy hats, even though he's already in.

A week after the Women's March in Paris, Claudine organizes a lecture at the French Coordination for the European Women's Lobby (C.L.E.F.). The C.L.E.F. represents 65 feminist organizations in France. Their building is located on a quiet street in the 9th arrondissement. It's not far, as the 18th sits on top of the 9th, but I'm in a rush to get out of the house, and I can't find my notebook.

The room is filled with thirty to forty primarily young women, all of whom have come to listen to Claudine speak. I'm so honored when Claudine calls me her "American daughter" to the two women I've started a conversation with.

After we've taken our seats and Claudine begins speaking, she again makes reference to me as a young American writer. Claudine is always my biggest advocate.

The talk is excellent, and I find it so inspiring to see a packed room come on a Saturday afternoon to discuss women's rights. The enthusiasm of the Women's March is translated here.

Claudine is talking about how feminist movements have always been taking place in different centuries but because their actions have not been transmitted and deleted from history, young feminists always think that their ideas are new. So we are not in the third or fourth wave of feminism, but actually the twentieth of the one hundredth. Feminism has been going on since the beginning of time. And as we've seen even within feminism, we've left people out or haven't heard their voices: Black women, transgender, non-binary, Indigenous, lesbians, queer. This is why the naming of Black feminism, of white feminism, is so important, of aligning our goals with Crenshaw's intersectional feminism.

In Bernardine Evaristo's Booker Prize-winning novel of 2019, *Girl, Woman, Other*, the character Yazz tells her mother, Amma

> *"nor is the child she raised to be a feminist calling herself one lately*
> *feminism is so herd-like, Yazz told her, to be honest, even being a woman is*
> *passé these days, we had a non-binary activist at uni called Morgan Malenga*
> *who opened my eyes, I reckon we're all going to be non-binary in the future,*

neither male nor female, which are gendered performances anyway, which
means your women's politics, Mumsy, will become redundant, and by the
way, I'm humanitarian, which is on a much higher plane than feminism
do you even know what that is?"

But we're not there yet. Even in 2020 in France, this idea of a third gender or no genders will not yet be folded into the cultural consciousness. I believe the acceptance of this is coming; it is what next. We have a long way to go, but maybe not as far as we think.

In 2018, a year later, we have moved to the South of France, and I write: Hard to believe that just last year I was marching with my mom and Anne-Louise in the freezing cold. Today we went to the beach and it was hot, the kids and I ran around without shoes in our tee-shirts. I feel so out of touch with what is happening in the States. Who would ever want to read my book now? How could I possibly make it relevant to American readers? Having no idea what is going on over there? But I do know what going on over here.

I have always said to Uber drivers, when they ask me why I live in France, as so many of them dream of going to America, that to me the major difference between France and the States is that France puts family first, whereas in America we put work first and then if we have time, we do family. There is also an inherent trust in the government here, that the government is there to protect you, which I never grew up with in the States. Ever since the Vietnam War, trust in the American government has declined. My generation not only grew up with our parents' ideology to never trust anyone over thirty, but also that the government existed to fuck us over, or that you really couldn't trust them, just as you couldn't trust cops in Los Angeles. (And other states, too, but Los Angeles is notorious for a sullied history of corrupt cops. Just read the Wikipedia entry on Los Angeles.)

In France, there is the sense that because we pay so much in taxes, the government is working for us so they'd better protect us. Healthcare is a given, as is five weeks' vacation, a minimum of three months' maternity leave, inexpensive daycare based on a sliding scale, and free education; all of which we don't have in the States.

MIGRANT MISCONCEPTIONS

This thinking of superiority of the French, because we have the "rights of man" is a stereotype which can be a trap. When I interview Marie-Paule Grossetête, who was born in Algeria in the 1950s and who migrated to Paris in 1971, we discuss the stereotypes of immigrants.

"I migrated to Paris in 1971 in order to study Life and Earth sciences there. I intended to become an agricultural engineer in Africa, my native continent. So my goal was not to live in France but to move back to North Africa or Central Africa. The fact is that I finally joined the Ecole Normale Supérieure de Fontenay aux roses at the time when these schools were single-sex. Once I earned my degree in Biology, I finally opted for scientific research and then higher education. I've always been a feminist, but in 2013 I joined the association "*Osez Féminismse!* Dare feminism," and in 2018, I was elected co-president of the CLEF (La Coordination Francaise pour le Lobby Europeen des femmes)." We have such a lovely discussion, but as she's also a writer, she sends me the following beautifully written passage about her work.

"My interest in migrant women and girls probably stems from the fact that I have found that all over the planet, women and girls are subject to male domination. So, if patriarchy is universal, the process of defending women's rights must also be done from a universal perspective, from a perspective of defending universal human rights. We therefore have to see migrant women as sisters in the struggle against patriarchy.

"However, in the media and in the collective imagination, they are invisible. We imagine migration through a male prism. The journey is so difficult that it is believed that there are only a few women and that those who migrate do so under "male protection." This is totally false. First, they are half of the migratory flow for both adults and children. Then, they very often leave without a companion because they are fleeing a situation of violence and danger. (We have about 1/3 of student migration, 1/3 of family reunification and also it is not always women who join their husbands, 1/3 of isolated migration for other reasons).

And then, if they are children, they are even more vulnerable due to the significant domestic and / or sexual exploitation of children. The pedocriminality in the prostitution of young girls is one of the scandals very widely tolerated and made invisible by societies, including those in so-called "host countries."

Immigrant women, those who are in France to settle there permanently, are perceived as having little education, "submissive" to their husbands, having too many (too many) children...

The reality is quite different. Studies show that they are almost as educated as native women. That their desire for independence, emancipation and participation in civic life is real. That their fertility, which was indeed higher than that of native women, joins that of natives in two or three generations. There are therefore many misconceptions to be overcome in order for migrant women to have a life of dignity.

As feminists, we demand in particular the application of the Istanbul Convention for the reception of refugees. We ask that the care of women and girls be the subject of specific care taking into account the violence suffered during their journey into exile. We also ask that the French administration starts enforcing the laws and helping them rather than treating them as people to be driven back to the border at the slightest administrative concern. In this, we can say that, as for native women victims of domestic violence, the police has to make great efforts to finally hear what the women say and to believe them. But to change that, we need a political will, which, at the moment, does not exist."

I suggest, "Perhaps what we need to call the immigrants expatriates instead. Because in fact we want these immigrants. They are the ones who are the most educated and they would contribute and want to contribute to our society and we should welcome them."

"Yes exactly!"

FEMINISTS IN THE CITY

écile Fara and Julie Marangé launch Feminists in the City in 2018 with their first Street Art and Feminism tour in the *Butte-aux-Cailles,* the 13th arrondissement of Paris. Since then they've expanded their vision and have had over six thousand people from around the world participate in their feminist tours such as *La chasse aux sorcières: les femmes puissantes de Paris (Witch Hunt and the powerful women of Paris)* in the Latin Quarter, *La libération sexuelle contée par des hystériques, (Sexual Liberation as told by hysterical women)* in Pigalle and Montmartre, and of course, *Dominé.e.s ? Jamais ! La vie de Simone de Beauvoir, Dominated? Never! The Life of Simone de Beauvoir* in the sixth arrondissement.

Julie and Cécile are friends who met in 2017, as they say on the benches of the *Sciences Po* in Paris, the equivalent of MIT in France, in ironically a class on entrepreneurship, which would come in handy. They developed what they call a "feminist crush" on each other. What's fascinating about both of them is that they really developed their feminist knowledge and activism whilst in college in the United Kingdom. .

Initially based in Paris, they quickly grew their business so that they currently run tours in Paris, Toulouse, Bordeaux, Lyon, and Marseille, as well as a very successful online lectures and masterclasses. Since the beginning of the confinement in France in April 2020, twenty-five hundred people have participated in online lectures on feminisms with guest speakers such as the historian Éliane Viennot, the President of FEMEN France Inna Shevchenko, the journalists Élise Thiébaut and Thomas Messias, the anthropologist Marie Serre, or the influencer and entrepreneur Camille Aumont Carnel. Usually with at least seventy people or more in attendance, they create a community of international engaged women and men who wouldn't have the chance to meet otherwise.

Claudine becomes their feminist godmother after going on one of their tours early in 2019 and will do several online events telling her stories with the women's Liberation movement, her life with Simone, and what is next for the future of feminism. The question they are most asked when they do events together is, *Who is the next Simone de Beauvoir?* Claudine will answer that there hasn't been allowed to be one, but in a way, this is a good thing. That we are the next voice, our diverse voices.

They are all about the sisterhood, and when they say it, I don't doubt their sincerity. In 2021, they will create a Summit of Sisterhood to discuss the solidarity between women. The question using the word sisterhood as is it inclusive enough, but in the end, they decide that sisterhood is what we need right now. I agree.

DIVING IN

At the crashing of the wave of the #MeToo movement I talk to my friend Nicole Brown for all things Hollywood and ask if thing have changed. "Yes and no," she sighs, "Women now feel more supported to speak up which is a beautiful thing. And men have to reflect, and think about how they can become allies and help contribute to environments for all to thrive equally...but there are still those that won't speak up, those who won't get called out, people who will abuse the privilege of speaking up, and bad habits that will linger...but all steps forward, big and small, are progress. Although we still have a lot of work to do, that we've arrived at this place of unity, support, awareness, and action brings me great pride."

The definition of a trailblazer, Nicole is by far one of the most driven of all of my friends. A double major a Columbia, with an incredible voice she stared in the film *Boyz N The Hood* at the age of ten and in the show *Kids Incorporated* about a young kids band. It was the highlight of my childhood going to watch her act in *Kids Incorporated*, I specifically remember being in awe of my friend. Watching her have her make-up put on in the mirror with lights. Singing on stage.

Nicole and I met twice, once at swim lessons when we were four. We were the ones that dived right in, no hesitation, not afraid. Later I'll be praised for this diving in at a pool in Miami Beach in December during Art Basel with my co-workers. I just dive right in. I hear them when I surface, "Did Augustine just dive right in?" My boss will say. "Yes" Kate, my friend will say. And I'll feel that same sense of pride. In love with myself, the way I've been in love with all my of girlfriends.

So Nicole and I met then, and then we meet in fifth grade when our parents don't come to the graduation for the older class. Why would they? Nicole and I still have one more year to go. So no one is watching us. We sneak off and talk deeply walking along the mini-stream and minor woods of our school. We fell in deep friendship love that day.

When my daughter turns five, I watch her experience this when she tells me her and her girlfriend did a "bisous sur la bouche." A kiss on the mouth. And they knew it was a special moment they made. The joyful exuberance of love. This is what I'm writing towards. I'm writing towards equality. I'm writing towards joy.

THE END OF MY BODY

Since December 2012, my body has been involved with something not its own.

Just shy of five years straight, my body has either been growing a human or feeding one. As I begin the arduous and emotional task of stopping breastfeeding, I try to embrace the joy of reclaiming my body as my own and my husband's. The French don't breastfeed for a long time, stating this exact reason—that their breasts are their husband's. What they really mean is that they are their own, the women's pleasure.

"My breasts are for me," is a common sentiment. The French women I've met have in fact breastfed for a while, but it's understood they are the exception.

There are not a lot of good articles on the Internet about stopping breastfeeding. Mommy blogs are about a lot of issues, but stopping breastfeeding doesn't seem to be one of them. I'm sure a more in-depth search would unearth a plethora, but I have neither the time nor the energy to do that. I'm still breastfeeding.

In fact, my time and energy ends here, as I'm sure I have to go breast-feed. And it's only when I eventually stop breastfeeding that I can then venture out on my own again unencumbered, which is how I'm able to travel to Strasbourg.

HÉLÈNE DE BEAUVOIR IN STRASBOURG

I'm in the car on the highway going from Strasbourg to the Würth Museum a week after Anthony Bourdain has died, It is June 2018. We drive by signs for Colmar, and I know that's where his body is still kept. I want to make a pilgrimage to the hotel, but I don't. I'm on a different adventure. I'm on my way to the Wurth Museum to see Hélène de Beauvoir's retrospective show.

It is an experience like no other. It is one of the first times I have ever gone to a museum and not already known the paintings ad infinitum, because unlike the van Goghs, Monets, and Picassos of the world, which have been printed on mousepads and coffee cups, Beauvoir's work is something new, something I have never seen before, a real discovery. Even though she was painted throughout the twentieth century, her work is fresh and exciting. I imagine this is what it must have been like when going to the newest exhibits was all the rage. And it makes such a difference that the artist is a woman. It is the first time I have ever been in a museum setting where the work is only by a woman. Yes, I went to *Elles at the Pompidou*, and that was interesting, but the difference of seeing an entire museum dedicated to one woman's work is astounding, and something I have never seen before.

The curator has done an excellent job, and has placed the most relevant work right at the entrance: Beauvoir's three paintings entitled, *La chasse aux sorcières est toujours ouverte (The witch hunt is still open)*; *Les femmes souffrent, les hommes jugent (Women suffer, men judge)*; and *Les mortifières (The mortifiers)*. This last one comes from the verb to mortify, but operates on a second level as it has the definition in French to tenderize meat. All three works were done in 1977, and they resonate with the renewed popularity of Margaret Atwood's *The Handmaid's Tale*. Later, I ask Claudine if Helene would've known about *The Handmaid's Tale*, but in fact Beauvoir is a precursor to Atwood's novel, which was published in 1985.

Claudine's painting of Simone de Beauvoir hangs next to a painting of the sisters in glass, followed by another portrait of Simone, which I think is just as good, if not better, than Picasso's classic portrait of Gertrude Stein.

After going through the exhibit, I am so moved. I'm amazed at what an impact art by a woman can have on me. We have lunch at the museum. It is quite a hot and sunny June day. We head back to the city of Strasbourg to take a nap before Claudine and I go out to dinner.

Strasbourg is a perfectly quaint and charming village, and it is a warm summer night. It is the first time I have been away from my kids, the first time I have travelled alone since before my son was born. It doesn't even seem possible when I say it. My sense of adventure and independence, which marked my everyday existence, returns. I remember how much I love exploring new places, how much I love to travel despite the severe claustrophobia on the plane to get here.

And it's here that Claudine and I have one of our best conversations over the classic Alsace dish: a flammekueche, which is essentially a thin-crust pizza with no tomato sauce and lots of cheese and bacon. The mood is relaxed, and we talk of Anthony Bourdain, of when I first came to France, of past love relationships, of our work and writing— it's a moment when I am so grateful to be just where I am. My gratitude feels immense for the friendship we've created.

PASSOVER, A LOVE STORY

We always left the door open for Elijah. So the cool desert Los Angeles night air would come in down the hall, past the picture of the rabbi and to the empty glass of wine on the table. Next to the Seder plate, brought down off the wall for this occasion.

We'd ask the four questions and eat reclining. The last question asks why? To recline in ancient days meant you were free. That was something I could get into–the sign that you're free.

One of the saddest parts about death being that you'll never eat her food again. The show *The Big Bang Theory* does this well, when Howard's Jewish Mother (she deserves a capital M) dies, they have a feast of all the frozen leftovers in the fridge, knowing this will be the last time he will taste her food as even with the recipe it won't be the same, because she won't have made it.

Still, I make the brisket on a bed of onions the way she taught me. (The cut of the meat isn't quite the same, I've never been able to adequately describe a "double decker" in French.) But the onions, that was the key, that was the secret. With a match in my mouth to keep from crying and I remember.

Passover was important to my Nana. It was one of the three holidays that our extended family got together. These Passovers, or Thanksgivings, or Hanukkahs around her dining room table blend together, or do I remember just one specific one?

The florescent violet color of the horseradish for the gefilte fish. The gelatinous gefilte fish that glistened and slightly jiggled on the lettuce leaf. The taste of which kind of grows on you because you only have it once a year. The pieces came in a jar of that same orange and green Manischewitz brand, the world's largest Matzo manufacturer, that comes to be recognized as a staple of Jewish cuisine.

As quintessential as leaving the cranberry sauce in the form of a can in a pretty serving dish. No denying its ready-made status. No hiding behind anything, as others of us might have been inclined to hide our true forms.

A cacophony of sounds of forks and glasses clanging, of mildly awkward conversations with relatives you don't often see, but have little in common with. Or maybe there is common ground, but you haven't found it yet.

The next night my daughter and I stand in the kitchen, eating the skin off a pintade (a guineafowl, or what I like to think of as a fancier French chicken). My husband has cooked it perfectly. The skin is crispy and that golden photographic brown, "with a touch of herbs de Provence, just how you like it," he says when he plates my food.

Now after dinner my daughter proclaims with certainty, "I love the skin, more skin."

How is she to know my aunt whom she is named after loved the skin, too? Sure, maybe lots of people love the skin, or maybe they don't. I don't really know. I have a handful of my family as a sample size. At most we were twelve, and it was particularly my aunt at Thanksgiving who requested extra skin on her plate.

But now my daughter and I are making new memories of standing in the kitchen together, like bandits relishing in their loot. Her on a stool surveying the carcass and pointing out the good parts to pillage. She says, "Mommy, you're so pretty," because I'm wearing a dress with butterflies, a dress of my mother's that I've literally worn since high school. We keep our clothes in my family just like inherited traits.

How is she to know she imitates mannerisms she never saw? How she holds up her pointer finger when she has something important to say is a spitting image of my Nana? And that she knows what she has to say is important and to be listened to she is truly herself.

CLIMAX

The China Club in Paris becomes one of my and my friends' places, so to speak. Located near Bastille, it's a convenient meeting spot for all of us. Also, it's just so damn sexy. The red velvet curtains, the black-and-white checkered floor. You feel sexy when you're there. It's the fantasy, the atmosphere rubs off on you. And of course it's the drinks, the absinthe sours and Hemingways. Though not convenient, anything in a martini glass has a way of making you feel more sophisticated, more cosmopolitan; perhaps that was the success of the cosmos of *Sex and the City*. But I'm getting off track. On an evening out with my girls—Olga, Sabrina, and Melis—we stand at the bar, and they are asking me, "But, yes, Augustine, what is the climax of your book?"

We talk a lot about the book I'm writing. About feminism and equality. I'm always slightly embarrassed. Am I really working? Am I really writing something of value?

And I didn't know. Every book has to have a climax, they tell me. I know this myself. So then I keep searching for that. *Could this be it? Could that?* I ask myself. *When will the book end?* Things keep happening. Keep needing to be added. I don't really believe my story has enough drama.

The climax comes years and years later. Wait for it. But it's worth it. The climax is when the book is finished. The climax is not when I find true love. Or when love finds me. Or when Eric says I love you. Or when we get married. Or when my children are born. All of this is life. But the real climax, for me, is when I can say with a smile that the book is finished. And know this is true. That it is its own entity, ready for the world. That it will survive on its own, without me but because of me. This is the orgasmic joy of accomplishing the one thing you set out to do. There is no other climax.

WHY I WRITE

I wrote my first story when I was nine years old. I remember the opening sentence: *Johanna's dress fluttered in the wind as she balanced on the white picket fence.* Or something like that. My parents couldn't believe it. I had written my first short story. After that, I was convinced I was good at this.

I wanted to be Harriet from the classic children's novel *Harriet the Spy*. I wore the blue-hooded zipper sweatshirt and carried my journal everywhere. I read all of Roald Dahl. The first book that made me cry was *Where the Red Fern Grows*. My mind was blown with *I Am the Cheese*. At ten, I started really keeping a journal; at eleven, I knew it was essential, and I haven't stopped since. So it feels like all my life I've wanted to be a writer, as even before that my mom and I would write down *The Adventures of Beary Bear* when I was four and six. The stuffed polar bear Nana bought me when I insisted, which was so soft, which I brought with me throughout Europe, when we lived at a Tuscan farmhouse in Italy for a summer while my dad taught.

The mom of my childhood was my superhero, looking so strong and fit in her leotard, literally like *Wonder Woman* if Wonder Woman wore a sports bra underneath a leotard and leggings with white bunched socks and Nike for the Greek Goddess sneakers. But she was so strong

—that is what I remember. Like the *50-Foot Woman*. That's how it felt looking up to her. She would take me to her classes, and I would sit and do homework and read and watch the women dancing in step. My mom is all about the endorphins, the high that kicks in with exercise. She just loves to dance. And to me, she is the best mom. So creative, so imaginative, and she makes the best Mamie because she's really kept her kid spirit alive.

It feels important to write this now as my son almost turns five and my daughter three. What will become influential in their life? What is already happening that will influence who they will become? For me, it was traveling to Italy and throughout Europe through France, Spain, and Amsterdam that gave me the desire to travel. To be an artist. How I would end up living in the south of France because it was where my parents took me as a child with a father obsessed with Picasso.

After that, I studied. I was always in Honors English, AP English. I was one of the only ones who read the entirety of *100 Years of Solitude* by Gabriel García Márquez over the summer of eighth grade. I did reports on Virginia Woolf and Adrienne Rich, but I know it was James Baldwin's *Another Country* that really solidified it for me. That book was a game changer. The language was so beautiful, and all I wanted to do was write as well as him. I was lucky to have inspired teachers who got us excited about the Romantics, poets and writers like Mary Shelley, who came up with Frankenstein at a party with her friends, Percy Shelley and Lord Byron. Books like *The Things They Carried* by Tim O'Brian taught me the freedom you could have as a writer. I'd never seen a book like that before.

But I think it was really the recognition of my own work, an essay I wrote on *Alice in Wonderland*, the real story versus the Disney version for art history, that my teacher thought was so good he kept it, and even when I saw him years and years later at Art Basil in Miami, he reminded me how good of an essay it was, how he was still impressed by it. "You really were talented, I could tell this was what you would do with your life." That has stayed with me.

MAMIE GÂTEAU

I 've just missed the 85 bus, so I have to wait ten minutes. I think of texting Claudine to tell her I'll be ten minutes late, but I don't want to be late, so I don't. I get off at the *Pont Neuf* at ten minutes to 4pm. There is no way I will make it in time.

Claudine is usually early, though since she stopped working, she tends to run ten minutes late, too. So when I get there, she hasn't yet arrived. It's a gorgeously sunny summer day in front of the *Bon Marche*. We decide to have a drink outside. We end up at the same place Claudine wanted to take me to all those years ago, and it's here I decide this is the end of the book. Right here on this street, where it all began. The restaurant has now doubled its size, and we have a table. The light is that perfect Parisian light.

"Bernard says I've terrorized them, so they know not to keep me waiting. They know how impatient I am."

"Yes, it's very un-French, Claudine."

"I know, I'm extremely impatient."

"I am too, Claudine."

"So, Augustine, I have to ask."

"Yes, I know, how is the work coming?"

"You said it, not me," Claudine says with a smile.

"Is that what you were going to ask?"

"Maybe you wait to send it now, though, because people will be going on vacation."

"Claudine, it's the States. No one goes on vacation."

"Yes, you're right, my dear. Still, I think you should wait until September, until your book is finished, to send the letters."

The waitress comes, and we order ice cream. Chocolate and vanilla for her, pistachio and coffee for me.

"Sylvie is trying to erase any existence of Helene." Sylvie is Sylvie Le-Bon de Beauvoir, the adopted daughter of Beauvoir. "My heart broke when she gave this Brazilian woman the letters. And I said to Bernard, they would surface again. It's three hundred thousand dollars for the four hundred letters. They go on auction at the end of the month. Helene was very nice to Sylvie, because she signed off on Simone adopting her and changing her inheritance."

"I always thought Helene was more of a kindred spirit to you than Simone."

"Helene was family. I think Simone was jealous of Helene and the relationship she had with Lionel, because Lionel wouldn't sleep with her and Sartre was so perverse. Some women get jealous when men don't want to sleep with them. I mean, I idolized their relationship, but once I saw them together, Sartre was awful."

"For such a strong feminist, it is strange she put up with that from Sartre."

"Yes, but then it was a different time." Claudine continues, "At the time, it was revolutionary. It was a different kind of relationship, and very brave to do. They had the intellectual link and the link of writing."

"So Claudine, you better save your notes, so that I can sell them on Christie's."

"Augustine, my notes are not worth three hundred thousand dollars,"

"You never know, Claudine."

"Well, you're very kind. But I must tell you this story so that you can use it in your book," Claudine says, "So I went to a conference at the UN and do you know who Christiane Taubira is?"

"No, unfortunately not."

"Well, she is an amazing woman. You'll look her up when you get home. She is currently the attorney general of France." She will be the one in charge of making same-sex marriage legal in France in 2013. "After she gave her speech at UNESCO, she walked through the crowd, and then she stopped at me. She said, 'Do I know you?' I said, 'Well, I worked with Simone de Beauvoir on the feminist movement.'

'Ah yes, Simone is here,' Christiane says, pounding her chest.' She hugged me, and then she walked away. But isn't that incredible? I was so moved."

"That's a beautiful story, Claudine, and it's true. Simone is here for us, too." I touch my heart.

"Yes, she's with us all the time." We enjoy this moment. "So, my dear, what is your next project?" Claudine asks.

"I have a few ideas," I smile. "I have a few ideas."

AFTERWORD

Writing a book about your life is a funny thing. It's an attempt to freeze a slice of your life, but your life doesn't freeze. You keep growing, changing. The world around you keeps changing, as does your place in it. I don't live in Paris anymore. It's been three years since I lived there. Around the time I moved to France, things started changing in America, and I watched from afar. The #MeToo movement came and went. White feminism was defined and challenged.

Intersectionality became a thing, but oh wait, it was invented by Kimberlé Crenshaw in 1989. No one had ever taught me that. No one had ever taught me about the Black feminists; oh wait, they didn't teach them to anyone. Angela Davis, yes. But I had to seek many of them out for myself. Slowly, then rapidly, Audre Lourde and bell hooks gained momentum.

We want to change the world. Full stop. We want to change the world. But how?

I like to call myself an optimistic feminist. There are many qualifiers of feminist: *Bad Feminist* via Roxane Gay, or a "Happy African Feminist Who Does Not Hate Men and Who Likes To Wear Lip Gloss And High Heels For Herself And Not For Men" via Chimananda Ngozi Adichie. A feminist with a disclaimer. I am an optimistic feminist because I hear the words of James Baldwin echo in my mind: "I can't be a pessimist because I'm alive."

There is that famous anecdote about Steve Jobs, that every day he asked himself, "If this were my last day alive, would I want to do what I'm doing today?"

What this means for me is making sure that I make love, write, and swim in the sea every day. And making love is not limited to just making love, though that's top priority, but making love is also expressing love to those I love, acting with love, coming from love.

When I write, I'm making love, so that's already two out of three on any given day that I wake up with the sunrise and embrace the quiet moment of the day by my pen. And even that sounds so cheesy and comically romantic that it makes me laugh and appreciate this ongoing fascination and love affair with myself.

For my husband, writing is replaced by playing guitar. And eventually, I'd love to add to my own daily habits playing piano, but for now, I maintain my optimism with these three. There are others that could be added to the list that are a given that don't need to be checked off, like cuddling with my children and telling them I love them, or reading. But three seemed an easy number.

And clearly, there are days when I don't do all three. There are days when I don't do any. And there are the glorious days where I do all three.

When I first moved to France in 2009 with the nebulous question of what I could do to help women, I didn't know that what I would do was document the evolution of feminism in the past decade from a French-American perspective.

I knew in my heart that women in the world weren't where they should be. We had made advances, and then stopped.

In 2009, I didn't know it yet, because it hadn't even really been defined and discussed when I started writing, though it certainly existed, but I'm a white feminist. If I was attempting humor, I'd say I'm, like, *totally* a classic white feminist—in a Valley Girl voice. This seems offensive on many levels, because the tone not only diminishes the severity of the claim, but also somehow makes it prideful. This is not far from the truth: there have been several studies indicating that the Valley Girl Voice is incredibly influential in our culture. Hence the impact of the teenage girls to create worldwide trends. If you've learned one thing it's to give the vocal fry credit.

I don't know it yet, but I'm a white feminist, and man, it sucks. I think I'm fighting the good fight, but as I will find out later, white feminism, as Rachel Cargle says, is just the patriarchy in heels.

As a white feminist—as any feminist—I have to contend with the fact that the feminist movement has some inherent problems and glaring omissions.

It didn't occur to me to question that my heroines, Simone de Beauvoir and Virginia Woolf, were white, brunette, child-free intellectuals. Why were they the women I was allowed to know?

As memoirists, we're only as good as our self-awareness, and when I first moved to France, I was completely oblivious to discrimination based on race, gender, and sexual orientation. This is not to say I wasn't guilty about it. I remember getting my apartment in Montmartre and feeling like the luckiest woman on the planet, and then later reading some article somewhere that said perhaps "luck" wasn't luck at all; perhaps it was because I was white and had a far easier time securing an apartment.

In writing this book, my greatest fear was getting written off as just some spoiled white girl—some pretty, cisgender, heterosexual-but-definitely-bi-curious middle-class trust fund woman just writing her little feminist stories. The trust fund bit isn't quite true, I don't actually have a trust fund, though at the time I started writing, my Nana was giving me and three other members of my family four thousand dollars a month, which is still the goal of what I'd like to make on my own. The point is that I was being financially supported. So what business did I have advising others on how to be "independent women?" What business did I have advising people on how to change the world? Still, I went and did it anyway. The irony is that it does become my business. And as Malcolm Gladwell writes in *Outliers,* when you do something for ten thousand hours, you become an expert. I have easily clocked ten thousand hours writing by now, so that I can teach it while keeping imposter syndrome at bay.

According to Netflix's *Feminists: What Were They Thinking?,* early feminists didn't even want lesbians in their feminist club, so that tells you something right there. You're supposed to be fighting for women's rights, but not all women were included.

I've done the journaling of Layla Saad's life-changing book, *Me and White Supremacy.* Gold stars for me. This sounds dismissive, but is meant to be self-deprecating to me; that's the least, literally the least, that I can do. The journey really starts there. When I was growing up, we were taught to be colorblind. Now we've figured out that, actually, that's not the greatest idea. Not seeing color is like not seeing the person.

OK, so that's an antiquated idea. When I grew up, I ended up saying Black as a whisper, as if you weren't supposed to notice that people were Black, or you weren't supposed to say it. In college, we were taught our prejudices because when describing people passing on the street you would say describe them as Black but for everyone else you wouldn't mention their ethnicity, because white was the default.

But there is no default.

Of course, I'm lucky to have Virginia Woolf and Simone de Beauvoir as my heroines, as some women didn't even grow up with any female heroines, and can't even name a woman they would aspire to be.

The irony is that in all my feminist reading, the key was to make money, and it wasn't until years later that I would figure out how to actually make money from what I knew, from doing what I love.

This meant that I was a fraud: here I was reading all about how the key to independence was your ability as a woman to make money, and I wasn't making any.

Not only was I not making any money, but when I first moved to France, my whole identity changed, because you can't schmooze if you can't speak the language. This made it very difficult to be myself. I love to chat with people and ask them about their stories, but when you can't say what you want to say, even at the marché, you grow quiet. You're self-silencing.

Studying feminism in all its forms—intersectional, intergenerational, and international—empowers women to become visible. To be afraid and do it anyway. The way to help women is be heard. To tell your story. To be visible.

I want to be visible, and I hope that, in reading my book, you will, too.

WORKS CONSULTED

Books

Adichie, Chimamanda Ngozi. *We Should All Be Feminists.*

Baldwin, James. *Collected Essays, Library of America.*

Beauvoir, Simone de. *The Second Sex.*

Berger, John. *Ways of Seeing.*

Bushnell, Candace. *Sex and the City.*

Callan, Jamie Cat. *French Women Don't Sleep Alone.*

Cavallo, Francesca and Elena Favilli. *Good Night Stories for Rebel Girls.*

Chicago, Judy. *The Dinner Party.*

_____. *Though The Flower.*

Colette. *The Pure and The Impure.*

Davis, Angela. *Women, Race & Class.*

Druckerman, Pamela. *Bringing Up Bebe: One American Mother Discovers the Wisdom of French Parenting.*

Evaristo, Bernardine. *Girl, Woman, Other.*

Fielding, Helen. *Bridget Jones Diary.*

Friedman, Jane. *The Business of Being A Writer.*

Gbowbee, Leymah. *Mighty Be There Powers.*

Gay, Roxane. *Bad Feminist.*

Gilbert, Elizabeth. *Big Magic.*

_____. *Eat, Pray, Love.*

Gladwell, Maxwell. *Outliers*

Guiliano, Mireille. *French Women Don't Get Fat.*

Hemingway, Ernest. *A Moveable Feast.*

hooks, bell. *Remembered Rapture.*

Jamison, Leslie. *The Empathy Exams.*

Jong, Erica. *Fear of Flying.*

Kristoff, Nicolas and Sheryl WuDunn. *Half The Sky: Turning Oppression into Opportunity for Women Worldwide.*

Lorde, Audre. *Sister Outsider.*

Maggs, Sam. *Wonder Women: 25 Innovators, Inventors, and Trailblazers Who Changed History.*

Mayes, Francis. *Under the Tuscan Sun.*

Monteil, Claudine. *The Beauvoir Sisters*

_____. *Éve Curie: L'autre fille de Pierre et Marie Curie.*

_____. *Simone de Beauvoir et les femmes aujourd'hui.*

_____. *Mémoires d'une jeune fille rebelle. Simone de Beauvoir: Le Mouvement des Femmes.*

Nelson, Maggie. *The Argonauts.*

Ollivier, Debra. *Entre Nous: A Woman's Guide To Finding Her Inner French Girl.*

Oluo, Ijoma. *So You Want To Talk About Race.*

Powell, Helena Frith. *All You Need To Be Impossibly French.*

Sandburg, Sheryl. *Lean In.*

Saad, Layla. *Me and White Supremacy.*

Schiff, Stacy. *Cleopatra.*

Sciolino, Elaine. *La Seduction: How the French Play the Game of Life.*

Shlain, Leonard. *The Alphabet Versus The Goddess: The Conflict between Word and Image.*

_____. *Sex, Time and Power: How Women's Sexuality Shaped Human Evolution.*

Smarsh, Sarah. *Heartland.*

Stimmler-Hall, Heather. *Naughty in Paris.*

Stein, Gertrude. *The Autobiography of Alice B. Toklas.*

Steinem, Gloria. *Outrageous Acts and Everyday Rebellions.*

Stone, Merlin. *When God Was A Woman.*

Vial, Véronique. *An American In Paris.*

Welscher, Toni. *Taking Charge of Your Fertility.*

Woolf, Virginia. *A Room of One's Own & Three Guineas.*

∼

Magazine Articles

Appiah, Kwame Anthony. "The Art of Social Change." *The New York Times*, 2010.

Armstrong, Carol."To Paint, To Point, To Pose" *Manet's 'Le Dejeuner sur l'herbe'* 2018.

Brooke, Eliza. "How to Sell a Billion-Dollar Myth Like a French Girl: The origins and consequences of everyone's favorite Parisian fantasy." *Vox*, Jul 5, 2017.

Cargle, Rachel. "When Feminism is White Supremacy in Heels." *Harper's Bazaar*, 2018.

DiAngelo, Robin. " White Fragility." *International Journal of Critical Pedagogy*, 2011.

Dionne, Evette "Women's Suffrage Leaders Left Out Black Women: Despite what you may have learned in school." *Teen Vogue,* August 18, 2017.

Druckerman, Pamela. "Perineal Re-education Rocks" *New York Times,* November 13, 2007.

Eisenhauer, Karen and Carmen Fought. "A Quantitative Analysis of Directives in Disney Princess Films" 2016.

Goldman, Andrew. "The Devil in Marina Abramovic." *New York Times,* June 13, 2012.

Hartley, Gemma. "Women Aren't Nags, We're Just Fed Up." *Harper's Bazaar,* September 27, 2017.

Hughes, Virginia. "Were the First Artists Mostly Women?" *National Geographic,* 2013.

Khazan, Olga. "Why Do Women Bully Each Other at Work?" *The Atlantic,* September, 2017.

Lundberg, Claire "The French Government Wants To Tone My Vagina: Inside my amazing and embarrassing postnatal "perineal re-education" class, paid for by la France," *Slate,* February 15, 2012.

Marie-Slaughter, Anne. "Why Women Still Can't Have It All." *The Atlantic,* July / August 2012.

Margulis, Lynn. "Interview with Dick Teresi" *Discover Magazine,* June 17, 2011.

National Geographic *"Women of Impact November 2019 Issue," "The Gender Issue January 2017."*

Peltier, Elian. "France Doubles Paid Paternity Leave to 28 Days, One of Europe's Most Generous Plans." *The New York Times,* Sept. 24, 2020.

Rosenthal, Elisabeth. "American Way of Birth, Costliest in the World." *The New York Times,* June 30, 2013.

Williams, Serena. "What my life-threatening experience taught me about giving birth." *CNN Opinion,* February 20, 2018

Wolf, Naomi. "Mommy, I want to Be A Princess" *The New York Times,* December 2, 2011.

∿

Musical and Dramatic Works

Adichie, Chimamanda Ngozi. "We Should All Be Feminists," "The Danger of a Single Story" *TED Talk.*

Beyoncé. "Run the World (Girls)," Video Music Awards performance of "Flawless" 2014.

Beirut. "Sunday Smile."

Cargle, Rachel. "Unpacking White Feminism."

Dave Matthews. "Satellite"

diFranco, Ani. "Untouchable Face."

Dylan, Bob. "Baby Let Me Follow You Down," "She Belongs to Me."

Feminists: What Were They Thinking? Directed by: Johanna Demetrakas

Franklin, Aretha. "Do Right Woman, Do Right Man."

Gainsbourg, Serge with Brigitte Bardot. "Bonnie and Clyde."

Gotye featuring Kimbra. "Somebody That I Used to Know."

Katz, Jackson. "Violence against women—it's a men's issue." *Ted Talk*.

The Magnetic Fields. "The Things We Did and Didn't Do," "Queen of the Savages."

Nirvana. "Teen Spirit."

Sly and the Family Stone. "If You Want Me To Stay."

Smith, Elliot. "Behind Bars."

Rage Against the Machine. (Album.)

The Rolling Stones. "Give Me Shelter," "Paint It Black," "Shattered."

ACKNOWLEDGMENTS

I'm so fortunate as there are so many amazingly talented people to thank who mean so much to me. I am forever grateful.

Thank you Michelle Heinz for reading this manuscript countless times, for being as invested in it as I am, and for always pushing me to clarity. Thank you Aysin Karaduman for reminding me to be curious, giving me new tools to change my life and for always being in my corner.

Thank you to my editor extraordinaire, Chantel Hamilton, your sharp-eye for detail and fabulous comments in the margins made editing fun. Thank you Yilin Wang, for your insightful notes which made the manuscript the best that it could be. Thank you Nicole Caputo, I'm so in love with this gorgeous cover! It was such a joy to collaborate with you—you made the book real. Thank you Sandy Kreps, your interior design is simply divine.

Thank you Doretta Lau and Dan White, your quotes continue to lift my spirits. Thank you Suzanne Lerner for bringing me to so many exceptional events and your remarkable support always. Thank you to my wonderful teachers over the years, Nicolas Christopher, Liz Harris, Sam Lipsyte, Richard Locke, Pamela Painter, Marc Simpson, Lauren Shaw, Ken Todd, Tony de los Reyes, and Allen Ziegler.

For my lovely ladies! Thank you to my sisters, Melis Arval, Olga Kuzmina, and Sabrina Casonato, for your amazing friendship and the endless hours listening to me at the cafe as I tried to hash out feminist theory and what my book was going to be "about." To my girlfriends and godmothers who have grown with me, Marienette Alberbide, Amber Banks, Kate Kurtz and Nancy Sadler. For my fellow writers who inspire me and champion my work, Clare Beams, Keri Bertino, Jennifer Estaris, Tupelo Hassman, Elaine Johanson, Kimberly King Parsons and Sarah Smarsh.

Les amis parisiennes: Rose and Funda Arval, Bernard Besson, Mariel Chatman and Thibaut Lassalle, Anne-Louise and Nick Craven, Penny-Lise, Marcelle and Christophe Guilloux, Suzanne and Sander de Klerk, Se-Woong Koo, Carolina Milanez, Natasha Nixon, Chris and Laetitia Pruszko, Katy Roberts, Rasul Siddik, Jarbas Silva, and Gosia Szyszka. Special shout out to the brilliant photographers Helene Beade, Barbara Bouyne, Marilia Destot, and Emmanuelle Tricore who helped make this adventure in Paris possible. And to all my neighbors and friends in our French town, thank you for making this home.

Thank you to my everlasting and faithful friends who've stuck by me through everything, Nicole Brown, Laila Contini, Rebecca Lerner, Evan Schoolnik, Adriana Shilton, Jackie Temkin, Shahirah Majumbar, Edie Nugent, and Michelle Zamplas.

Diane Boureston, thank you for your wisdom, love and guidance over many years.

For my grandparents and great-grandparents, Boby and Jakey Kubernick, Eva and George Tobman, for creating the solid foundation I stand on and providing an education I couldn't have received otherwise. To Irl Hazard Blaisdell for being an inspiration to me and my father always. For my namesake, Frances Augusta Redmond, I know you've been with me all the way.

Thank you to my family: Erin Blaisdell, Thomas and Shana Murray-wolf, the Rothner Clan—Herbie, Anita, Glenn, Maggie, Jacobo, Kurt, Kathi, Amy, Colleen, Erin, Hannah, Hailey, and Matthew, Marc and

Dominique Simon, and to the Wolfs—Pearl, Linda, Jory, Jessica, Tom, Ryan, Sami, Mason, Kate, Brendan, Eula, Aylwyn and Solas.

Thank you Delene Wolf, a true feminist. Russ Rothner, for calling me the real deal, I wish you were still here. Andrew Rothner, for inspiring Noah to rock climb. Richard Blaisdell for your eternal poetic mind. Marilyn Braiser for your humor and insight.

Thank you to all the inspiring women who have taken my classes— your momentum for change encourages me. Especially Jean Holmes, Neelima Goel, Laurah Lou, Wynter Mitchell, Martina Oettl, and Sneha Rooh. Thank you to to everyone who gave their time and brilliance to be interviewed for this book: Sheila Aminmadani, Bernice du Bois, Gisèle Bourquin, Judy Chicago, Cécile Fara, Marie-Paule Grossetête, Pascale Jeandroz, Colette Kreder, Sheila Malovany-Chevallier, Julie Marangé, Danielle Michel-Chich, Hélène de Monferrand, Hélène Monties, Jaqueline Pasquier, Nathalie Pilhes, Elena Rossini, Moïra Sauvage, Tina Tangalakis, Eliane Viennot, Marie-Helene Vincent and Catherine Zviloff.

My eternal gratitude goes to Claudine Monteil, for our immeasurable conversations—without your encouragement, friendship and love this book may never have come to fruition.

To Andrea Frison, for raising a thoughtful and caring son and father to our children. To Barbara, I miss you every day and you still make me laugh. To Auntie Lissa, for introducing me to sushi and all the wonders of the world and for showing me how to be independent.

For my parents, Karen and Don, for inspiring me to realize my dreams, for teaching me how to live a creative life, and of course for your love.

My husband, Eric, I'm more in love with you than when I first met you, if that's even possible. Thank you for reading all the feminists books, for wanting to marry a writer and all that entails—though perhaps we didn't realize I'd be working on this project for twelve years—you've always had infinite faith in me.

To my children, Noah and Evalie—everything I do I do for you. I hope this book inspires you to follow your passions and teaches you to lead a feminist life.

ABOUT THE AUTHOR

Augustine Blaisdell earned her MFA in creative writing at Columbia University. Now, fluent in French, she also studied at the Sorbonne and lived in Paris for nine years. She is a member of the French associations *Femmes au-delà des Mers* and *Femmes d'ici et allieurs*. Blaisdell leads an international literary salon online as well as teaches the courses *French Feminists on the Beach, Counterpoint,* and *Writing Into the Known*. Originally from Los Angeles, California, she currently lives in the Côte d'Azur. *Women À La Mode* is her first book. For more information or to sign up for her weekly newsletter go to www. augustineblaisdell.com.

© Karen Blaisdell

Printed in Poland
by Amazon Fulfillment
Poland Sp. z o.o., Wrocław

71843219R00247